A Culture of Engagen

SELECTED TITLES FROM THE MORAL TRADITIONS SERIES

David Cloutier, Kristin Heyer, Andrea Vicini, SJ, *Series Editors*
James F. Keenan, SJ, *Founding Editor*

A Culture of Engagement
Law, Religion, and Morality

Cathleen Kaveny

Georgetown University Press
Washington, DC

Library of Congress Cataloging-in-Publication Data

Kaveny, Cathleen, author.
  A culture of engagement : law, religion, and morality / Cathleen Kaveny.
    pages   cm — (The moral traditions series)
  Includes bibliographical references and index.
  ISBN 978-1-62616-303-4 (hardcover : alk. paper) — ISBN 978-1-62616-302-7 (pbk. : alk. paper) — ISBN 978-1-62616-304-1 (ebook)
  1. Christian ethics—United States. 2. Catholic Church—United States—Doctrines. 3. Law—Moral and ethical aspects—United States. 4. Freedom of religion—United States. 5. Culture conflict—United States. I. Title. II. Series: Moral traditions series.
  BJ1249.K367 2016
  261'.1—dc23
  2015025211

♾ This book is printed on acid-free paper meeting the requirements of the American National Standard for Permanence in Paper for Printed Library Materials.

17 16   9 8 7 6 5 4 3 2 First printing

Printed in the United States of America

Cover design by Faceout Studio
Cover image by Lisette Poole/Bloomberg via Getty Images

To my brother and sisters
John Kaveny, Meg Kaveny, and Lee Kaveny
who taught me so much about what it means to
take care of people

Contents

Acknowledgments

The reflections in this volume are the fruits of my longtime relationship with *Commonweal* magazine, whose "mission is to provide a forum for civil, reasoned debate on the interaction of faith with contemporary politics and culture." I am deeply grateful to Paul Baumann, *Commonweal*'s editor, for inviting me to become a regular columnist and teaching me how to do the job. I am also happy to acknowledge my debts to the extremely talented associate editors I have had the privilege to work closely with over the past few years, especially Patrick Jordan, Grant Gallicho, Mathew Boudway, and Mollie Wilson O'Reilly. They have all helped me to become a better thinker and writer.

I began this project while on the faculty at the University of Notre Dame. I would like to extend my appreciation to my longtime administrative assistant, Lu Ann Nate, for her steady help on this and many other projects. I would also like to thank Craig Iffland, a doctoral student in the Department of Theology at Notre Dame, who served as my research assistant during my final two years at Notre Dame. The project is coming to its end as I begin my second full academic year on the faculty of Boston College. Many thanks as well to Dan DiLeo, also my research assistant and a doctoral student in the Theology Department at Boston College. Conversations with both Craig and Dan about the topics discussed in these chapters have left me very hopeful about the future of Christian ethics. Marissa Marandola, a member of the Boston College class of 2016, provided expert help in finalizing the manuscript.

Finally, I want to thank my friends and colleagues at Notre Dame and Boston College, as well as friends and family throughout the country. I am very grateful to them all for their time, their conversation, and their wisdom in helping me think through the implications of the pressing issues of the day.

Introduction

Life in the Crisscross

Nearly four decades ago, the brilliant sociologist John Murray Cuddihy argued that American civil religion is actually "the religion of civility."[1] The core belief of that civil religion is that it is impolite to impose commitments or beliefs appropriate in one sphere of life upon people one happens to meet in other spheres. The religion of civility recognizes that it is good to be religious—provided that we are not too religious, or religious in the wrong context. So piety is perfectly acceptable on Sunday at church, but not at the water cooler on Monday or at the ballot box on the first Tuesday of November.

Cuddihy argues that what makes American civility a workable project is a strong, even if tacit, commitment to living a compartmentalized life. American cultural stability is not due to the creation of a single overarching loyalty binding upon everyone, such as a national political party to which everyone belongs. Instead, it is the cultivation of a multitude of intermediate loyalties that tug at each of us, ranging from the bowling club, to the Rotary, to the Knights of Columbus. These loyalties, said Cuddihy, sometimes overlap and sometimes conflict. It is because Americans tend to be characterized by a patchwork of disjointed commitments, rather than by an array of coordinating ones, that the country has been so successful in avoiding fanaticism. Americans are free of the absolute battle of "us" versus "them," because those categories change from context to context. Rather than developing loyalties that run all the way down, we are encouraged by the culture to mix and match them. So millions of American happily worship with others whose political candidate they hope is defeated and whose football team they root against in the Superbowl.

Cuddihy's phrase for the web of conflicting and converging loyalties that characterizes American culture is "crisscross." It is a practice that has its psychic costs, particularly for persons coming from religious

1

traditions that have long offered its adherents a total worldview, such as Orthodox Judaism and Roman Catholicism. What happens to us, Cuddihy wonders, when "we internalize the crisscrossed web of organic solidarity that constitutes the modernizing world?"[2] He argues that the conflicts themselves do not disappear; instead, they become internalized. Our psyches become compartmentalized and fractured. The price that each of us pays for civil peace, he claims, is to forfeit a coherent and seamless sense of our own identity that is integrated across the various spheres of our social lives. In his view, the personal statement, "I happen to be Protestant [or Catholic or Jewish]" conveys the slogan of the successful practitioners of crisscross. Such persons treat religion as part of their identity, but only as one part. Without denying their religious commitments, civil Americans do not place too much emphasis on them.

Cuddihy was writing in the mid-1970s, at what was arguably the high point of the influence of crisscross in American life. The smile he used to symbolize the civilizing operations of crisscross was the smile of President Jimmy Carter, a devout Baptist personally opposed to abortion who nonetheless won the nation's elected highest office as a prochoice Democrat in 1976. Although he sometimes suggests that the civilizing crisscross is an irreversible phenomenon in American life, Cuddihy actually knew better, as do we—Jimmy Carter could never be elected president in the twenty-first century.

In fact, the appeal of crisscross in the American political context appears to be cyclical. A few short years after Jimmy Carter's election, Ronald Reagan was swept to power by a newly energized conservative majority, which included Evangelical Protestants determined to resist socially liberal developments in the name of the distinctive claims of their faith. In the early 1990s, the country elected Bill Clinton to the presidency, who put his Southern Baptist upbringing in one compartment while governing the country according to the tenets of the policy analysis he first encountered as a Rhodes Scholar and student at Yale Law School. After eight years of the Clinton administration, the country installed George W. Bush in the White House, in part because of a well-coordinated appeal to Evangelical Protestants and Roman Catholics, who together constituted about one-half the nation's population. Eight years of Bush's mixture of religion and politics have yielded to eight years of Barak Obama's cerebral and largely secular style of governance.

There also seems to be a cyclical appeal to crisscross within religious communities. In the mid-twentieth century, it appeared that a liberal Judaism, which focused its identity on its political support for the State of Israel, was becoming dominant in the Jewish community. Emphasizing Israel's strategic importance to the United States along with its status as the only democracy in the Middle East, liberal Jews reconciled loyalty to the Jewish state with a fully American identity. In more recent years, however, the fastest-growing segment of the American Jewish population in recent years has been the ultra-Orthodox, many of whom not only set themselves apart from broader American culture but also deny the religious legitimacy of the state of Israel.

The Culture of Openness

The Roman Catholic community in the United States has witnessed a roughly analogous phenomenon. Cuddihy highlights the towering influence of the Jesuit priest John Courtney Murray on the Second Vatican Council and on the sensibilities of American Catholics. Murray helped to reconcile Catholic values and American values by drawing heavily upon the experience of religious pluralism in America to advocate for Vatican II's astounding endorsement of religious liberty in *Dignitatis Humanae*.[3] Murray both catalyzed and symbolized what I call "the culture of openness" in the Catholic Church in the United States, in which American Catholics abandoned their geographical and intellectual enclaves in order to become more fully integrated into American life. The election of John F. Kennedy in 1960 to the presidency had demonstrated that Catholics could also be fully American. The vindication of John Courtney Murray's view on religious liberty in 1965 confirmed that American values could also be fully Catholic.

The culture of openness is marked by an emphasis upon *aggiornamento*—a process of bringing the church up to date—as the dominant purpose of the Second Vatican Council.[4] Its key text was *Gaudium et spes* (1965), Vatican II's Pastoral Constitution on the church and the Modern World. Rather than emphasizing what sets the church apart from the broader culture, the culture of openness stresses commonalities, as the opening lines of *Gaudium et spes* proclaim: "The joys and the hopes, the griefs and the anxieties of the men of this age, especially those who are poor or in any way afflicted, these are the joys and hopes, the griefs and anxieties of the followers of Christ. Indeed, nothing genuinely human fails to raise an echo in their hearts."[5] Many of those whose sensibilities resonated with the culture of openness assumed that there would be a strong basis of cooperation among Catholics and a wide range of persons of goodwill, particularly on matters of social justice. This assumption was pragmatic as well as principled; the horrifying prospect of a nuclear holocaust made international cooperation a matter of the highest urgency. Moreover, *Gaudium et spes* set a moral and political agenda for protest and reform that many Catholics assumed could command wide acceptance: The Council Fathers condemned a wide range of practices as "infamies," ranging from "murder, genocide and abortion" to "prostitution, the selling of women and children, as well as disgraceful working conditions."[6] The culture of openness fostered optimism about the possibility of cooperation across religious, cultural, and national boundaries to combat these infamies.

The Culture of Identity

Whether Catholics knew it or not, the election of Pope John Paul II in 1978 marked the beginning of the end of the culture of openness. At least in the United States, however, the seeds of its demise had been sown over a decade earlier, when official church teaching and mainstream American values decisively began to diverge. In 1965, the Supreme Court of the United States had declared that married couples had a constitutional right to use contraception.[7] In 1966, the Pontifical Commission on Birth Control, whose members had been appointed by Pope Paul VI, issued a majority report concluding that the use of artificial birth control was not an intrinsically evil act. This report raised many hopes (and some fears) that the Catholic Church would "update" its teaching on contraception, just as it had on religious liberty. Those expectations were dashed, however, in 1968, when Paul VI formally rejected the findings of his own commission and reaffirmed the traditional Catholic moral prohibition against contraception.[8]

A discernable rift, therefore, had opened up between American values and Catholic values: the highest court in the country had deemed the use of contraception to be a constitutional right, while the highest authority in the church continued to maintain it was an intrinsically immoral act. That rift became a chasm in 1973, when the Supreme Court declared that women had a constitutionally protected right to choose abortion rather than carrying their pregnancies to term.[9] To many Catholics, including those who had supported a change in church teaching on contraception, the Supreme Court's decision announcing a broad and secure right to abortion was almost unthinkable.

The idea of a "right" to abortion was also unthinkable for Pope John Paul II. Adamantly opposed to contraception as well as abortion and euthanasia, Pope John Paul II urged the church to defend a "culture of life" against a secularized Western "culture of death" that denied the existence of absolute truth and devalued the vulnerable, particularly the very young, those afflicted with severe disabilities, and the very old.[10] Accordingly, younger people (and others) who identify themselves as "JP II Catholics" tended to stress the practices and beliefs that set Catholicism apart from contemporary American culture, not points of consonance. They emphasized the importance of a full-bodied, distinctively Catholic commitment that permeates and orders all aspects of one's life, including one's political activities. Rejecting compartmentalization, they prioritized the cultivation of religious integrity, whose elements were often defined in sharp contrast to the values of the secular, materialistic, culture.[11]

In my terms, these JP II Catholics participated in the "culture of identity," which strongly influenced the American bishops appointed by both Pope John Paul II and Pope Benedict XVI. They feared that adherents of the culture of openness risked losing important Catholic commitments by chasing the fads of secular society. They valued the distinctive patterns, practices, and moral beliefs found within the Catholic tradition, including some practices that fell into disuse after the Second Vatican Council, such as Eucharistic Adoration. Adherents of the culture of identity were inclined to approach the broader culture, and those spoke for it or governed it, with a great deal of suspicion. They tended to trust the magisterial pronouncements of John Paul II and Benedict XVI. In interpreting the Second Vatican Council, they tended to prioritize *resourcement*—the retrieval and renewal of the tradition on its own terms. At the same time, they often viewed any appeal to the sense of the faithful with suspicion, in part because they believed the faithful had been inadequately catechized in the tumultuous times of the post–Vatican II church. That does not, mean, however, that all adherents of the culture of identity totally withdrew from American politics. Some may have done so. Many others, however, prioritized political opposition to abortion and same-sex marriage and offered their support to the Republican Party in order to combat the "culture of death," which they associated with the Democrats.

The patterns may be shifting again. Several studies suggest that the emerging generation of "millennial" Americans are detaching themselves from organized religion, in significant part because they are repelled by the militant social conservatism of its most vocal proponents.[12] They are appalled by its seeming hostility to equal rights for women, as well as gays and lesbians. They are disheartened by the failure of many religious leaders to attend to emerging issues of global import such as climate change. This generation, in other words, has become wary of totalizing religious worldviews, because of the harm believers inflict upon others in the name of those worldviews.

Is there a way to escape these cyclical reversals of approach to religion and culture? Is there a way forward for religious believers, in other words, that involves neither capitulating to the call to assimilate, nor reacting against that call by attempting to build a complete religious world in distinction, defiance, or even in outright opposition to the broader culture? This seems to me to be an important question for adherents of religious traditions to ask, for two reasons.

First, it is all too easy for the culture of openness to shade into uncritical assimilation of the broader social context, and for the culture of identity to shift into adamant resistance to that context. Both uncritical assimilation and adamant resistance, therefore, take their cues from the broader culture; the only difference is the tenor of their response. Uncritical assimilation is defined by what attracts it, while adamant resistance is defined by what repels it. Moreover, the cyclical appearances of the two stances suggest that each reacts to the excesses of the other, as much as to the surrounding culture.

Second, while the appearances may be cyclical, the orbits that they trace seem to be degrading toward loss of religious belief. The number of Roman Catholics in the United States dropped in the two decades following the Second Vatican Council (1965–1985), arguably a period of assimilation. Yet the subsequent two decades, marked by Pope John Paul II's efforts to recover a distinct sense of Catholic identity, did not stem the tide. A rough measure of the strength of the Catholic community is the number of its members who choose to marry within the church. That number has continued to fall precipitously.[13]

Toward a Culture of Engagement

In my view, a different approach to the problem of religious identity in American culture needs to be forged. While I am deeply indebted to Cuddihy, I would like to offer another, more positive interpretation of the experience of American "crisscross." I would like to suggest that it can be viewed as an intricate mode of interaction, as in a tapestry. Crisscross can bring the threads of different traditions, in different spheres of discussion, into proximity. In some cases, they can add illuminating nuance, depth, and color to each other. In other cases, the threads from one tradition can unsettle the gaze of the observer who is looking upon another conversation by highlighting problematic premises or placing unanticipated problems in bold relief. I call this sort of interaction and interrelation the "culture of engagement."

The process of engagement is rarely simple or unproblematic. The movement of ideas from one tradition to another does not run only in one direction. It is tempting, however, to assume that it does. On the one hand, some people who emphasize the need for religious traditions to accommodate themselves to the contemporary era tend to assume that all religious beliefs need to be resized and reshaped within the framework of the dominant culture. On the other hand, some of those who prioritize a holistic religious identity frequently suggest that their religious tradition rightly functions as the measure of American culture. While some identity-focused believers withdraw from the public square in order to preserve the integrity of their religious lives, others attempt to remake it to fit the tenets of their faith.[14]

In my judgment, however, critical conversations between religious traditions and the broader culture inevitably go both ways, and run in both directions. What would a helpful conversation look like between America's secular, liberal democratic tradition and a religious tradition like Roman Catholicism, with its roots in premodernity? What is necessary in order to make this conversation fruitful? In addressing these questions, I think the work of the philosopher Alasdair MacIntyre can be very helpful. This suggestion may appear odd to some

readers, because MacIntyre's thought has been most vocally appro-
priated by those who emphasize the importance of maintaining a distinct religious identity over and against the surrounding culture. They
have seized with great enthusiasm upon the famous last paragraph
of *After Virtue*, in which MacIntyre suggests that religious believers
would do well to cultivate new forms of monastic communities.[15] Living immured from the broader liberal culture, they hope to nurture
a whole, seamless identity shaped by their religious tradition and un-
tainted by the incoherence of life in modern liberal democracies such
as the United States. In Cuddihy's terms, they would try to cope with
modern American life by refusing to undergo its characteristic ordeal
of civility, by opting out of the crisscross.[16]

MacIntyre's thought, however, is far from reducible to the provoca-
tive last paragraph of *After Virtue*. In *Whose Justice? Which Rationality?*, MacIntyre does the hard work of showing how specific moral
traditions are constituted, develop, and sometimes even decay. He
also shows how different moral and cultural traditions might encounter one another, challenge one another, contribute to one another, and
correct one another.[17] Most strikingly, he contends that negotiating
the claims posed by rival traditions requires a kind of bilingual skill.
Persons who can speak two languages can translate back and forth
between the two. Moreover, and perhaps more importantly, they
know which concepts and expressions escape translation. So too with
people who move back and forth between moral traditions. The role
model for Christians inspired by *Whose Justice? Which Rationality?* is
neither a culture warrior nor a monk, but rather a diplomat.

I think MacIntyre's idea of translation is true to the intellectual
history of the West. Like languages, moral traditions are not imper-
meable. Their adherents regularly pick up expressions, ideas, and intellectual frameworks from other contexts, and revise and refurbish
them to meet their current needs. Thomas Aquinas, for example,
famously borrowed from both Greek and Muslim philosophy to reframe, refurbish, and re-present Catholic Christian thought. Intellectual historians of late antiquity have demonstrated how both Jewish
and Christian thinkers adapted Greek and Roman concepts in order
to present and advance their own traditions. Scripture scholars have
shown how key stories in the Hebrew Bible/Old Testament have

significant points of consonance with the literature of other peoples in the Ancient Near East.

It is impossible, I think, to insulate a religious tradition from the intellectual and experiential currents of the culture in which believers are living out their faith commitments. What is possible, I believe, is to reflect critically and constructively upon the terms of the engagement. But there is no neutral, objective point from which to analyze and orchestrate the proper relationship of religious traditions and cultural contexts. Cultural and religious critics cannot escape the fact that we are participants as well as observers in the communities to which we belong. Most American Catholics participate not only in their religious tradition, but also in the secular, liberal, democratic rights-based tradition that currently dominates American political life. We cannot stand completely outside either our American identity or our Roman Catholic identity. The best we can do is to achieve some critical distance in order to evaluate the strengths and weaknesses of both identities. My goal in the pages that follow is to do just that.

Pope Francis and the Culture of Encounter

Advocates of the culture of engagement have taken great encouragement from both the words and example of Pope Francis. Since his election to the papacy in April 2013, Francis has manifested a willingness to interact with people in a manner that is not hemmed in by the formalities of church protocol. He has given a wide range of interviews and extemporaneous talks that make plain his affection and concern for human beings in a wide range of situations, even those that are morally compromised according to official church teaching. His paramount concern is not to preserve the church's boundaries in pristine integrity, but to reach out to encounter human beings made by God in Christ's image. The importance of personal "encounter," particularly encountering those who are different and who are suffering is a key theme of his papacy. Moreover, Francis's actions speak louder than his words. For example, he has regularly ignored the liturgical rules that say that Holy Thursday's ritual foot-washing ceremony should be performed by the pope only on Catholic men, preferably priests. Instead, the world watched as Pope Francis visited Rome's main prison on Holy Thursday, bending over in order to wash the feet of both male and female prisoners, some of whom were Muslim.[18]

Pope Francis's more official writings leave no doubt that his actions are not merely a matter of personal taste, but rather spring from a deep vision of the purpose and promise of the Catholic Church. One image from his apostolic exhortation, *Evangelii gaudium* (*The Joy of the Gospel*) strikes me as particularly important. He imagines the contemporary church as doing its work in the messy vitality of a cosmopolitan city (such as Buenos Aires), rather than in the serenity of a rural village. Cities are cacophonous but alive, dangerous but energizing; they create common interests by attracting very diverse persons to live in a common space. Francis writes: "What is called for is an evangelization capable of shedding light on these new ways of relating to God, to others and to the world around us, and inspiring essential values. It must reach the places where new narratives and paradigms are being formed, bringing the word of Jesus to the inmost soul of our cities."[19]

Francis is not, of course, advocating that the church simply turn to the secular world for its marching orders. He is not attempting to revivify the culture of openness. He is acutely aware, for example, of the dangers of a "throwaway" culture, especially for the poor and vulnerable.[20] So he situates his concern for the unborn in the context of a broader advocacy for those whom a globalized capitalism considers disposable. At the same time, it does seem that he is reacting against the excesses of the culture of identity that cropped up under his two predecessors. He pointedly observes: "In some people we see an ostentatious preoccupation for the liturgy, for doctrine and for the Church's prestige, but without any concern that the Gospel have a real impact on God's faithful people and the concrete needs of the present time. In this way, the life of the Church turns into a museum piece or something which is the property of a select few."[21]

Pope Francis does not think the church must isolate itself in a defensive posture in order to maintain its integrity. The church, after all, is the body of Christ, who did no such thing. He bluntly asserts: "I prefer a Church which is bruised, hurting and dirty because it has been out on the streets, rather than a Church which is unhealthy from being confined and from clinging to its own security."[22] His words amount,

I think, to a papal blessing—or at least papal encouragement—for the culture of engagement.

A Culture of Engagement on Same-Sex Marriage?

On June 26, 2015, a closely divided Supreme Court handed down *Obergefell v. Hodges*,[23] which legalized same-sex marriage throughout the United States. Writing for the five-justice majority, Justice Anthony Kennedy held that the Fourteenth Amendment to the Constitution prohibited states from limiting the benefits and privileges of marriage to opposite-sex couples. The right to marry, wrote Kennedy, is a fundamental right protected by the Due Process Clause of the Fourteenth Amendment because "the right to personal choice regarding marriage is inherent in the concept of individual autonomy."[24] Depriving same-sex couples of that right also violates the Fourteenth Amendment's Equal Protection Clause. "Especially against a long history of disapproval of their relationships, this denial to same-sex couples of the right to marry works a grave and continuing harm. The imposition of this disability on gays and lesbians serves to disrespect and subordinate them."[25]

Obergefell can be challenged on a number of fronts. The most obvious critique has to do with the content of the decision: those who do not think that extending marriage to same-sex couples is socially beneficial will find the decision conferring constitutional protection upon such relationships to be thoroughly mistaken. Others will have legal or procedural objections to the jurisprudential means used, even if they accept or applaud the end result. For example, many jurists believe that development of a new moral consensus on socially controversial issues is a task that belongs to the people themselves, not to unelected judges. In his dissenting opinion, Chief Justice John Roberts strongly hinted that he supported the extension of the institution of marriage to same-sex couples. At the same time, he expressed deep reservations about whether that extension is mandated by the Constitution itself. Roberts does not think that judges appointed for life should take it upon themselves to elaborate new substantive constitutional rights, which they then use to strike down democratically enacted laws. Haunting Roberts and others opposed to the jurisprudential method used in the *Obergefell* majority opinion is *Roe v. Wade* (1973), which found a right to abortion in the "penumbras" of the Constitution. *Roe* did not settle the issue, but rather inflamed the culture wars that have been raging for the past forty years.

The various objections to *Obergefell* notwithstanding, it is clear that same-sex marriage is now the law of the land. Moreover, commitment to securing equal rights for gays and lesbians is growing stronger in the American population, especially among younger people. At the same time, some religious traditions, including the Roman Catholic tradition, remain officially and adamantly opposed to extending the institution of marriage to same-sex couples. Even within such traditions, however, a range of reactions to *Obergefell* can be discerned. For example, Joseph Kurtz, the Archbishop of Louisville, Kentucky, and president of the United States Conference of Catholic Bishops, called the decision "a tragic error that harms the common good and most vulnerable among us."[26] Kurtz's approach seems to contemplate the formation of a new anti-same-sex marriage movement modeled on the anti-abortion movement: "Just as *Roe v. Wade* did not settle the question of abortion over forty years ago, *Obergefell v. Hodges* does not settle the question of marriage today. Neither decision is rooted in the truth, and as a result, both will eventually fail."

In contrast, Blase Cupich, the Archbishop of Chicago, was more about distinguishing the new secular understanding of marriage than opposing it. His statement was far less confrontational than Kurtz's. After reminding his readers that "the Catholic Church has an abiding concern for the dignity of gay persons," Cupich, who was appointed by Pope Francis, emphasized that the "Supreme Court's redefinition of civil marriage has no bearing on the Catholic Sacrament of Matrimony, in which the marriage of man and woman is a sign of the union of Christ and the Church."[27] Cupich's statement could be read as suggesting an amicable divorce, so to speak, between the nature and purposes of civil marriage, on the one hand, and those of Catholic marriage, on the other. Such an approach could provide the blueprint of a separate peace. While it does not suggest an ongoing cultural battle, it does not encourage ongoing interaction and engagement, either.

In my view, however, it is a mistake to segregate the Catholic understanding of marriage too sharply from the understanding operating in the broader civil society. The sacramental understanding of marriage has in fact developed alongside and in conversation with the shifting role the institution has played in changing secular society. St. Augustine famously specified that the goods of marriage included *fides*, *proles*, and *sacramentum*.[28] Over centuries, the good of *fides*, or faithfulness, has developed in the tradition from a rather narrow focus on sexual fidelity to encompass a life of mutual support and help between the spouses. The good of *proles*, or progeny, has similarly expanded over the centuries to include the education of children as well as their procreation.[29]

Is it possible to have a broad and wide-ranging conversation that includes advocates of same-sex marriage as well as advocates of traditional marriage about what the goods of *fides* and *proles* might look like in the twenty-first century? After all, opposite-sex couples and same-sex couples face many of the same challenges in maintaining a life-long commitment. For example, many couples in prosperous Westernized countries will spend nearly as many years in retirement together as they did actively raising children. In this later period of life, the harshest tests of faithfulness may not involve sexual temptation, but rather the temptation to demean, isolate, or abandon a partner with an increasingly compromised physical or mental state and increasingly complex and expensive medical needs.

Moreover, precisely because the years of active child-rearing do not consume most of the years of a modern couple's partnership, one can also reasonably ask what marital fruitfulness consists in after the children are raised. Can we, for example, identify a responsibility to serve as a surrogate "mother" or "father" to other young people in one's life, which can be viewed as a natural extension of marital fruitfulness? While the focus on natural law in the Catholic tradition has understandably meant that it has given much attention to biological parenthood, it is important to remember that a key model of that role and relationship in the New Testament is the Pauline notion of "adoption," which is heavily influenced by Roman law and custom. We tend to think of adoption as a process best designed to imitate the modern nuclear family, in which young infertile couples adopt babies or small children, frequently preferring those that can pass as their biological offspring. In Roman times, however, adoption was not a closed transaction, but rather an open social and familial arrangement that had its own value. Moreover, adults could even adopt other adults, a fact that is tacitly presupposed by Paul's claim that God views us in Jesus Christ no longer as slaves, but as adopted sons and daughters.[30]

What about the sacramental good of marriage? Here, I think, we can discover a potential for the Catholic tradition to critique *Obergefell* in a constructive way that challenges both same-sex and opposite-sex couples. The most morally troubling aspect of the opinion is its understanding of the nature and purpose of marriage itself. Kennedy's opinion in *Obergefell* portrays marriage in exaltedly individualist terms, as an institution primarily designed to secure the existential fulfilment of the two partners to the relationship. Yet marriage in the Christian tradition is not meant to be so completely inward-looking; it constitutes a relationship that also finds fruition in enriching the broader community. The late theologian Karl Rahner maintained that the purpose of the sacrament of marriage was not simply to improve the spiritual life of the recipients in isolation, but in so doing to orient them in love and service toward the needs of the broader community, particularly the least among us.[31] What, concretely, this communal orientation would require from married couples in our time and place is a question that might fruitfully be pondered by both same-sex and opposite-sex Christian couples who are open to thinking about their marriages in sacramental terms.

Is such a conversation among Christians who hold different views about same-sex marriage about *fides*, *proles*, and *sacramentum* in twenty-first-century first-world democracies possible? It depends. If the price of entry into such conversation is full agreement about the moral status of homosexual acts, then probably not. Yet if participants are allowed to prescind from that question in order to grapple with common challenges facing same-sex and opposite-sex couples, then conversational engagement may proceed in rich and unexpected ways.

The Contents of This Book

I am by training and long practice both an American law professor familiar with the normative commitments of a liberal democratic polity and a Christian ethicist working out of the Roman Catholic tradition. I have acquired, I think, fluency in both traditions, enabling me to move back and forth between them in the way that MacIntyre describes in *Whose Justice? Which Rationality?*. As MacIntyre would also say, however, participating in a normative tradition is not only a matter of academic study. It also requires living within its practices and institutions, as well as grappling with the specific challenges and questions it faces in a specific place and time.

Fortunately, both the American legal tradition and the Roman Catholic moral tradition have many resources for addressing vexing moral problems. Grounded in English common law, American law frequently develops its general normative principles through its consideration of particular cases. Those general normative principles develop over time, tested by and responsive to their effect on the lives of actual persons and communities. The Roman Catholic tradition of moral reflection, rooted for so long in the practice of sacramental confession, also takes the particular challenges of life very seriously. Despite their significant differences, both the American legal tradition and the Catholic moral tradition recognize that the merit of general rules and principles cannot be divorced from the way in which they handle particular situations.

The book's five parts reflect these commitments to the mutually informing relationship of general principles and particular situations. They deal with topics at the intersection of law, culture, and religious commitments in the United States of America in the early decades of the twenty-first century. I use particular questions to raise issues of broader concern. Part 1, "Law as a Teacher," grapples with the topic of whether and how law can function as a moral teacher in a pluralistic society. In addition to considering more general matters such as the role of empathy in judicial decision-making, I also look at specific questions confronting contemporary American legal practice, such as the changing nature of the institution of marriage, the legalization of assisted suicide in Montana, and the resort to torture by the US government in order to expose ongoing terrorist plots after the devastating events of September 11, 2001.

The second part, "Religious Liberty and Its Limits," offers commentary on an emerging and ongoing issue in American life. American law has long honored the right to free exercise of religion. Until recently, that right has been claimed by distinct and vulnerable religious minorities, such as the Amish. Now, however, large and powerful religious groups, such as Roman Catholics and evangelicals, are claiming the right to be exempt from generally applicable laws such as the contraception mandate in the regulations implementing the Affordable Care Act. Are such claims legitimate? Or do they constitute an unfair "second bite at the apple" for the losers in controversial political battles? It is not only political and moral conservatives who can claim their moral beliefs are motivated by religious commitments. If the losers in every morally fraught political battle can raise the stakes by invoking the First Amendment, what will happen to the rule of law? These are the questions that animate my reflections in Part 2.

Part 3, "Conversations about Culture," shifts the focus to broader American social life, which of course reflects and exerts pressure upon both the American legal system and the religious institutions situated in this country. A key theme is the polarization brought on by the culture wars, and a key goal is to resist the black-and-white framework that a culture war mentality produces. My resistance to the culture-war frame is prompted in part by an awareness of the historical and conceptual gaps between the Roman Catholic tradition and the American traditions.[32] From the time of the Puritans, American moral-political rhetoric has been dominated by a strong strand of prophetic indictment, which tends to draw sharp lines between the pure and the tainted, and the righteous and the damned. In contrast, dominant strands of the Catholic tradition have resisted such absolute divisions. Instead, they have long emphasized that it can be difficult to distinguish between the wheat and the tares, which will in any case grow together until the end of time. Consequently, I repeatedly suggest that it is important to draw careful distinctions, rather than to issue absolute indictments that absolutely block all forms of co-operation with fellow citizens with whom we disagree. This does not mean we cannot make moral judgments about personal or political actions or policies—far from it. It does mean, however, that making such judgments in a sound manner will require a nuanced assessment of the facts and circumstances of particular cases.

In Part 4, "Conversations about Belief," I turn to the discussions and controversies that have been taking place between and among American Catholics. Many of the particular issues considered lie at the intersection of Catholic polity, American culture, and civil law. Moreover, they illustrate the fact that challenging questions come from both directions. It was the outrage of the broader culture—Catholics and non-Catholics alike—about clergy sexual abuse and its cover-up that pressured the Catholic church in the United States to revise its policies. With the increasing acceptance of same-sex marriage in the United States, new conflicts have developed between civil laws and policies banning discrimination on the basis of sexual orientation, on the one hand, and strong civil commitment to the autonomy of religious institutions, on the other. These tensions in American law impinge upon discussions among Catholics in complicated ways. One group of Catholics, including most American bishops, continues to object to same-sex marriage as a betrayal of the natural purpose of the institution of marriage. Another group of Catholics believes that church teaching can and will develop on the question of homosexuality, just as it did previously on slavery and religious liberty. On this issue of same-sex marriage, as on so many others, it is not possible to assign neat and clearly delineated positions either to American culture or to the church. The crisscross is far more complicated, difficult, and finally, rich.

The final part, "Cases and Controversies," engages in what is sometimes called casuistry—a venerable practice in many religious traditions as well as in the secular law. At its core, casuistry involves close analysis of the moral issues raised by particular situations. Casuistry has been criticized, most famously by Blaise Pascal, as a technique for developing deceptive and self-serving justifications of wrongful practices. The pejorative understanding of casuistry is widespread; in fact, it is frequently included in the first definition offered in various dictionaries. Yet the practice of casuistry cannot be reduced to its abuses. At its best, casuistry can hold our principles and norms accountable to the messy details of our lives; it can test the soundness and probe the boundaries of our moral concepts. In cases involving competing values, it can help us clarify our priorities. Moreover, it is through casuistry that we extend our concepts to deal with situations we have not yet encountered or even imagined. In this part, I look at some hard cases involving conflicting values in American life. I explore, for example, whether there is a possibility of compromise on the increasingly (and improbably) controversial issue of contraception as part of a basic health care package. I try to show that even for philosophers and theologians who consider themselves "prolife," there are hard questions at the boundaries in deciding who counts as a human being. And I draw upon a horrific crime in Connecticut to test moral opposition to the death penalty.

Most of the chapters began life as columns or blog posts for *Commonweal*, a magazine whose "mission is to provide a forum for civil, reasoned debate on the interaction of faith with contemporary politics and culture." I have revised many of the columns to make them less time-specific, as well as to provide more background or context when necessary. Chapters that began life as blog posts have been significantly reworked. Edited by lay Catholics since its founding in 1924, *Commonweal* is read not only by Catholics, but also by persons from many other faith traditions, as well as by those who profess no religious belief. Its mission of fostering open-ended debate and dialogue on a host of issues is consistent with my own beliefs about the importance of civil discourse about law, morality, and culture. *Commonweal's* refusal to narrow its focus to political issues is also congenial, because it is consistent with MacIntyre's insight that moral reasoning takes place within full-bodied traditions that include the practices of art, music, and literature, as well as academic reasoning about right and wrong.

The opportunity to write on a regular basis for *Commonweal* has allowed me to refine my views on the role of religious discourse in the public square, and the relevance of religious traditions to an increasingly secular, pluralist liberal democracy. The periodic nature of the columns has encouraged me to relate general principles to topical questions. As anyone familiar with academic writing knows, it can be tempting for professors to wrap the inconsistencies and uncertainties in their thought in a fog of verbiage. By helping me to resist this temptation, the editors of *Commonweal* have prompted me to develop my thinking in a clearer and more rigorous way. I hope all these fruits of my long association with *Commonweal* can be found in the forthcoming pages, and that this volume invites, encourages, and contributes to future conversations at the intersection of faith, law, politics and culture.

Notes

1. John Murray Cuddihy, *No Offense: Civil Religion and Protestant Taste* (New York: Seabury Press, 1978).
2. Ibid., 185.
3. Vatican II, *Dignitatis humanae* (1965). For more details, see, e.g., Barry Hudock, *Struggle, Condemnation, Vindication: John Courtney Murray's Journey toward Vatican II* (Collegeville, MN: Liturgical Press, 2015).

4. The term came from a speech that Pope John XXIII gave on January 25, 1959; the term was used in reference to the "updating" of canon law. The speech is available in Italian at http://w2.vatican.va/content/john-xxiii/it/speeches/1959/documents /hf_j-xxiii_spe_19590125_annuncio.html.

5. Vatican II, *Gaudium et spes* (1965).

6. Ibid., para. 27.

7. *Griswold v. Connecticut*, 381 U.S. 479 (1965)

8. Pope Paul VI, *Humanae vitae* (1968).

9. *Roe v. Wade*, 410 U.S. 113 (1973).

10. John Paul II, *Evangelium vitae* (1995).

11. See, e.g., Colleen Carroll Campbell, *The New Faithful: Why Young Adults Are Embracing Christian Orthodoxy* (Chicago, IL: Loyola Press, 2002). The book does not represent an unbiased sociological assessment of the religious beliefs of a particular age cohort, but instead articulates the vision of a distinct subgroup within the Catholic Church.

12. See, e.g., Pew Research: Religion & Public Life Project, "Religion among the Millennials," February 17, 2010. Available at http://www.pewforum.org/2010/02/17 /religion-among-the-millennials/. See also Pew Research: Religion and Public Life Project, "America's Changing Religious Landscape: Christians Decline Sharply as Share of Population; Unaffiliated and Other Faiths Continue to Grow," May 12, 2015. Available at http://www.pewforum.org/2015/05/12/americas-changing -religious -landscape/.

13. According to statistics drawn from the Official Catholic Directory in the United States, there were 352,458 Catholic "marriages in previous year" reported in 1965, 261,626 reported in the year 2000, and 154,450 reported in 2014. See CARA, "Frequently Requested Church Statistics," http://cara.georgetown.edu /CARAServices/requestedchurchstats.html. The problem is not unique to the United States. See, e.g., David V. Barrett, "New Figures Show Stark Decline in Catholic Baptisms, Ordinations, and Marriages," *Catholic Herald*, May 17, 2013. Available at http://www.catholicherald.co.uk/news/2013/05/17/new-figures-show -stark-decline-in-catholic-baptism-ordinations-and-marriages/.

14. While many are politically conservative, identity-focused Catholics can be found on both ends of the political spectrum. Politically progressive Catholics such as Michael Sean Winters and John Carr have, on occasion, wistfully noted that no party fully accords with Catholic teaching, and encourage fellow believers to assess the whole sweep of American policy in terms of current magisterial teaching. See, e.g., Michael Sean Winters, "Catholics Need to Risk Being Political Party Insurgents," *National Catholic Reporter*, May 21, 2014. See NPR, "Keeping the Faith in the Catholic Church," interview with John Carr, February 15, 2013, http://www.npr.org/2013/02/15/172102690/keeping-the-faith-in-the-catholic -church.

15. "This time however the barbarians are not waiting beyond the frontiers; they have already been governing us for quite some time. And it is our lack of consciousness of this that constitutes part of our predicament. We are waiting

not for a Godot, but for another—doubtless very different—St. Benedict." Alasdair MacIntyre, *After Virtue: A Study in Moral Theory*, 3rd ed. (Notre Dame, IN: University of Notre Dame Press, 2007). Archbishop Chaput commends this passage in "Law and Morality in Public Discourse: How Christians Can Rebuild Our Culture," *Public Discourse*, August 7, 2014. Available at http://www.thepublicdiscourse.com/2014/08/13612/.

16. See John Murray Cuddihy, *The Ordeal of Civility: Freud, Marx, Lévi-Strauss and the Jewish Struggle with Modernity*, 2nd ed. (Boston: Beacon Press, 1987).

17. Alasdair MacIntyre, *Whose Justice? Which Rationality?* (Notre Dame, IN: University of Notre Dame Press, 1988).

18. Associated Press, "Pope Francis Washes Feet of Prisoners, Baby during Holy Week Ceremony," Daily News, April 4, 2015. Available at http://www.nydailynews.com/news/world/pope-francis-washes-feet-prisoners-baby-holy-week-article-1.2173180.

19. Pope Francis, *Evangelii gaudium* (2013), para. 74.

20. Ibid., para. 53.

21. Ibid., para. 95.

22. Ibid., para. 49.

23. *Obergefell v. Hodges*, 576 U.S. ___, 135 S. Ct. 2584 (2015).

24. *Obergefell*, 135 S. Ct. at 2599.

25. *Obergefell*, 135 S. Ct. at 2604.

26. United States Conference of Catholic Bishops, "Supreme Court Decision on Marriage a 'Tragic Error' Says President of Catholic Bishops' Conference," June 26, 2015, available at http://www.usccb.org/news/2015/15-103.cfm.

27. Archdiocese of Chicago, Statement of Archbishop Blase J. Cupich, Archbishop of Chicago, June 28, 2015, available at http://www.archchicago.org/news_releases/news_2015/stmnt_150628.html.

28. St. Augustine, *The Literal Meaning of Genesis*, Bk IX, chap. 7.

29. See, for example, Pope Paul VI, *Humanae Vitae* (1968).

30. See, generally, St. Paul's Letters to the Galatians and the Romans.

31. Karl Rahner, "Marriage as a Sacrament." In Karl Rahner, *Theological Investigations*, vol. 10, trans. David Bourke (New York: Herder and Herder, 1973), 199–221. Thanks to David Hollenbach, SJ, for bringing this point to my attention.

32. I address these questions in more detail in *Prophecy without Contempt: Religious Discourse in the Public Square* (Cambridge, MA: Harvard University Press, 2016).

Part 1

Law as a Teacher

This part explores the purpose and function of law in a pluralistic society. In the United States, we take the rule of law very seriously; in fact, most of our most acerbic debates over the years have involved questions of what the law should require or prohibit in order to promote the overall good of the community. These are complicated questions, because they involve a difficult mixture of morality and pragmatism. The law functions by regulating actions in an immediate way, by attaching penalties (e.g., prison time) or rewards (e.g., tax breaks) to certain kinds of activities. It also functions, however, in a less immediate and less direct way, by encouraging the citizenry to view the actions it regulates in a certain moral light. Law, in other words, has an important pedagogical function.[1] It shapes our political and moral values, including our response to other human beings.

We cannot forget, for example, the terrible regime of "Jim Crow" laws, which imposed a harsh regime of segregation and degradation upon African-Americans in the South for a century after the Civil War. As civil rights activists such as Martin Luther King, Jr. well understood, the corrosive effect of those laws extended beyond their actual requirements and prohibitions. The values propelling the Jim Crow regime wormed their way into the hearts and minds of the citizenry, not only encouraging Caucasians to view themselves as superior to their African-American neighbors, but also inculcating a sense of inferiority and helplessness in African-Americans themselves. As historians of the Civil Rights movement have pointed out, it was the black churches that enabled African-Americans in the South to reclaim their sense of authority, agency, and integrity. This experience, in turn, empowered many people to overturn Jim Crow and secure the passage of the Civil Rights Acts.

Why not take the experience of the Civil Rights Movement as a stellar example supporting the position that civil law should always correspond as closely as possible with true moral judgments? Unfortunately, the question is far more complicated, as another example from America's past illustrates. Alcoholism was a pressing social problem in the late nineteenth and early twentieth centuries, particularly in cities teeming with immigrants. Alcohol exacerbated poverty, as breadwinners often spent their paltry salaries on liquor rather than their struggling families. Alcohol sparked domestic violence, as inebriated men released their anger and frustration upon their wives and children. Social reformers, therefore, had good reason to think that banning alcohol would improve social welfare. The influence of temperance groups reached its zenith in 1919, when Congress ratified the Eighteenth Amendment to the Constitution, which prohibited the manufacture, sale, or transportation of intoxicating liquor within the United States and its territories. While the law was enforced in some areas of the country, such as the South, it was defied and circumvented in others, such as the Northeast. Large quantities of alcohol were smuggled into the country, as a black market was created and maintained by organized crime. No matter what its moral merits were, in the end, Prohibition failed for two reasons: it was practically unworkable, and it lacked the moral support of a significant number of Americans, who did not think that consumption of alcohol was always wrong. Increasingly unpopular as the country entered the Great Depression, Prohibition was repealed by the Twenty-First Amendment in 1933.

Quoting the fifth-century Isidore of Seville (d. 636), St. Thomas Aquinas (d.1274) neatly encapsulated the several qualities that sound law must demonstrate: "Law shall be virtuous, just, possible to nature, according to the custom of the country, suitable to place and time, necessary, useful; clearly expressed, lest by its obscurity it lead to misunderstanding; framed for no private benefit, but for the common good."[2] While it is important for law to accord with virtue and justice, it is equally essential for it to be "possible to nature" and "according to the custom of the country." Otherwise, as the lessons of Prohibition demonstrate, a widespread backlash may undermine not only the particular law in question, but commitment to the rule of law itself. Law, as Aquinas himself recognized, can lead persons to moral virtue only gradually.

In more recent times, Pope Francis has recognized the need to balance the pedagogical ideals of the law with sensitivity to the actual situation of the people that the law purports to govern. Law, he recognizes, is not an end in itself. Taking the law that governed the ancient Hebrews as an example, he criticized the perennial temptation among the legal scholars to see the law they study as a perfect, closed system. Instead, Pope Francis views law in a more pragmatic and flexible manner, rather like a map for a long trip that will undoubtedly result in unexpected surprises and even setbacks. He observed that the scholars of the Jewish law "had forgotten that they were a people on a journey. And when one is on a journey one always finds new things, things one does not know." The law, like the journey, is not an end in itself. It is a path, "a pedagogy," toward "the definitive manifestation of the Lord."[3] Good lawmakers, whether they are dealing with religious or secular matters, need to keep the ultimate purpose of the law in mind. At the same time, they need to remain flexible about its implementation in order best to achieve that purpose.

The chapters in this part attempt to grapple with the tensions between the pedagogical and pragmatic qualities of law across a range of contemporary topics with both religious and secular significance, including abortion, assisted suicide, immigration policy, the death penalty, and torture. An implicit topic running throughout the chapters is a challenge to the pedagogical function of law that Aquinas was never forced to face: the significant and growing moral pluralism that characterizes our liberal democracy. This problem is compounded by the fact that our federal government is limited; plenary power to work out the details of day-to-day life remains in the states. So, for example, until the recent Supreme Court decision giving constitutional protection to same-sex marriage, some states permitted the practice while others did not. Some states practice the death penalty while others have removed it from the available list of punishments. How do we decide which policy variations are permissible among the several states, and which must be rejected, like slavery and segregation, as lethal threats to our common commitment to human dignity? As the following chapters illustrate, this is a question that admits of no easy resolution.

Notes

1. I discuss the nature and limits of the pedagogical function of law at more length in *Law's Virtues: Fostering Autonomy and Solidarity in American Society* (Washington, DC: Georgetown University Press, 2012).

2. Isidore of Seville, Etymologies, v., 21, quoted in Thomas Aquinas, *Summa Theologica*, I-II, q. 95, art. 3, ob. 1.

3. Pope Francis, "The God of Surprises," Morning Meditation in the Chapel of Domus Sanctae Marthae, October 13, 2014, available at http://w2.vatican.va/con tent/francesco/en/cotidie/2014/documents/papa-francesco-cotidie_20141013 _the-god-of-surprises.html.

Rules Are Not Enough
Why Judges Need Empathy

During the first year of his presidency, Barack Obama said he judged "empathy" to be a desirable quality in a Supreme Court appointee. He set off a discussion that was as confused as it was contentious. But it raised an important and enduring question: What exactly is "empathy," and how does it relate to the task of a judge?

Obama himself described it as a quality that allows judges to take into consideration the concrete effects of their rulings, especially on ordinary people. He said in an interview that he "will seek someone who understands that justice isn't about some abstract legal theory or footnote in a case book. It is also about how our laws affect the daily realities of people's lives—whether they can make a living and care for their families; whether they feel safe in their homes and welcome in their own nation."

Obama's critics worried that "empathy" is not merely undesirable, but inconsistent with the fundamental obligations of a judge. Republican Senator Orrin Hatch feared it is a code word for judicial "activism," a potent political issue, if a notoriously elusive concept. In an opinion piece in the *Washington Times*, Wendy Long argued that empathy was inconsistent with impartiality. She truculently accused Obama of being "the first president in American history to make lawlessness an explicit standard for Supreme Court justices."

Despite appearances, this debate is not simply a partisan skirmish. It involves important and enduring questions about what it means to be a good judge. Jurist and Catholic moralist John Noonan tackled the question head-on in *Persons and Masks of the Law: Cardozo, Holmes, Jefferson, and Wythe as Makers of Masks.*

Noonan argues that at the heart of the legal system are two equally essential components: rules and persons. We all know the importance of rules—they are impersonal, they are impartial, they are framed with a concern for the larger good of the whole community. Neglecting the claims made by rules produces judicial "monsters" who strangle justice with bribery, arbitrariness, or bias. As Noonan notes, the Book of Deuteronomy describes God as a judge who "regardeth not persons nor taketh rewards." A good judge must have due regard for the rules.

But rules are not enough. "There is no reason to suppose that justice is the only virtue required of a lawyer, legislator, or judge," Noonan writes. "If [judges] are not to cease to be human, they must cultivate the other virtues of humanity." Without these other virtues, the application of rules can become "merciless and inhuman." Playing on the dual meaning of the Latin word *persona* as both "person" and "mask," Noonan argues that rules can become masks that conceal the human faces—and human needs—of the persons to whom they apply. A judge can hide behind rules to escape responsibility for the harm he or she is causing to other human beings.

In my favorite chapter in the book, Noonan examines the persons and rules behind the most famous case in American tort law, *Palsgraf v. Long Island Railroad* (1928). Helen Palsgraf, a middle-aged custodian taking her two daughters to the beach on a hot summer day, was injured in a freak accident on a train platform. She sued the railroad for negligence, winning $6,000 (a sum equal to fourteen times her annual income) in damages in a jury trial. Reversing the verdict on appeal, the eminent judge Benjamin Cardozo took the money away from her. He articulated a rule under which the railroad was not negligent, because it could not have reasonably foreseen the harm to Palsgraf. Noonan wonders why Cardozo thought it was preferable to announce a rule that makes a single unlucky passenger bear the entire loss from an accident instead of assigning it to the railroad, which could distribute the cost of compensating the injured person among all passengers by slightly raising ticket prices. Noonan reserves his greatest censure, however, for Cardozo's decision to impose the costs of the litigation on Palsgraf—costs that equaled an entire year of her income. In principle, imposing the costs of litigation on a plaintiff or defendant was done at the discretion of a judge. In practice, costs were routinely imposed on the losing party. By mechanically following that rule, Cardozo completely masked the real circumstances of Helen Palsgraf's life. Perversely, the penalty imposed on Palsgraf for seeking justice through the courts was to deprive her, a single mother, of the ability to support her children.

Judges must pay attention to both rules and persons. Needless to say, no rule can tell us how the balance should be struck in a particular case. The decision must be made by judges who are not only committed to the rule of law, but who also have the imaginative capacity to identify with the parties before them when interpreting and applying the rules. One source of that capacity is direct personal experience. Still, no one judge can have every relevant experience. All judges, however, can develop empathy. And in telling the story of Helen Palsgraf, Judge Noonan makes a good case for why they should.

Sources

Long, Wendy. "Opening of a Sorry Chapter." *Washington Times*, May 4, 2009.

Noonan, John T., Jr. *Persons and Masks of the Law: Cardozo, Holmes, Jefferson, and Wythe as Makers of Masks.* 2nd ed. Berkeley, CA: University of California Press, 2002.

Palsgraf v. Long Island Railroad Co., 248 N.Y. 339 (1928).

Teacher or Remedy
What Is the Law for?

Many clashes about law and public policy reflect not deep, principled divisions about moral values, but different ways of prioritizing two purposes of the law: its pedagogical function, which encourages people to do good and avoid evil, and its remedial function, which tries to clean up the mess when people fail to do so.

Watts v. Watts, a 1987 Wisconsin Supreme Court case I teach to my first-year law students, nicely illustrates this tension. Sue Ann and James Watts lived together for twelve years and had two children. Although Sue Ann took James's last name and the two filed joint tax returns and maintained joint bank accounts, they never legally married. Yet he listed her as his wife on his medical- and life-insurance policies; and, in addition to her duties as a homemaker, she spent about twenty-five hours a week helping him get his landscaping business off the ground. The business flourished, and by the time the couple separated in December 1981, it was worth well over a million dollars.

Unfortunately for Sue Ann, most of the assets were in James's name—and after the couple split up, he refused to share the wealth. So she sued him. Arguing that the two had established something "tantamount to a marital family except for a legal marriage," she maintained she was entitled to the same division of property that would follow a legal divorce in Wisconsin: an equal portion of the assets accumulated during the relationship.

Needless to say, James rejected her claim. Because the two weren't legally married, he argued, they couldn't be divorced under the law. Emerging as a passionate defender of the institution of marriage, he maintained that granting Sue Ann's request for division of property in accordance with Wisconsin's marriage law would subvert the intention of the legislature. Furthermore—implying that his relationship with Sue Ann had in fact been immoral—he argued that for the court to award recovery to her under any *other* legal theory, such as contract or restitution, would violate public policy.

Year after year, *Watts v. Watts* generates a lot of heat among my students. Those who embrace the pedagogical function of the law don't want to award Sue Ann any money. In their view, when the legislature enacted marriage and divorce laws, it clearly signaled that legal marriage is preferable for couples, their children, and society at large. Making an example of Sue Ann Watts, however sad for her personally, might deter countless other women from cohabiting without a wedding ring—in the long run, a better outcome for society as a whole. And so we need to be cruel to be kind.

In contrast, students who favor law's remedial function want to fix the damage created when the Watts split up. To do that by denying Sue Ann her share of the couple's assets, they believe, is deeply unfair. After all, James was no less guilty of flouting Wisconsin's public policy on marriage than she was—so why should her missteps cost her everything, while his bring a huge windfall? Both parties voluntarily held themselves out as a legally married couple for many years; doing justice requires treating them as a legally divorced couple, even if they never did have a marriage certificate.

In its actual ruling, the Wisconsin Supreme Court attempted to split the difference, gesturing at both pedagogy and remedy. While the court did not allow recovery under the state's marriage and divorce laws, it did allow Sue Ann to sue both for recovery under contract law (claiming she and James had an agreement to share property acquired in the relationship), and for restitution (claiming he needed to reimburse her for the services she rendered his business). Upon rehearing by the lower court, the jury awarded Sue Ann a sum nowhere near equal to half of James's assets. Her years with him were acknowledged—but only in her function as housekeeper and bookkeeper, not as a life partner who provided love and support.

Clashes about what to do with the Watts can be passionate. We can all agree that legal marriage, with its protections and guarantees, should be encouraged and that James Watts ought not to benefit at Sue Ann's expense. Reasonable people can differ about how the law ought to prioritize those insights in particular, and the primary function of law in general. When courts try to reach a compromise between such contending views and interests, the result can be murky—rather like marriage itself.

Source

Watts v. Watts, 137 Wisc.2d 506 (1987).

3

Letter versus Spirit
Why the Constitution Needs Interpreting

When discussing Supreme Court nominees, Republican presidential candidates such as George W. Bush have long repeated the mantra: they want judges, who "will strictly apply the Constitution and laws, not legislate from the bench." They think that Associate Supreme Court Justice Antonin Scalia's textualist approach should be the standard. Yet their mantra sets up a false dichotomy. Good judges do far more than apply the law; they also interpret it, that is, they give a specific meaning to a general legal term or phrase in the context of deciding a case. In so doing, they're not "legislating from the bench"—they're simply doing their job as judges. The real question isn't whether a Supreme Court justice will interpret the Constitution; it is impossible to avoid doing so. The real question is how a justice will approach the task of constitutional interpretation.

For many people, the right approach is defined solely in terms of the outcome. If the main focus is getting rid of *Roe v. Wade*, one might argue as follows: in interpreting the Constitution, a justice should be bound by the text of the document and the intentions of the text's framers. The Constitution does not mention, or explicitly protect, a right to privacy, let alone a right to abortion. Furthermore, the framers of the Constitution, and of the relevant constitutional amendments, certainly did not mean to legalize abortion. In fact, in nineteenth-century America, the practice of abortion violated the statutory or the common law of most states. Consequently, in articulating a constitutional right to privacy which includes a right to abortion, the *Roe* majority was engaged in an act of "raw judicial power."

If you only care about prolife issues, then this approach to constitutional interpretation works just fine. If you think other issues are important too, you immediately run into difficulties. Consider racial segregation in public schools. Is it unconstitutional? The key text is

31

the Fourteenth Amendment to the Constitution, which provides that no state shall "deny to any person within its jurisdiction the equal protection of the laws." Bush's mantra notwithstanding, we can't simply "apply" the law. Interpretation is required. What counts as "equal protection"?

In 1896, in *Plessy v. Ferguson*, the Supreme Court held that "separate but equal" facilities, especially in the school system, do not run afoul of the Constitution. The argument, like the anti-*Roe* argument above, was based on the text of the document and the intent of the framers. According to the *Plessy* majority:

> The object of the [Fourteenth] Amendment was undoubtedly to enforce the absolute equality of the two races before the law, but in the nature of things it could not have been intended to abolish distinctions based upon color, or to enforce social, as distinguished from political, equality, or a commingling of the two races upon terms unsatisfactory to either. Laws permitting, and even requiring, their separation in places where they are likely to be brought into contact do not necessarily imply the inferiority of either race to the other, and have been generally, if not universally, recognized as within the competency of the state legislatures in the exercise of their police power.

Plessy was the law of the land for nearly fifty years. But in *Brown v. Board of Education* (1954), Chief Justice Earl Warren wrote that "in the field of public education the doctrine of 'separate but equal' has no place." What was the basis of this holding? Not the text of the Constitution, which says nothing about segregation. Not the intent of those who adopted the Fourteenth Amendment, whose views Warren maintains were at best "inconclusive." Some wanted only to end slavery, others wanted to abolish every difference based on race. In any case, Warren contends, their intentions are not decisive: "In approaching this problem, we cannot turn the clock back to 1868 when the Amendment was adopted, or even to 1896 when *Plessy v. Ferguson* was written. We must consider public education in the light of its full development and its present place in American life throughout the nation." Key factors considered by the *Brown* Court were the increasing role that education plays in a successful life, and the demonstrated inferiority of racially segregated schools. But the most important factor was the moral insight that racial segregation in public schools could not be distinguished from a poisonous racism that cannot but infect the hearts and minds of schoolchildren, particularly black schoolchildren. "Separate educational facilities," wrote Warren, "are inherently unequal."

It is a mistake to build a theory of constitutional interpretation around just one case, especially a case as controversial as *Roe*. We have to ask how we should make sense of the "basic law" of our country today, which faces responsibilities and challenges the Founding Fathers could never have imagined. An approach rigidly focused on the explicit provisions of the text and the intention of the framers is both theoretically and practically inadequate. The general approach of the Court in *Brown*, which assesses basic constitutional values in light of current political and social realities, seems better able to deal with the challenges of the twenty-first century. Does adopting this general approach mean you can't criticize *Roe*? Absolutely not. But it means that you criticize *Roe* not because it cast its interpretive net too widely, but because it did not cast its net widely enough. *Roe* rightly took into account new social insights about the full equality of women and the special burdens women face in carrying unwanted pregnancies to term. But in holding that the unborn are not legal "persons," the Court failed to consider the dangers to democracy of separating "personhood" from humanity—a lesson that the holocausts of the twentieth century drove home to us again and again.

Sources

Brown v. Board of Education, 347 U.S. 483 (1954).

Plessy v. Ferguson, 163 U.S. 537 (1896).

Roe v. Wade, 410 U.S. 113 (1973).

Scalia, Antonin. *A Matter of Interpretation: Federal Courts and the Law*. Edited by Amy Gutmann. Princeton, NJ: Princeton University Press, 1997.

Remember the Mormons
Thinking about the Nature of Marriage

Few activists on either side of the same-sex marriage debate have paid much attention to the nineteenth-century campaign to suppress Mormon polygamy. Why? In my view, that campaign—our first great battle over the nature of marriage—is full of uncomfortable ironies for both sides.

As Richard Van Wagoner describes in his fascinating book, *Mormon Polygamy*, Joseph Smith Jr., the founder of Mormonism, appears to have practiced polygamy from the early 1830s, although he did not announce his "Revelation on Celestial Marriage" until 1843. According to Mormon theology, polygamy was no mere alternative lifestyle choice; it was an essential aspect of the divine plan, to be set aside by the faithful at their eternal peril. To say that the world did not applaud Smith's theological revelation would be an understatement. The 1856 Republican Party platform denounced slavery and polygamy as "the twin relics of barbarism."

In 1862, Congress passed the Morrill Act, which made bigamy a criminal offense. Subsequent legislation not only attempted to stamp out polygamy, but also tried to destroy the Church of Jesus Christ of Latter Day Saints. "Unlawful cohabitation," easier to prove than polygamy, was made a crime. "Cohab hunts" were conducted on a regular basis, forcing polygamous men to abandon their wives and children to go underground. Polygamists were excluded from juries, deprived of the right to vote, and denied any "place of public trust, honor, or emolument." Wives were forced to testify against their husbands in polygamy trials. Children of plural marriages were disinherited. The Mormon Church itself was stripped of its status as a law-abiding corporation and treated almost as a criminal conspiracy. According to Van Wagoner, the church finally capitulated to the government's unrelenting pressure in 1890, when its leader announced that he "had sought the will of the Lord, and the Holy Spirit had revealed that it was necessary for the church to relinquish the practice of that principle for which the brethren had been willing to lay down their lives."

How might we compare the protagonists in the current debate about marriage with those in the earlier one? The natural move would be to put the proponents of same-sex marriage in the shoes of the proponents of polygamy. But many secular (and religious) supporters of same-sex marriage would oppose polygamy, because it is not consistent with women's equality. Equality-minded proponents of same-sex marriage could not support the federal government's role in the polygamy controversy either. Many Mormon women supported polygamy, and as a consequence Congress abolished women's suffrage in the Utah territory. In *Davis v. Beason* (1890), the Supreme Court warmly endorsed the traditional view of marriage held by all "civilized and Christian countries."

Choosing a side in the past debate isn't any easier for contemporary opponents of same-sex marriage. It would be hard for those opposed to same-sex marriage to find either religious or secular grounds to support polygamy. They also wouldn't be comfortable backing the government. That would put them in the shoes of ruthless oppressors of religious believers sincerely committed to doing God's will—not a comfortable stance for Christians who oppose same-sex marriage precisely because of their own commitment to doing God's will. Moreover, in upholding the constitutionality of the Morrill Act, the Supreme Court proclaimed that the First Amendment protects only freedom of religious belief, not freedom of religiously motivated actions. That narrow view of religious freedom would have allowed prohibitionists to outlaw all alcoholic beverages without making an exception for Communion wine as the Volstead Act did.

Some themes of the same-sex marriage debate echo themes in the debate over polygamy. Now, opponents of same-sex marriage portray the homosexual lifestyle as promiscuous, while its proponents point to the ordinary domesticity of many same-sex couples. Then, opponents of plural marriage portrayed the polygamous lifestyle as lascivious, while its proponents pointed to the ordinary domesticity of many polygamous unions. Now, opponents of same-sex marriage argue that such unions are psychologically detrimental to any children raised within them; then, opponents of polygamy argued that the detriment to children was physical.

Yet there is at least one stark difference. The polygamy debate centered on the practice of polygamy—not its status before the civil law. Mormons were not seeking federal recognition of polygamous marriages; they simply wanted to enter them without federal obstruction. But the federal government wanted to put an end to polygamous cohabitation. In contrast, the same-sex marriage debate centers on the legal recognition of homosexual unions. No one is seriously arguing that homosexual cohabitation should be stopped; indeed, the Supreme Court struck down anti-sodomy laws as unconstitutional. Our debate is not mainly about the *coercive* function of the law; it is about its *pedagogical* function. What should the law teach about the moral status of homosexual unions?

If there is someday a third great national debate on marriage, will anyone wholeheartedly endorse either side of our current debate? I have my doubts. I suspect that the proponents of both polygamy and same-sex marriage will seem too rash about radically altering a fundamental societal institution responsible for socializing the next generation. At the same time, their opponents will seem too callous about the well-being of the people actually involved in polygamous or same-sex relationships. But perhaps these tensions are involved in any battle for social change.

Sources

Davis v. Beason, 133 U.S. 333 (1890).

Morrill Anti-Bigamy Act (1862), 37th United States Congress, Sess. 2, ch. 126, 12 Stat. 501.

National Prohibition Act (Volstead Act) (1919), Pub. L. No. 66-66.

Reynolds v. United States, 98 U.S. (8 Otto.) 145 (1878).

Van Wagoner, Richard S. *Mormon Polygamy: A History.* Salt Lake City, UT: Signature Books, 1989.

Regulating Abortion
What Did the Roberts Court Do?

In *Gonzales v. Carhart*, the Supreme Court upheld the Partial Birth Abortion Act of 2003, a federal law banning a specific type of late-term abortion procedure in which a physician delivers the baby partway, then kills it while it is still in the vaginal passage before completing the delivery. Although the law made an exception for cases in which the procedure is necessary to preserve the life of the mother, it made no exception for her health.

Predictably, the decision prompted jubilation on the part of pro-life activists and angry despair on the part of prochoice activists. In response, legal scholars emphasized the narrowness of the decision: the federal law in question does not ban all late-term abortions, only a specific type that is rarely performed. Its impact, they say, is largely symbolic. And therein lies the problem. From a symbolic perspective, the law in question pits the core concern of the prolife side—the human dignity of the unborn child—directly against the core concern of the prochoice side—the bodily health and integrity of the mother. Here is a capsule summary of the conflict.

From the perspective of prolifers, the core concern is the human dignity of unborn life. The most objectionable aspect of *Roe v. Wade* is its holding that the unborn aren't persons under the law. Legal personhood, according to *Roe*, doesn't begin until the baby is born. According to prolifers, this dividing line is particularly arbitrary and cruel; it turns on the baby's physical location, not on any aspect of its physical development. Consequently, they see the partial-birth abortion procedure as a ruthless exploitation of that arbitrary line: the physician partially delivers the baby, then kills it in a particularly gruesome manner, collapsing or crushing its skull immediately before birth. No procedure better exemplifies the fact that there is no intrinsic difference between a late-term fetus and a newborn baby. Prolifers see the law as striking a blow for the personhood of the unborn by prohibiting a procedure that is on the very verge of infanticide.

From the perspective of prochoicers, the core concern is the physical integrity and well-being of the mother. They see the law as striking a blow against this concern by excluding a health exception. The personhood of the unborn and the brutality of the procedure are not, for them, conclusive factors. Pregnancy involves the bodily dependence of the unborn child on its mother; in many cases, it entails a significant physical burden. To legally require a woman to continue a pregnancy—or to deliver a baby—when doing so harms her own body is to treat her as a mere means to the well-being of the child she carries. There is no other instance where U.S. law requires one person to provide bodily life support to another person. The law does not require parents to rescue children when doing so puts their own safety at risk. A father is not required to rush into a burning building, nor is a mother required to donate a kidney. To require a woman to carry a pregnancy to term when doing so risks her health confirms the worst fears of the prochoice movement: it's not simply that pregnant women have no autonomy, it's that pregnant women have no right to protect the fundamental integrity of their own bodily existence.

So why no exception for the health of the mother? Practically speaking, prolifers introduced weighty medical testimony that the procedure was never medically necessary to preserve the mother's physical health. Furthermore, prolifers had learned to mistrust the "health of the mother" clause as an exception that swallows the rule. If "health" encompasses "mental health," and "mental health" is broadly defined, virtually any abortion strongly desired by the mother could fall into the loophole. So for symbolic and pedagogical as well as practical reasons, they argued that the law could not make an exception for health.

What's the prochoice response? Medical testimony was not unanimous. Some physicians testified that in certain cases, the procedure was better able to preserve the mother's health than the alternatives. When experts disagree, who do we want making decisions about what best serves our health? The physician at the bedside, or politicians and judges thousands of miles away? This question encapsulates a basic fear of many Americans, not only about abortion, but about health care in general. Upholding the constitutionality of the law, Justice

Anthony Kennedy's opinion nonetheless acknowledged this fear, indicating his willingness to consider a challenge to the law "as applied" in a case or set of cases where the woman's health is indeed at risk.

Life versus choice. Personhood versus bodily health and integrity. Women versus unborn children. Are we in for endless abortion wars? I think the Court was right in upholding the act's constitutionality. At the same time, I think the law itself will exacerbate conflict over core values rather than ameliorate that conflict. But maybe there's another way. Is it possible, for example, to design a law that prohibits a range of late-term abortions, while at the same time including a clear and defined health exception? Would the Roberts Court uphold such a law? Perhaps. Such a law would not satisfy activists on either side. But it would nod toward both sets of core values: it would highlight the humanity of unborn life while recognizing that secular law should not require a woman to sacrifice her fundamental physical integrity to carry her baby to term. Maybe that's a step toward a workable compromise. But I'm not holding my breath.

Sources

Gonzales v. Carhart, 550 U.S. 124 (2007).
Roe v. Wade, 410 U.S. 113 (1973).

6

Caught in the Gap
What Hostility to Health-Care Reform Has Wrought

In 2012, the Supreme Court upheld the Affordable Care Act's requirement that most Americans obtain health insurance or pay a penalty.
In so doing, the Court preserved the law's backbone. As we are now
discovering, however, the same Supreme Court decision also cut out
the ACA's heart: the justices struck down the law's requirement that
the states expand their Medicaid programs to cover all adults at or
below 138 percent of the poverty level. The requirement is now an option. Each state can choose whether to expand its Medicaid program
or keep it as it is. As of March 2014, twenty-four states had refused to
expand their programs—despite the fact that the federal government
promised to pick up more than 90 percent of the costs for the next
decade. Most of these are "Red States" in the Southeast and Mountain
regions, along with the vertical line of states from South Dakota to
Texas.

We soon began to see the consequences of Red State hostility to
health-care reform, and they were devastating for the poor. According to an April 2014 report from the Kaiser Family Foundation, nearly
5 million people below the poverty line would now be ineligible both
for Medicaid and for the subsidies available for the new health-care
exchanges. The door to health-care coverage is doubly barred for the
most vulnerable of our fellow Americans.

How can this be? We need to begin with a realistic picture of Medicaid. Many Americans believe all poor people already receive health-
care coverage through Medicaid, just as all elderly people receive
coverage through Medicare. But that's not true. Most of the states
that are refusing to expand Medicaid provide no coverage whatsoever to nondisabled adults who don't have dependent children. And
in many of these states, parents of dependent children don't fare much
better. Only the poorest of poor parents are covered. In Alabama, for

instance, parents are covered only if their annual income does not exceed 16 percent of the federal poverty level—in 2014 dollars, that was $3,221 for a family of three. In Texas, the eligibility limit is 19 percent of the federal poverty level, which is particularly problematic given that state's large uninsured population. The average cutoff for the twenty-four states that have refused to expand Medicaid is 46 percent of the federal poverty level, which was about $9,000 for a family of three.

And that's not the worst of it. Many adults who exceed the state Medicaid limits are too poor to purchase insurance on the new health-insurance exchanges, which were designed to subsidize insurance for working and middle-class Americans making up to four times the poverty level. These insurance policies are completely unavailable to adults earning below the federal poverty level, because lawmakers assumed such people would be covered by the expansion of Medicaid. A family of three with a 2014 household income of more than $9,000 and less than $20,000 will be out of luck in many parts of the country.

Why did the Supreme Court strike down the Medicaid expansion mandate? In a nutshell, seven justices held that threatening the states with the loss of all their Medicaid funding unless they expanded the program was too "coercive," and that it therefore exceeded Congress's power under the Spending Clause. But the Spending Clause confers broad authority on Congress to distribute federal funds. No state is entitled to federal funds from year to year. And Congress regularly uses money as both a carrot and a stick to secure state compliance with federal programs. Given the fact that the federal government is subsidizing nearly all the costs of the Medicaid expansion, it's hard to see this as constitutionally impermissible coercion.

Why did some states refuse to expand Medicaid? Most point to the cost of doing so. But that is short-sighted on the part of cost-conscious governors and legislatures. First, it now looks as though expanding Medicaid won't cost as much as the federal government initially expected it to. Second, by expanding Medicaid, states avoid the cost of treating the uninsured in hospital emergency rooms, which is not only expensive but also breathtakingly inefficient. So it's hard to make sense of the refusal to expand Medicaid on financial grounds; it looks more like ideological opposition to President Obama and health-care reform.

Let's hope the poor in these states have better access to polling booths than they do to doctors. According to the Kaiser Foundation's report, 86 percent of all poor, uninsured non-elderly adults fall into the Medicaid coverage gap. That's not just a gap. That's a sinkhole. The Supreme Court opened it up, and Red State governors and legislatures pushed their poor people into it.

Sources

Kaiser Commission on Medicaid and the Uninsured. "The Coverage Gap: Uninsured Poor Adults in States That Do Not Expand Medicaid." April 2, 2014. Available at http://kff.org/health-reform/issue-brief/the-coverage-gap -uninsured-poor-adults-in-states-that-do-not-expand-medicaid/.
National Federation of Independent Business v. Sebelius, 567 U.S. __, 132 S.Ct. 2566 (2012).

"Peaceful and Private"

Montana's Supreme Court Rules on Assisted Suicide

At the beginning of every year, the attention of most prolife activists is understandably focused on beginning-of-life questions, as they make preparations for the Right-to-Life March in Washington, D.C., that occurs annually around the anniversary of *Roe v. Wade* (January 22). But it is important not to ignore developments related to other prolife issues. On December 31, 2009, a troublesome development occurred with respect to end-of-life questions—the other prolife issue. The Montana Supreme Court issued its decision in *Baxter v. Montana*, holding that physician-assisted suicide (PAS) did not violate state law, making Montana the third state (after Oregon and Washington) to legalize PAS.

The *Baxter* decision did not garner much attention at the time it was issued. It did not even rate a mention on the U.S. Conference of Catholic Bishops Web site. Doubtless, that neglect was due in part to the decision's holiday release and the urgency of the debate about health-care reform and abortion and contraception coverage that year. But I fear that it was also due in part to a perception that the decision was "not as bad as it could have been"—as one Montana prolife leader told the press.

It's understandable why some people might think that. I did myself until I actually read the opinion. After all, the court did not declare PAS to be a right under the state constitution but merely held that it did not violate current Montana law. No constitution-bending judicial activism of the *Roe v. Wade* sort was involved. And if outside observers haven't gotten around to reading the opinion yet, they might assume that Montana law is idiosyncratic. We all know that cowboys and other fiercely independent types live in Montana.

But prejudices are just that—prejudices. Judicial activism also includes twisting statutes beyond recognition to achieve political ends.

Far from being idiosyncratic, the relevant Montana law is very similar to the law in most states. Montana criminalizes homicide but not suicide. It does criminalize assisting in the suicide of another and, if the attempt is successful, elevates the charge to homicide. But like most states, Montana treats the consent of the victim as a defense to some crimes—unless doing so violates public policy as reflected in state law. Thus the question the Montana Supreme Court set itself in *Baxter* was whether the physician's assistance in a patient's suicide violated the state's public policy. It answered no, for two reasons, both of which are highly flawed.

First, the majority recognized that in Montana (as elsewhere) public policy does not allow the victim to give legally valid consent to crimes destructive of the person, such as assault. The majority attempted to distinguish this situation from PAS by saying that the public-policy exception applied centrally to "violent, public altercations [that] breach public peace and endanger others in the vicinity." In contrast, it argued, death by PAS is "peaceful and private."

This line of reasoning fundamentally misconstrues what counts as "private." Our legal tradition has always recognized that when one member of the community seriously injures or takes the life of another, it is always an issue of public concern—no matter where it might take place or how serene the action itself might appear. The opinion's requirement that the consensual attack be "private" and "peaceful" doesn't hold up under examination. An assault consisting of a consensual strangling in a hotel room won't spark a riot, nor will the consensual smothering of one sleeping spouse by the other. But these are still matters of public concern.

Second, the majority opinion points to Montana law as requiring doctors to withdraw life-sustaining treatment at the request of the patient or surrogate decision-maker. It asks how PAS can be against public policy when withdrawal of treatment isn't.

There is a significant distinction between a doctor's respecting the wishes of a patient or surrogate to withhold or withdraw treatment, on the one hand, and assisted suicide and euthanasia on the other, as the U.S. Supreme Court has recognized. Doctors cannot force competent patients to receive treatment they don't want, no matter what the reason. But that is a far cry from saying they can help patients kill themselves with legal impunity.

Should prolifers worry? Can't the Montana legislature undo the decision by passing a new law? Yes, but that is harder than it seems. The burden of action has now shifted. People who would be unwilling to pass a law legalizing PAS may also be unwilling to pass a law criminalizing it. Uncertainty and ambivalence favor the status quo—whatever it is. Especially in this time of spiraling health costs and economic uncertainty, people may think, "I'll hold on to the possibility of PAS—just in case."

The *Baxter* decision is radical: it says that intentional killing isn't always a matter of public concern. It is stealthy. By refraining from finding a state constitutional right to assisted suicide, it avoided immediate criticism for judicial activism. It is politically canny. It put the burden of action on opponents. Most troubling of all, its strategy is portable. There's no reason its contorted logic can't be exported to other states by euthanasia activists.

Physician-assisted suicide is expanding its reach. In 2008 it was prohibited everywhere but in the state of Oregon. As of October 2015, it has been legalized in five states: Oregon, Washington, Montana, California, and Vermont. The New Mexico Supreme Court is considering the issue. Additionally, a referendum to legalize the practice was narrowly defeated in Massachusetts in 2012. Those who value the equal dignity of all human beings can no longer consider the fight against euthanasia and physician-assisted suicide to be a part-time job.

Sources

Baxter v. Montana, 354 Mont. 234 (2009).

Eckholm, Erik. "'Aid in Dying' Movement Takes Hold in Some States." *New York Times*, February 8, 2014.

8

More Than a Refuge
Why Immigration Officials Should Steer Clear of Churches

Is it morally acceptable for agents of Immigration and Customs Enforcement (ICE)—or local police, for that matter—to station themselves outside places of worship in order to identify and capture illegal immigrants?

When I gave a paper at Duke University in the fall of 2010, I learned about a controversy involving the Iglesia de Dios's Catedral de Jesus in Zebulon, North Carolina. In April of that year, church members charged that local law-enforcement officers posted license checkpoints outside the church immediately following services. They claimed that the police detained only drivers who appeared to be Latino, while allowing Caucasian and African-American drivers to pass through freely. Suspecting that the real goal of the checkpoints was to catch illegal immigrants, church members filed a complaint with the local branch of the ACLU, which launched an investigation of this and similar incidents in the state.

In late September 2011, after concluding its investigation, the ACLU issued an apology to the police department—it appeared, among other things, that the checkpoints were not as close to the church as was first thought. But I found myself wondering: What exactly would be the problem if they were close?

Many people, I think, would find such a strategy of enforcing immigration law intuitively distasteful, no matter how cost-effective it might be. In a 2008 memorandum, ICE itself acknowledges this sensibility, stating that it is not agency policy to target churches, schools, and other "sensitive" locations, absent exigent circumstances such as threats of terrorism or other forms of violence. But why are these locations considered "sensitive"? ICE does not say, other than to note that "children and their families might be present."

In the past several years, Catholics have heard a lot about "intrinsically evil" acts—acts that are always and everywhere wrong. But our moral tradition also has much to say about acts that are wrong in certain circumstances—in some times and in some places. What does it tell us about why houses of worship might be "sensitive" locations for immigration enforcement?

In the Christian West, houses of worship have long been considered places of sanctuary, although the law has not always recognized that claim. A friend who is an expert in early Christianity suggests that the root concern was not to harbor the guilty, but rather to prevent the defilement of the altar by violence and bloodshed in the pursuit and capture of the fugitive. Moving from cultic to theological concerns, it is also clear that doing violence to someone—whether guilty or innocent—in a church subverts a central message of the gospel: Jesus Christ came to save sinners, offering us all redemption from the sentence of death that sin brought into the world. No matter who the victim, an act of violence is more heinous if it is committed in a place of worship. The 1963 bombing of the 16th Street Baptist Church in Birmingham, Alabama, which killed four young African-American girls, was an act of sacrilege. So too was the 2009 shooting of the abortionist doctor Craig Tiller in Reformation Lutheran Church in Wichita, Kansas.

In the 1980s, the Sanctuary Movement attempted to protest U.S. policy toward undocumented refugees from Central America. Invoking analogies to the Underground Railroad, a network of churches offered physical sanctuary to refugees, even as the same congregations worked to gain sanctuary seekers better treatment under federal immigration law. More recently, the "New Sanctuary Movement" has emerged to provide similar protection for today's illegal immigrants. Most famously, in 2007, thirty-one-year-old Elvira Arellano took refuge in the United Methodist Church in Chicago rather than be deported to Mexico and separated from her son. Declining to pursue her into the sanctuary, ICE waited for over a year to arrest her. She was detained for deportation only after she had traveled to Los Angeles to speak at a rally. For the New Sanctuary Movement, the church is not merely a place but how a congregation responds to the call to obey God's law rather than man's.

Someone might object that the prospect of immigration checkpoints directly outside churches does not raise the specter of a defiled sanctuary, nor does it challenge the church as a locus of political protest. That is true. But it does raise a danger, less dramatic perhaps but more fundamental. For it threatens to reduce undocumented immigrants to their immigration status, thereby occluding their common humanity. First and foremost, those in the country illegally are human beings made in the image and likeness of God—just like us. They love their children and they give praise to God—just like us. One way of keeping the humanity of the undocumented before us is for law-enforcement officials to stand a respectful distance from places where humanity is most fully enacted and welcomed. The "sensitivity" that ICE justly respects in refraining from targeting churches and schools in enforcement practices is actually nothing less than sensitivity to our common humanity.

Sources

Minnick, Beau. "Groups Accuse Zebulon Police of Racial Profiling." WRAL.com. May 1, 2010. Available at http://www.wral.com/news/local/story/7525932/.

Morton, John. "Memorandum For: Field Office Directors, Special Agents in Charge, Chief Counsel. Subject: Enforcement Actions at or Focused on Sensitive Locations." U.S. Immigration and Customs Enforcement. October 24, 2011. Available at http://webcache.googleusercontent.com/search?q =cache:zB7erkKvNdAJ:www.ice.gov/doclib/ero-outreach/pdf/10029.2-policy .pdf+&cd=1&hl=en&ct=clnk&gl=us.

Singular, Stephen. *A Death in Wichita: Abortion Doctor George Tiller and the New American Civil War.* New York: St. Martin's Press, 2012.

Thorne, T.K. *Last Chance for Justice: How Relentless Investigators Uncovered New Evidence Convicting the Birmingham Church Bombers.* Chicago, IL: Chicago Review Press, 2013.

9

Justice or Vengeance
Is the Death Penalty Cruel and Unusual?

Botched executions do occur. On April 29, 2014, an Oklahoma inmate died of a heart attack after the execution went horribly awry. He began to writhe and gasp in pain after he was injected with the first drug of the three-drug cocktail used by Oklahoma, which was supposed to render him deeply unconscious. It turns out that the state had revised its protocol after some of the drugs it normally used became unavailable. In January 2014, a revised drug protocol had caused an Ohio inmate to take twenty-five minutes to die, while gasping for air.

Does the risk of a botched execution caused by a particular method of causing death make the death penalty unconstitutional, because it violates the Eighth Amendment to the Constitution, which prohibits "cruel and unusual punishment?" The Supreme Court addressed this question in 2008 in *Baze v. Reese*, a case in which the petitioners were Kentucky prisoners on death row, facing execution by the three-drug cocktail then used by virtually all states. The Supreme Court upheld Kentucky's method of lethal injection, by a 7-2 vote. But there was no majority opinion.

After the events in Oklahoma and Ohio, I found myself pondering a larger moral question: Why should a decent society ban "cruel and unusual punishment" in the first place? So I went back to the briefs in *Baze*. Reading them, you might get the sense that the purpose of the prohibition is narrow: to eliminate physical pain from punishment. The legal question is whether the Eighth Amendment prohibits all "unnecessary risk of pain and suffering" in the imposition of the death penalty, or simply the "substantial risk of wanton and unnecessary pain, torture, or lingering death." The prisoners claim that if the administration of the three-drug cocktail is botched, they will die in an excruciating fashion. Because this risk is unnecessary—it could, for example, be eliminated by using a single lethal overdose of barbiturates—it is also unconstitutional. The state responded by outlining the safeguards taken by Kentucky, arguing that the three-drug method does not impose a *substantial risk* of severe pain on the condemned prisoner.

I don't think that the purpose of the prohibition against cruel and unusual punishment can be reduced to the minimization of physical pain. History does not support such a claim. In prohibiting "cruel and unusual punishment," the American Bill of Rights (1791) echoed the English Bill of Rights (1689). In England, execution—often by hanging or another painful method—was a common punishment for many crimes well into the nineteenth century. Indeed, for some crimes, severe pain was part of the penalty. The English did not abolish drawing and quartering as a punishment for treason until 1814. Common punishments in colonial America for noncapital crimes included the stockade, the pillory, flogging, and branding. For many years, the infliction of physical pain, sometimes significant physical pain, was considered neither "cruel" nor "unusual."

So what is the purpose of a prohibition against "cruel and unusual punishment"? Here's my take: The conjunction "and" is important. If the state imposes penalties that are both cruel and unusual, it risks undermining the primary goal and rationale of those penalties: the communal exercise of retributive justice. As the image of the blindfolded woman holding a scale implies, retributive justice aims to restore balance to the community by imposing a cool, measured, and fair punishment on the transgressor. Theoretically, at least, the focus is positive: once the criminal has "paid his debt" to society, he is reintegrated into the fold—even if only in memory after his execution. A punishment that is both cruel and unusual doesn't further retributive justice. It does, however, advance two other objectives that are frequently confused with retributive justice: private revenge and social control through deterrence.

Cruel and unusual punishment satisfies the desire for private vengeance. We are all inclined to evaluate harms to ourselves and our loved ones as more serious, and deserving of more punishment, than injury to others. We see ourselves as unique and the injustices we suffer as uniquely horrible. So from the not-so-disinterested perspective of the victims and those who love them, a cruel-and-unusual punishment for a crime can easily seem quite fitting. It has taken humanity a long time to uncouple justice from vengeance. Biblical scholars remind us that the *lex talionis* was intended to be a limitation on punishment, not a call for greater harshness: *only* an eye for an eye, *only* a tooth for a tooth.

Cruel and unusual punishment is also used as an instrument of social control. My students are frequently surprised to discover that the utilitarian Jeremy Bentham, who was dedicated to promoting pleasure and avoiding pain, was a vigorous supporter of harsh and inexorable punishment for certain crimes. Why? Because harsh punishment publicly administered can function as an effective deterrent. The pain inflicted by cutting off one thief's hand is far outweighed by the pain avoided if a hundred potential thieves are deterred by the gory example.

How, then, should we think about *Baze*? From a moral perspective, the real question isn't whether the Eighth Amendment prohibits methods of execution that impose "unnecessary risk" of severe pain, or merely "a substantial risk" of severe pain. The question is whether the death penalty itself continues to serve the goals of retributive justice, rather than merely vengeance or deterrence. While the Supreme Court decided in the 1970s that the death penalty need not violate the Constitution, there is no reason that state legislatures cannot judge for themselves that it constitutes "cruel and unusual punishment." Times change, and with them our moral sentiments. If enough states abolish the death penalty, eventually the Constitution will catch up.

Sources

Baze v. Rees, 553 U.S. 35 (2008).

Connor, Tracy. "Oklahoma Execution: What Went Wrong and What Happens Now?" NBC News. April 30, 2014. Available at http://www.nbcnews.com /storyline/lethal-injection/oklahoma-execution-what-went-wrong-what -happens-now-n93556.

Eckholm, Erik. "One Execution Botched, Oklahoma Delays the Next." *New York Times*, April 29, 2014.

Gregg v. Georgia, 428 U.S. 153 (1976).

Undue Process
The Evisceration of Habeas Corpus

Halfway through his second term, President George W. Bush signed the Military Commissions Act of 2006, which gave him the power to identify unlawful enemy combatants, to order harsh interrogation of them, and to detain them indefinitely. American forces can snatch an Iraqi man from his bed, shackle him, and ship him off to Guantánamo Bay as a suspected terrorist, where he has no right to a speedy trial.

But what if he's innocent—what if his detention is a mistake caused by the fog of war and the confusion of clashing cultures? The law provides that if a Combatant Status Review Tribunal—or other tribunal established by the president or the secretary of defense—finds that the detainee is an unlawful enemy combatant, that finding is "dispositive." It seems that he can only appeal it to the United States Court of Appeals for the District of Columbia Circuit. If he manages to, it is not clear what good that will do him. Many legal scholars believe the review process has been so hemmed in by Congress that it has little real independent value. But whatever its value, that process is his one shot. Congress has stripped every court in the United States of the power to hear a petition for a writ of habeas corpus on behalf of an alien deemed to be an unlawful enemy combatant. Once his status as an "unlawful" enemy combatant has been determined, no independent court has jurisdiction to hear any claim "relating to any aspect of the detention, transfer, treatment, trial, or conditions of confinement." He has no right to a timely resolution of his case; as Robert C. Weaver, Jr.'s article in *Commonweal* demonstrates, a detainee can languish in jail for years before facing the charges against him. What exactly is the writ of habeas corpus?

This situation raises serious questions with respect to the writ of habeas corpus. The writ's name, which means "you should have the body" in Latin, gives some clue as to its purpose. In sixteenth-century

England, a court issuing the writ ordered a sheriff or warden to produce the prisoner in court, and to show good cause why the prisoner should not be set free. As the writ developed, it became clear that its focus was due process, broadly construed: its goal was to ensure that the trial, detention, and punishment of a prisoner were conducted in a fair way that did not conflict with fundamental moral and political rights.

How should Christians think about this? Are the protections that the writ of habeas corpus offers a matter of man-made law that can be wiped away with the stroke of a legislator's pen, as Congress just did? Or is it a requirement of natural law, based in natural justice? In my opinion, Christians should take the latter view.

The writ reflects five fundamental moral insights. First, individuals are not mere creatures of the state, to be preserved or discarded as political leaders find convenient. Second, individuals possess a basic right to freedom that is not subject to abrogation at the whim of the government. The government needs to have a good reason for depriving individuals of their liberty. Third, an elemental requirement of procedural justice—of due process—is the giving of reasons for the state's actions against a person before a disinterested third party. Fourth, justice needs to be timely. It's cold comfort to tell an innocent man that he's innocent after he's spent twenty years incarcerated while "awaiting" trial. Fifth, a detainee hasn't lost his humanity. Conditions of detention—and interrogation—need to be humane.

There are, of course, objections. The writ of habeas corpus has been suspended in the past, most notably by Abraham Lincoln during the Civil War. It seems to me, however, that this objection can be countered by drawing some distinctions. It is one thing to suspend the writ for a limited period of time in situations of complete social chaos (such as the Civil War), where the government does not have the resources to maintain the type of legal system that would process habeas applications in an orderly manner. It is another thing entirely to abolish the writ indefinitely because government officials don't want the inconvenience—or the embarrassment—of having to justify their actions in the light of day. The "war on terror" is now a chronic condition of our body politic, not an acute one. We need to find a way to incorporate our fundamental values into the ongoing processing of suspects.

A second objection pertains to a detainee's citizenship status. The Supreme Court has ruled, and Congress has accepted, that American citizens held as unlawful enemy combatants cannot be deprived of access to habeas proceedings in federal court. The new law specifically denies the same right to aliens. Is this legal distinction morally justified? I think the key here is to apply the Golden Rule, which is arguably a requirement of the natural law as well as the gospel.

Suppose that you were in the wrong place at the wrong time, and were rounded up by foreign soldiers with an entirely different language, culture, and religion. Wouldn't you want the chance to explain yourself? Wouldn't you want an impartial third party to assess your captors' explanation of why your detention is justifiable? Then do unto others as you would have them do unto you. Extend the protections of the writ of habeas corpus to aliens as well as American citizens detained in the "war on terror."

In *Boumediene v. Bush* (2008), the U.S. Supreme Court held in a 5–4 decision that prisoners at Guantánamo Bay had a right to habeas corpus, which the Military Commissions Act of 2006 had unconstitutionally suspended. President Obama signed into law the Military Commissions Act of 2009, which provided new protections for defendants in the handling of commission trials. Sometimes the Golden Rule wins.

Sources

Boumediene v. Bush, 553 U.S. 723 (2008).

Lind, Douglas W. *Lincoln's Suspension of Habeas Corpus: The Pamphlet Literature and Congressional Debate.* Getzville, NY: William S. Hein & Co., 2012.

Military Commissions Act of 2006, Pub. L. 109-366 (2006), 120 Stat. 2600.

Military Commissions Act of 2009, Pub. L. 111-84 (2009), 123 Stat. 2190.

Weaver, Robert C. "No Man's Land: Report from Guantánamo," *Commonweal*, October 6, 2006.

Bad Evidence
Not Only Is Torture Immoral, It Doesn't Work

Puritans in Salem, Massachusetts, in the summer of 1692 must have viewed the threat of witchcraft in much the same way Americans today view the prospect of another attack by Al Qaeda. Witches were, so to speak, supernatural terrorists. They blended into the population and attacked the innocent without warning. In covenant with Satan himself, they aimed to destroy the godly. Witches had to be stopped. In the end, however, the means employed in Salem's life-and-death struggle against the Devil ended by harming the very community they were supposed to preserve. As the historian Perry Miller observed, the witchcraft trials, which led to nineteen deaths by hanging, were a "blot on New England's fame" which, over time, were "enlarged, as much by friends as by foes, into its greatest disgrace." There is a lesson here for our own "war on terror," which has a similar problem with means: the use of torture to obtain information from suspected terrorists.

The Puritans cannot be faulted for believing that witches posed a threat. It was a view held not only in Massachusetts but in the entire Christian West. Consequently, the Puritans acted reasonably in making witchcraft—entering into a covenant with the Devil—a crime. They can, however, be faulted for their reliance on "spectral evidence" in convicting the accused. Under the influence of the presiding judge, Lieutenant Governor William Stoughton, the court operated on the assumption that the Devil could not appropriate the shape of a person who did not consent to work with him. Consequently, the court admitted testimony from victims claiming to have seen a defendant's "specter" even though the defendant was physically present elsewhere.

But the Devil is the father of lies. Why wouldn't he take the spectral form of innocent persons in order to destroy godly individuals and communities? Prominent members of the Puritan clergy, such as

Increase Mather, expressed theological and practical doubts about the reliability of spectral evidence. But their doubts were not expressed with sufficient force to bring the process to an early conclusion. Historian Francis Bremer suggests that the religious leaders hesitated to bring pressure on the governor to stop the madness for fear of jeopardizing their own political influence in the colony.

What about our own "war on terror"? As the attacks of September 11, 2001 showed, the threat of terrorism on American soil is very real. We cannot be faulted for responding aggressively. Yet, in our zeal to identify our furtive enemies, we became entangled in our own "spectral evidence" problem. Leaving aside the moral questions, there is good reason to doubt that torture can produce reliable information about future terrorist attacks or past perpetrators.

At a June 2008 forum sponsored by the group Human Rights First, fifteen experienced former interrogators issued a statement affirming that "the use of torture and other inhumane and abusive treatment results in false and misleading information, loss of critical intelligence, and has caused serious damage to the reputation and standing of the United States." That conclusion echoes the judgment of Senator Jay Rockefeller (D-W. Va.), then chair of the Senate Intelligence Committee, quoted by Jane Mayer in her book *The Dark Side*: "I have heard nothing to suggest that information obtained from enhanced interrogation techniques has prevented an imminent terrorist attack. . . . I do know that coercive interrogation can lead detainees to provide false information to make the interrogation stop." Mayer offers a blunt summary: "In other words, according to one of the few U.S. officials with full access to the details, the drastic 'ticking time bomb' threat used to justify what many Americans would otherwise consider indefensible tactics, had never actually occurred, other than on the TV sets of those watching Fox-T.V.'s terrorism fantasy show *24*."

If a community sees itself as locked in a life-and-death battle with an evil and implacable enemy, it is likely to lose moral perspective on its own actions. Years later, when the threat has passed, the next generation will look back at some actions with shame. At the end of her book, Mayer quotes Philip Zelikow, director of the 9/11 Commission, who predicted that in time the Bush administration's turn to torture would be compared to President Franklin D. Roosevelt's internment of the Japanese during World War II: "Fear and anxiety were exploited by zealots and fools."

We cannot step out of the fear and anxiety endemic to our times any more than the Puritans could. But we can learn from their mistakes. The best defense against moral blindness—and the reprobation of future generations—is close attention to the relationship between evidence and truth. The "evidence" produced by torture is finally no more reliable than a ghost sighting.

Sources

Bremer, Francis J. *The Puritan Experiment: New England Society from Bradford to Edwards*. Hanover, NH: University Press of New England, 1995.

Human Rights First. "Top Interrogators Declare Torture Ineffective in Intelligence Gathering." June 24, 2008. Available at http://www.humanrightsfirst .org/2008/06/24top-interrogators-declare-torture-ineffective-in-intelligence -gathering.

Mayer, Jane. *The Dark Side: The Inside Story of How the War on Terror Turned into a War on American Ideals*. New York: Anchor Books, 2009.

Miller, Perry. "The Judgment of the Witches." In *The New England Mind: The Seventeenth Century*, 191–208. Cambridge, MA: Belknap Press of Harvard University Press, 1981.

Perverted Logic
Behind the Bush Administration's "Torture Memo"

In the Bush administration's most infamous "torture memo," dated August 1, 2002, Assistant Attorney General Jay Bybee wrote to then–White House Counsel Alberto Gonzales: "Physical pain amounting to torture must be equivalent in intensity to the pain accompanying serious physical injury, such as organ failure, impairment of bodily function, or even death." An American interrogator who inflicted anything short of this level of pain on a detainee in the war on terror would not be committing torture, he argued, and therefore could not be charged with that crime under the federal anti-torture law.

Bybee's purpose in adopting such a definition of torture was clearly to give interrogators maximum leeway to inflict physical pain in order to obtain information. Where did his definition originate? In international law? No. From scholarly commentary on torture? No, again. Bybee drew on an entirely unrelated body of law, federal health-care law, which mandates the *alleviation* of pain rather than justifying its *infliction*. In my judgment, Bybee's reasoning is not simply faulty, it is perverse. It exemplifies the sort of reasoning that has given us lawyers a bad name.

The federal anti-torture law prohibits acts "specifically intended to inflict severe physical or mental pain or suffering," but leaves those terms undefined. Seeking a definition, Bybee did not turn to the most obvious sources for interpreting the statute, such as the UN Convention against Torture and Other Cruel, Inhuman, and Degrading Treatment, which the U.S. anti-torture law was designed to implement, or to the significant body of international case law and scholarly commentary interpreting that convention. Instead, he seems to have googled the entire thirty-eight-volume United States Code in search of the phrase "severe pain." He discovered several general statutory provisions, but none dealt with torture or international law more generally. In fact, they all fell under the heading of health-care law; as Bybee acknowledges, they "defin[e] an emergency medical condition for the purpose of providing health benefits." What Bybee does not acknowledge is that the central example of the provisions he cites is found in the Emergency Medical Treatment and Active Labor Act, colloquially known as the "antidumping law."

That law was passed by Congress in 1986, in response to public outcry after hospital emergency rooms were found to be turning away or "dumping" seriously ill patients who were not able to pay for treatment. The law requires every hospital that receives funds from federal programs such as Medicare to perform a medical evaluation of each person who seeks treatment in its ER. If the individual has an "emergency medical condition," the hospital must stabilize that condition before discharging the patient, or arrange for a transfer to another facility. What is an "emergency medical condition"? It is a condition that manifests acute symptoms of such severity (including severe pain) that "the absence of immediate medical attention could reasonably be expected to result in placing the health of the individual . . . in serious jeopardy;" "serious impairment to bodily functions;" or "serious dysfunction of any bodily organ or part."

By manipulating this definition of "emergency medical condition," Bybee concocted his definition of torture as severe pain "equivalent in intensity to the pain accompanying serious physical injury, such as organ failure, impairment of bodily function, or even death." How did he manage it? In a nutshell, Bybee rearranged the elements of an "emergency medical condition" found in the antidumping law to define the term "severe pain," and then reasoned that when it came to interrogating alleged terrorists, anything up to that threshold did not count as torture. But Bybee's attempted definition of "severe pain" is totally spurious, and not simply because it is circular. Bybee also distorts the elements of an "emergency medical condition" that he invokes: the antidumping law requires *serious dysfunction* of an organ or body part, not *organ failure*, as Bybee alleges; and it speaks of serious jeopardy to *health*, rather than the threat of *death*.

What is most objectionable in Bybee's misuse of the definition of an "emergency medical condition" is his utter insensitivity to the larger moral purpose of the statutory provisions he is interpreting, for the bottom line of the antidumping law and its corollaries is that severe pain constitutes an emergency medical condition that demands immediate treatment. Respect for our common humanity means that virtually nothing is more important than alleviating such suffering. Efficiency is not more important: Medicare HMOs cannot require prior authorization from enrollees who seek emergency treatment for severe pain. Nor is money more important: hospital ERs are legally obliged to treat patients who are in severe pain, regardless of their ability to pay. Even immigration status can't trump treatment: in 2004, the U.S. House of Representatives balked at proposed legislation that would exclude illegal aliens from the protection of the antidumping law.

For Bybee (now a Bush-appointed judge on the U.S. Court of Appeals) to use a group of statutory provisions designed to alleviate physical pain in order to justify inflicting pain is literally perverse (*perversus*)—it is argument turned the wrong way 'round. His twisted attempt to limit the prohibition against torture by drawing on bits and pieces of a definition of "emergency medical condition" fashioned for an entirely different purpose undermines the fundamental moral insight the antidumping and anti-torture laws have in common: the conviction that fellow human beings experiencing great physical suffering exert a moral claim on us. Turning our faces away when we have the power to alleviate the grave pain of others not only derides their human dignity, but it also compromises our own. Intentionally inflicting such pain, even as a means to a very important political end, is an unspeakable crime.

Sources

Bybee, Jay. "Memorandum for Alberto R. Gonzales, Counsel to the President Re: Standards of Conduct for Interrogation under 18 U.S.C. §§ 2340-2340A." In *Torture Memos: Rationalizing the Unthinkable*, edited by David Cole, 42–105. New York: The New Press, 2009.

Emergency Medical Treatment and Active Labor Act (1986), 42 U.S.C. § 1395dd.

United Nations General Assembly. "United Nations General Assembly. Convention against Torture and Other Cruel, Inhuman or Degrading Treatment or Punishment. A/RES/39/46." Originally published December 10, 1984. Accessed May 27, 2014. http://www.un.org/documents/ga/res/39/a39r046.htm.

Regret Is Not Enough
Why the President Should Read Paul Ramsey

In late December 2011, President Barack Obama signed the National Defense Authorization Act into law, despite having "serious reservations" about provisions allowing those suspected of terrorist connections to be detained indefinitely without trial—including U.S. citizens arrested on American soil.

Obama expressed a similarly ambivalent attitude toward the darker side of statecraft in his 2009 Nobel Peace Prize acceptance speech, where he asserted that war is both "necessary" and an "expression of human folly." Such ambivalence is a hallmark of the political theology of Reinhold Niebuhr, whose influence Obama first acknowledged in an interview with David Brooks in 2007.

I found Obama's decision to sign NDAA despite his well-founded reservations deeply troubling. So, I hope that he adds another great twentieth-century Protestant political moralist to his reading list: Paul Ramsey. Ramsey once said that his goal in writing was to "propose an extension within the Christian realism of Reinhold Niebuhr." And by "extension," Ramsey meant "necessary theological correction."

If Martin Luther's motto is "sin boldly," Niebuhr's would be "sin humbly—but effectively." As a "Christian realist," Niebuhr insisted that statesmen don't have the moral luxury of refusing to get their hands dirty. At the same time, he held that leaders ought to resist the delusion that the comparative justice of their cause whitewashes their methods—or their hearts, for that matter. By critiquing American self-righteousness, Niebuhr presented himself as a strong critic of American exceptionalism.

What Ramsey allows us to see, however, is that Niebuhr's framework ultimately provided American exceptionalism with its best defense mechanism yet. It encourages us to deceive ourselves into believing that the regret and doubt we experience over the use of morally questionable means only proves our morally superior status. Ultimately, American exceptionalism and moral consequentialism go together hand in glove—the moral self-examination and self-recrimination only make the glove fit like a second skin.

How, then, to curb the pride and self-righteousness that Niebuhr perceived to be at the heart of American exceptionalism? Ramsey rightly saw that it is necessary not only to be appropriately measured about the political goals we set, but also to be appropriately limited in the means we use to achieve them. We escape the snare of excessive self-regard by honoring absolute moral norms that respect the humanity of our enemies, who are equally beloved by God, not by wringing our hands before we violate these norms.

Ramsey argued, for example, that the justification for waging war and the limits restricting how we wage it arise from the same source—Christian love of neighbor. Following Augustine, he maintained that when we are unjustly attacked as individuals, we ought to turn the other cheek. When our innocent neighbors are attacked, however, love requires that we take up arms and defend them. But this justification immediately generates its own limit: Ramsey insisted we cannot consistently claim to be motivated by Christian love and a concern to protect the weak and vulnerable if we target our weapons at just such groups of people. And so he defended the principle of discrimination as part of the just war criteria: the absolute immunity of noncombatants from direct attack.

I also think there is a strong Ramseyan argument against indefinite detention of terrorist suspects without trial. Not only does indefinite detention violate American constitutional norms, particularly the norm of due process, it also violates the norms of Christian neighbor love, because the idea of personal moral accountability and just judgment is at the heart of Christianity. We recite in the creed that Jesus will come again to judge the living and the dead; we know that if we are consigned to hell, it will be on the basis of our own actions for which we are fairly judged.

The Christian belief in the possibility of just judgment in the end times undergirds our efforts to hold ourselves and one another morally accountable in these times—including in times of war. To detain prisoners indefinitely without a fair trial doesn't merely consign them to an earthly hell without first hearing their case. Perhaps more troubling, it treats them as animals to be contained and controlled, rather than moral agents to be judged and held accountable for their actions—and *only* for their actions.

Does it matter that Obama promised not to authorize indefinite military detention without trial of American citizens? On this question, I think both Niebuhr and Ramsey would agree that the answer is "not much." It is not merely a matter of what Obama himself will do if he is presented with circumstances he perceives as sufficiently exigent; it is also a question of what his successors in office will do. Both Ramsey and Niebuhr would say that the human capacity for self-deception and self-justification is nearly boundless—especially among the powerful.

Sources

National Defense Authorization Act for Fiscal Year 2012, Pub. L. No. 112-81.

Niebuhr, Reinhold. *The Essential Reinhold Niebuhr: Selected Essays and Addresses.* Edited by Robert McAfee Brown. New Haven, CT: Yale University Press, 1986.

Obama, Barack H. "Remarks on Accepting the Nobel Prize in Oslo, December 10, 2009." *Public Papers of the Presidents of the United States,* 2009, bk. 2, 1799–1804.

Ramsey, Paul. *The Essential Paul Ramsey.* Edited by William Werpehowski and Stephen D. Crocco. New Haven, CT: Yale University Press, 1994.

Part 2

Religious Liberty and Its Limits

The First Amendment to the Constitution specifies in part that "Congress shall make no law respecting an establishment of religion, or prohibiting the free exercise thereof." The first part of that provision, usually called the Establishment Clause, prohibits the government from holding one particular set of religious beliefs up for honor and influence upon law and policy. The provision's second part, commonly called the Free Exercise Clause, prohibits the government from using its power to target religious activities for diminishment or destruction. While the religion clauses apply by their terms only to the federal government, the Supreme Court of the United States extended their reach to the states in the middle part of the twentieth century.[1]

Interpreting the religion clauses is no easy task. What counts as "establishing" religion? Inviting a member of the local clergy to offer a prayer before a meeting of the city council?[2] What about school officials inviting a clergyperson to pray at a public high school graduation?[3] How far does the reach of the Establishment Clause extend? Religious beliefs and practices do not always exist in a hermetically sealed bubble, but can permeate both the common culture and the common morality. Generally speaking, the courts have found that reasonable efforts to promote a common morality and a common culture do not violate the Establishment Clause, provided that those efforts are not put forth with the explicit intention of promoting a particular religion. It is permissible for the government to encourage a common day of rest; in a community composed primarily of Jews, that day will be Saturday; in a community whose members are primarily Christian, that day will be Sunday. Similarly, the courts have recognized that many moral prohibitions and requirements have roots in religious traditions; provided those moral prohibitions and requirements are widely shared, no Establishment Clause problem applies.

Criminal laws against murder are not unconstitutional, for example, simply because it appears in the Ten Commandments.

Establishment Clause jurisprudence, therefore, tacitly recognizes a "common morality" that is both necessary to the proper functioning of society, and does not raise any particular problems of religious endorsement. The converse was also true with respect to Free Exercise Clause jurisprudence: the general steps taken to promote a common culture and support a common moral vision were not viewed as an impermissible violation of the religious liberty rights of those who were not in step with that culture or morality. In the nineteenth century, the Supreme Court rejected arguments that anti-polygamy laws violated the Free Exercise Clause, because it prevented members of the Church of Jesus Christ and Latter Day Saints from establishing the polygamous families commended by their religion.[4]

This sort of First Amendment equilibrium can function quite well as long as there is a broadly shared common morality among different communities of faith. It is significantly threatened, however, as the social consensus begins to break down—as what was once part of unquestioned, nonsectarian morality begins to become contested, and eventually, a new consensus begins to form. This is precisely what has happened in the past fifty years, particularly in the realm of sex, marriage, and family life. So, for example, until about 1930, most branches of Christianity were officially opposed to contraception. Now, not even a century later, contraception is widely accepted as a morally permissible option. Until recent years, sexual relationships outside of marriage, including sexual relationships between persons of the same sex, were considered to be morally unacceptable by most people, no matter what their religious views. Now, most people, including most young people, do not believe that to be the case.[5]

Moreover, over the past five decades, the changing sexual morality has increasingly been reflected in American law and policy. In 1965, the Supreme Court conferred constitutional protection upon the right of married couples to use contraception in the privacy of their bedrooms;[6] in 1968, it extended that right to cover the rights of all adults, married or unmarried, to purchase contraception.[7] In 1973, *Roe v. Wade* extended the constitutional privacy to cover a pregnant woman's decision to choose whether to have an abortion or to give birth.[8] The latest developments, however, have been in the realm of equal rights for homosexuals. In 2003, the Supreme Court struck down laws prohibiting sodomy;[9] a decade later, same-sex relationships were not merely tolerated, but protected by the status of marriage in nineteen states. In 2013, the Supreme Court struck down a section of the Federal Defense of Marriage Act, which limited federal benefits conferred on married couples to heterosexual married couples.[10] In early 2015, same-sex marriage was permitted by 37 states. It seems that a new social consensus is forming about the morality of same-sex relationships, which is leaving behind traditional religious views on the topic. This shift in social morals gained added force and momentum in June 2015, when the Supreme Court held that the Fourteenth Amendment to the Constitution, which guarantees equal protection of the law, demands that all fifty states extend the benefits and responsibilities of marriage to same-sex couples.[11]

At the same time, this emerging new consensus is putting powerful religious groups who advocate for a traditional sexual morality in a difficult position. Such groups used to be part of the moral consensus, a powerful voice in mainstream public policy and law. They have suddenly found themselves on the outside—part of a moral minority. What are they to do? On the one hand, they have not given up hope of reestablishing a social consensus and reflecting their views in the law. And indeed, social conservatives continue to constitute a powerful political force in this country. On the other hand, many social conservatives increasingly believe that they may lose the broader social battle, at least in the short term. Therefore, they want to secure some sort of refuge for themselves.

This second goal has led some groups, including the United States Conference of Catholic Bishops, to turn to the Free Exercise Clause of the Constitution for protection. They have claimed, for example, that the federal regulations requiring employers to subsidize contraception as part of a basic health care benefit package violate the religious freedom of employers religiously opposed to contraception. One can easily imagine Catholics and Evangelical Protestants making a similar claim to exemption from anti-discrimination laws requiring them to provide equal benefits to same-sex married couples.

This is a highly innovative approach to the Free Exercise Clause. Until this point in time, the claimants under the Free Exercise Clause have largely been discrete religious minorities who seek to protect their distinctive way of life or manner of worship against encroachment by majority legislation. The Free Exercise Clause has been invoked (often unsuccessfully) to protect minority groups who do not have enough power or influence to participate in political battles. It has not been treated as providing a fallback option to influential players who happen to lose political battles, even morally and religiously important ones.

The chapters in this section articulate my reactions to this innovative use of the Free Exercise Clause. They were written in real time; they trace my reactions to the claims of bishops and others that the contraception mandate violates the right to religious liberty. Three key themes run throughout. First, how will the rule of law prevail if powerful minorities who lose a particular legislative battle can circumvent a law by invoking religious freedom? Second, how do we account for the legitimate claims of all those affected by the law in question? For example, how do we balance an employer's objections to contraception against an employee's religious and moral beliefs that contraception is appropriate? Finally, I consider the price that may be exacted from religious communities that invoke the protection of religious freedom jurisprudence. That jurisprudence, in my view, tends to frame religious beliefs as idiosyncratic and irrational—as inaccessible to the claims of ordinary practical morality. While this frame may be comfortable for many religious traditions, it requires significant contortion from others. The Roman Catholic tradition, for example, has steadily presented its moral teaching (including on contraception and abortion) as part of the natural law, and therefore as accessible to and applicable to everyone.

Needless to say, these issues are controversial. Different readers will have different opinions upon how to balance the various values involved in these cases. Nonetheless, I think that more thorough reflection on and engagement with the structure and logic of many current Free Exercise Clause appeals can only benefit our discussion. These essays represent my own efforts toward these ends.

Finally, a strong disclaimer is in order. Whatever one thinks about the threats to religious liberty in the United States, we ought to be able to agree that our troubles pale in comparison to the terrible sufferings inflicted upon Christians around the world on account of their faith. Pope Francis reminded us not to forget our sisters and brothers in the faith in an address he delivered at an international conference on religious liberty sponsored by the Centers for Law and Religion and for International and Comparative Law at St. John's University and the Department of Law at the Libera Università Maria SS. Assunta (LUMSA). He rightly observed: "Persecution against Christians today is actually worse than in the first centuries of the Church, and there are more Christian martyrs today than in that era. This is happening more than 1,700 years after the edict of Constantine, which gave Christians the freedom to publicly profess their faith."[12]

While the debates about religious freedom in the United States are important, I do not want anything I say in the following pages to be interpreted as dismissing or detracting from the plight of religious believers, particularly Christians, in the rest of the world.

Notes

1. *Everson v. Board of Education*, 330 U.S. 1 (1947).

2. Not always—see *Town of Greece v. Galloway*, 572 U.S. ___, 134 S.Ct. 1811 (2014).

3. It is not permissible for school officials to invite outside speakers to pray at graduation ceremonies. See *Lee v. Weisman*, 506 U.S. 577 (1992). Students offering their own prayers raise a different set of issues.

4. *Reynolds v. United States*, 98 U.S. (8 Otto.) 145 (1878).

5. See, e.g., Frank Newport and Igor Himmelfarb, "In U.S. Record-High Say Gay, Lesbian Relations Morally OK: Americans' Tolerance of a Number of Moral Issues Up since 2001," Gallup Politics, May 20, 2013, available at http://www.gallup.com/poll/162689/record-high-say-gay-lesbian-relations-morally.aspx.

6. *Griswold v. Connecticut*, 381 U.S. 479 (1981).

7. *Eisenstadt v. Baird*, 405 U.S. 438 (1972).

8. *Roe v. Wade*, 410 U.S. 113 (1973).

9. *Lawrence v. Texas*, 539 U.S. 558 (2003).

10. *United States v. Windsor*, 570 U.S. ___, 133 S. Ct. 2675 (2013).

11. *Obergefell v. Hodges* 576 U.S. (2015).

12. Pope Francis, Address to Participants in the Conference on "International Religious Freedom and the Global Clash of Values," June 20, 2014, available at http://w2.vatican.va/content/francesco/en/speeches/2014/june/documents/papa-francesco_20140620_liberta-religiosa.html.

The Right to Refuse
How Broad Should Conscience Protections Be?

Do health-care providers have a right to refuse to be involved in medical procedures that they believe to be immoral? If so, how broad is that right? These are the questions raised by the eleventh-hour decision of the outgoing Bush administration to enact a federal regulation confirming a right of both individual and corporate health-care providers to refuse involvement in some procedures they believe to be immoral. The regulation was placed under review by the Obama administration, which expressed concern about its breadth.

Three federal laws have long tied the receipt of government funding to respect for the consciences of both corporate and individual health-care providers. The Church Amendment (1973) protects the right of hospitals and individuals to refuse to participate in abortion or sterilization procedures on moral grounds, and safeguards conscientious objectors from discrimination. The Coats/Snowe Amendment (1996) prohibits discrimination against medical training programs and medical students refusing to participate in induced abortions. The Hyde/Weldon Amendment (2004) protects health-care entities, including insurance companies, from being forced to perform, pay for, and refer for abortions.

In December 2008, just before Barack Obama assumed the presidency, the Bush administration issued a set of regulations that it claimed were merely an interpretation of these laws. Supporters, such as the Catholic Health Association, claimed the regulation is necessary because faith-based providers are under increasing pressure to provide or refer for morally objectionable services, such as abortion. Their rights need to be clarified and enforced. Opponents, such as the American Academy of Pediatrics, argued that the regulations were not mere clarifications; they unacceptably broadened the law in at least two ways. They expanded the services to which one could conscientiously object, covering not only abortion and sterilization, but also contraception. And they expanded the class of people who can object, covering not only those directly involved in patient care, but also ancillary workers, such as receptionists and operating-room custodial staff. The Obama administration agreed with the view that the Bush regulations were overly broad. In 2011, it tightened them up, while still preserving the conscience rights of providers with respect to abortion.

It will be tempting for some people to treat this controversy as another partisan skirmish accompanying a shift in political power. But that would be a mistake. In our society, both increasingly pluralistic and increasingly centralized, questions of conscience are bound to become more prevalent and to cover a wider array of topics. We need to grapple with the underlying moral and political issues.

Those claiming conscience-clause protections must ask themselves a basic question: Am I committed to protecting conscience for its own sake, or simply because it's the best fallback option in what I consider to be a fundamentally immoral, even evil, legal and political situation? Many prolife arguments for abortion conscience clauses take this form: "A decent society ought to ban abortion, but at the very least, it ought to protect those morally courageous doctors who refuse to perform it." This appeal to conscience is provisional. When we are in political power, we will try to ban abortion, when we are out of power, we will claim the protections of conscience. Needless to say, that argument will not persuade prochoice advocates, who think their own position is about respecting the consciences of pregnant women.

In evaluating laws to protect conscientious refusals, we also have to think about the implications for cases in which we believe refusals to perform certain professional responsibilities are morally unjustified. A broad right to refuse to perform *any* medical procedure based on sincere moral or religious objections will protect an Evangelical or Catholic doctor who refuses to perform an abortion. But it will also protect a biblical fundamentalist nurse who refuses to give anesthesia to a woman in labor on the grounds that the Bible condemns all women to suffer in childbirth. Are we prepared to honor that personal decision as well?

Sound legislation will also need to consider to what degree the conscientious objector has a duty to avoid the conflict. We sympathize with the moral plight of a drafted pacifist, but we think a pacifist who voluntarily joins a combat unit in Iraq has created her own moral problem. What, then, do we say to the analogous argument that people who morally object to abortion or euthanasia simply shouldn't go into medicine? Here the argument inevitably shifts from the nature of conscience to the nature of the medical profession. Prolife advocates will need to defend the proposition that medicine can simply never be defined in a way that mandates intentional killing.

Finally, sound legislation needs to take into account the interests of vulnerable third parties. For example, in 2007, some Muslim cab drivers at the Minneapolis airport objected to transporting passengers who carried alcohol in their luggage. In this case, as far as the law is concerned, the vulnerability of travelers trumps the consciences of cabbies. Analogously, we need to ask whether there are cases in which the vulnerability of a patient trumps or qualifies the conscience of a health-care provider.

I think we ought to protect the doctor who refuses to perform the abortion, but not the nurse who refuses the anesthesia to a woman in labor. Why? I'm not sure. I can identify some important theoretical questions, but I can't yet answer them fully. These questions need sustained attention from practitioners and scholars, including but not limited to Catholic theologians and lawyers.

Sources

American Academy of Pediatrics. "Right of Conscience Regulation Dangerous Policy." December 19, 2008. Available at http://webcache.googleusercontent .com/search?q=cache:F4l8fLDrzDIJ:www2.aap.org/advocacy/washing /AAP%2520SAM%2520release_Right%2520of%2520Conscience_FINAL .pdf+&cd=1&hl=en&ct=clnk&gl=us

Catholic Health Association. "DHHS's 'Rights of Conscience' Regulation," *Health Care Ethics USA*, vol. 17, no. 1 (Winter 2009): 23–24.

Church Amendments, 42 U.S.C. §300a-7.

Coats/Snowe Amendment, 42 U.S.C. § 238n.

Desmond, Joan Frawley. "Obama Rescinds Bush-Era Conscience Regs." *National Catholic Register*, February 23, 2011. Available at http://www.ncregister.com /daily-news/obama-rescinds-bush-era-conscience-regs.

"Ensuring That Department of Health and Human Services Funds Do Not Support Coercive or Discriminatory Policies or Practices in Violation of Federal Law," 73 Fed. Reg. 78072 (December 19, 2008).

Gibson, David. "Obama Administration Returns to Earlier Conscience Protections for Health Workers." *Politics Daily*, February 18, 2012. Available at http://www.politicsdaily.com/2011/02/18/obama-administration-returns-to-earlier-conscience -protections-f/.

Hyde/Weldon Conscience Protection Amendment. A version has been passed on a yearly basis in the annual budget appropriations legislation. See, e.g., Consolidated Appropriations Act, P.L. 113-76 (2014), div. H, tit. 5 §§506–507.

"Regulation for the Enforcement of Federal Health Care Provider Conscience Protection Laws," 76 Fed. Reg. 9968 (February 23, 2011). The current regulation is found at: 45 CFR 88.1–2.

The Bishops and Religious Liberty
Are Catholics Becoming a Sect?

"Our First, Most Cherished Liberty" reflects the bishops' deep ambivalence about whether they prefer the protection afforded a religious minority in the United States or whether they want to be an influential force in the moral mainstream. The first option will likely require them to accept some marginalization, while the second exposes them to uncomfortable pushback from opposing forces. Their statement suggests they want to have it both ways, but that outcome seems highly unlikely, at least within the American legal and political framework.

The bishops tend to frame their complaint in terms of religious liberty. Yet most religious-liberty cases involve minority religious groups seeking to be left alone to pursue holiness as they see fit, free from the baleful attention or coercion of the majority. They want to worship as they wish (*Church of Lukumi Babalu Aye v. City of Hialeah*, 1993) or educate their children as they think faith requires (*Wisconsin v. Yoder*, 1972). Recognizing themselves as religious and moral minorities, most religious liberty plaintiffs do not try to influence the broader community. Nor do they attempt to recast American society in their own image.

Of course, unlike the Amish in the *Yoder* case, the bishops do not want to withdraw into a sectarian corner. As many passages in the bishops' statement make clear, they want to participate more broadly in American life, and to shape the American ethos in accordance with their own values. For example, the bishops proclaim, "what is at stake is . . . whether the state alone will determine who gets to contribute to the common good, and how they get to do it."

This impetus toward public influence seems to be operating in the bishops' dubious claim that "it is essential to understand the distinction between conscientious objection and an unjust law. Conscientious

75

objection permits some relief to those who object to a just law for reasons of conscience—conscription being the best known example. An
unjust law is 'no law at all.' It cannot be obeyed, and therefore one does
not seek relief from it, but rather its repeal."

It seems to me that this line of reasoning about unjust law is at
the heart of the bishops' stance on the contraception mandate. They
flatly rejected the administration's attempts to insulate Catholic employers from the mandate by requiring third parties to pay for and
provide contraception coverage to employees of nonexempt Catholic
institutions. Nor did the bishops propose any accommodations themselves. Instead, they claimed the only moral option is the complete
repeal of the mandate. Why is the mandate an unjust law? Because,
according to the US Catholic Bishops, contraception is intrinsically
immoral. This position is consistent with the Catholic view that the
magisterium is the authoritative interpreter of the natural law. But it
goes far beyond the American understanding of religious liberty. Of
course, there are constitutional limits, but generally in a representative democracy such as ours, the majority has the power to determine
through the legislative process what counts as a wise and just law.
In the United States, I think, justice includes a concern of fairness—
we ask whether all people are being treated respectfully, not merely
those who share our moral and religious viewpoints. So any hint of an
idea that the bishops get to articulate the moral law for all Americans
without taking into account the very many people who hold different
views in good faith is a non-starter.

There are other problems with the statement. Several of the examples of religious oppression cited by the bishops do not stand up
to close scrutiny. For example, the bishops cite a 2009 bill in the Connecticut legislature that would have forced Catholic parishes to be
restructured according to a Congregationalist model. What the bishops fail to note is that a chorus of legal experts immediately shot the
bill down as flagrantly unconstitutional. It was killed by a unanimous
committee vote two weeks after it was proposed.

The bishops note that several states have passed laws that prohibit
"harboring" undocumented immigrants, "and what the church deems
Christian charity and pastoral care to those immigrants." They point
in particular to Alabama's 2011 law targeting the undocumented as

"perhaps the most egregious." Yet they fail to inform the reader that the Obama administration immediately challenged the Alabama law on the grounds that it conflicted with federal immigration law, which is far more humane. A federal district court quickly issued a preliminary injunction barring enforcement of those aspects of the statute to which the bishops objected. Why are the bishops providing the faithful with only half the story?

Two other examples are more complicated. The bishops highlight the refusal of several states and municipalities to grant licenses to Catholic adoption agencies that would not place children with same-sex couples. Also mentioned is the decision not to renew the federal contract of the USCCB's Migration and Refugee Services because it would not provide or refer for contraceptive or abortion services for victims of human trafficking.

I do not think these are examples of the government infringing on the religious liberty of the Catholic Church. Instead, the bishops are dealing with the difficult problem of finding a modus vivendi with a fast evolving moral consensus that conflicts with traditional Catholic teachings. As a matter of public morality, the country increasingly rejects discrimination on the basis of sexual orientation. Most people understand this to be the logical extension of protections already provided to individuals on the basis of sex, race, and religion. So it is not entirely surprising that Catholic Charities is refused a license because it won't place a child with same-sex couples. Atheist Charities would be refused a license, too, if it made the same decision—or if it refused to place a child with Catholics, for that matter.

The situation involving the contract for victims of human trafficking also reflects the conflict between Catholic moral teaching and the broader moral consensus. The federal government is using government funds—taxpayer money—to hire someone to act on its behalf in serving a vulnerable population. Contraception and abortion are, in fact, not only legally protected, but constitutionally protected choices. Victims of human trafficking may not have a clear idea about how to access these services on their own; they may not even speak English. Is it really outrageous for the government to give "strong preference" to organizations that will at least offer referrals for the "full range of legally permissible gynecological and obstetric care"?

What about the fact that the bishops' Migration and Refugee Services has a sterling track record? That fact complicates the picture, but it does not settle the question. Consider a hypothetical that raises a mirror-image problem. Suppose the Freedom from Religion Foundation also provided excellent care to victims, but refused to give them information or help finding local churches or religious support groups. Would the bishops be upset if the government ruled them out as a contractor on the grounds that they were hampering the exercise of the victims' right to freely worship as they see fit? Probably not, but what's the difference between the two? Catholics need to think hard about what neutral principle the government should apply in making distinctions in cases like these. To be frank, I'm not sure there is one.

Finally, the most striking aspect of the bishops' claims about religious liberty is the absolute nature of their assertions. They give the reader virtually no hint that such questions must be assessed in a framework of competing rights and duties, particularly the duty to promote the common good. This is ironic from a theological perspective. Vatican II's *Declaration on Religious Freedom* recognizes that there are "due limits" on the exercise of religious freedom, including the need to promote a "just public order," and preserve the "equality of the citizens before the law." For years, Catholic moralists and lawyers have railed against the assertion of rights claims without any consideration of relational responsibilities. Nor does the bishops' rights absolutism make much sense as a legal strategy. American law does not treat religious freedom as an absolute right. The leading case interpreting the Free Exercise Clause, *Employment Division v. Smith* (1990), holds that the Constitution does not require lawmakers to give religious exemptions to neutral laws of general applicability, provided no other constitutional rights are involved. Even under the stricter, "compelling state interest" test that governed in the pre-*Smith* era, religious freedom was never an absolute right, but had to be balanced against competing state interests. Moreover, those interests must be assessed from the vantage point of the lawmakers, not the religious objector.

The case that seems most on point with regard to the contraception mandate is *United States v. Lee* (1982). It was decided under the stricter test that the Religious Freedom Restoration Act still applies to federal regulations such as the mandate. In that instance, the

Supreme Court held that it was constitutionally permissible for the federal government to force Amish employers to pay Social Security taxes for their employees, although both the payment and receipt of Social Security taxes violated their religious beliefs, and although the employees in question were Amish themselves.

Why should it be permissible to force Amish employers to pay Social Security taxes but not to force Catholic employers to pay for contraception? I don't see a compelling distinction between the two cases. In *Lee*, the Court noted that "the Social Security system in the United States serves the public interest by providing a comprehensive insurance system with a variety of benefits available to all participants, with costs shared by employers and employees." A similar claim could be made about employer-based health reform.

Moreover, the Court noted "it would be difficult to accommodate the comprehensive Social Security system with myriad exceptions flowing from a wide variety of religious beliefs." The administrative difficulty would be even greater with comprehensive health reform, since objections would run not merely to payment, but to various and sundry covered services.

Noting that Congress had made an exemption for self-employed Amish, the *Lee* Court stated it need not go further by making an accommodation for Amish who employ other Amish, such as the plaintiff. The reasoning is instructive:

> When followers of a particular sect enter into commercial activity as a matter of choice, the limits they accept on their own conduct as a matter of conscience and faith are not to be superimposed on the statutory schemes that are binding on others in that activity. Granting an exemption from Social Security taxes to an employer operates to impose the employer's religious faith on the employees (p. 261).

It seems to me that this last point is decisive with respect to the contraception mandate. The vast majority of Americans do not believe that the use of contraception is intrinsically immoral. In fact, they think it is a morally appropriate way to fulfill their responsibilities to themselves and to their families. In this context, granting an exemption to Catholic institutions would effectively impose the Catholic employer's understanding of morality on the employee just as surely as granting a Social Security tax exemption to Amish employers would.

Congress did eventually grant Social Security tax exemptions to the Amish hiring their coreligionists, since both employer and employee rejected the costs and benefits of Social Security. That exemption was not constitutionally required. It was, however, constitutionally permitted and even constitutionally sensible. I think the same thing could be said about the latest attempt on the part of the Obama administration to accommodate Catholic employers, such as universities and hospitals, which do not meet the strict criteria for the exemption. On the one hand, such employers will not be required to provide or arrange for contraception coverage. On the other, employees will have access to such coverage through insurance companies or third-party administrators. I see no reason to disbelieve the actuaries who say that it is revenue-neutral to do so, since it reduces the rate of unexpected pregnancies across covered populations.

According to *Lee*, "To maintain an organized society that guarantees religious freedom to a great variety of faiths requires that some practices yield to the common good." The bishops do not agree, of course, that expanding access to contraception will in fact contribute to the common good. And they are free to make that argument in the public square. But just as a member of Peace Church cannot politically demand that the only way to respect his or her religious liberty is to end a war for everyone, so the bishops cannot insist that "the only way to respect our religious liberty is to repeal the contraceptive mandate for everyone." It just doesn't work that way.

Sources

Church of Lukumi Babalu Aye v. City of Hialeah, 508 U.S. 520 (1993).

Connecticut General Assembly, Jan. Sess. 2009, R.B. 1098, LCO 4528, "An Act Modifying Corporate Laws Relating to Certain Religious Corporations."

Employment Division v. Smith, 494 U.S. 872 (1990).

Religion Clause Blog. "Connecticut Bill Would Reform Financial Management of Catholic Parishes." May 9, 2009. Available at http://religionclause .blogspot.com/2009/03/connecticut-bill-would-reform-financial.html.

Sadowski, Dennis. "HHS Defends Decision on Funding Trafficking Victims Program to Congress." *Catholic News Service*, December 2, 2011. Available at http://www.catholicnews.com/data/stories/cns/1104711.htm.

United States Conference of Catholic Bishops. "Our First, Most Cherished Liberty." March 2012. Available at http://www.usccb.org/issues-and-action /religious-liberty/our-first-most-cherished-liberty.cfm.

United States v. Lee, 455 U.S. 252 (1982).

Vatican II. *Dignitatis humanae* (1965).

Wisconsin v. Yoder, 406 U.S. 205 (1972).

Is the Government "Defining Religion"?
The Bishops' Case against the Mandate

The Patient Protection and Affordable Care Act was enacted into law in 2010. Despite strong support in Catholic social teaching for access to basic health care for all persons, the U.S. Conference of Catholic Bishops continued actively to oppose the Affordable Care Act. In large part, the USCCB objected to the Department of Health and Human Services' imposition of requirements to cover contraceptive services as part of an array of mandated women's preventive health services. Moreover, while the Administration carved out an exemption for those employers who had religious objections to subsidizing contraception for their employees, the bishops did not think it was broad enough. In particular, the USCCB was not only worried about what the law might force these institutions to *do*, such as pay for contraceptive coverage. It was also worried what it might say about who they *are*. In a statement issued in 2012 the USCCB Administrative Committee protested: "Government has no place defining religion and religious ministry . . . . HHS thus creates and enforces a new distinction—alien both to our Catholic tradition and to federal law—between our houses of worship and our great ministries of service to our neighbors, namely, the poor, the homeless, the sick, the students in our schools and universities, and others in need, of any faith community or none."

I think the USCCB's criticism is rooted in a mistaken assumption about how our law operates. The HHS regulations don't define religion—they define exemptions to the mandate applicable to institutions that certify themselves as religious, while balancing competing concerns in light of the purposes of the particular law they are implementing. Institutions, in other words, *define themselves* as religious. But the fact that an institution is religious does not settle the question about whether it gets an exemption. There are other interests and concerns involved, related to the objectives of the law.

What is the purpose of the controversial contraception mandate? The ACA requires total coverage of many preventive health services because studies have shown that even small copayments deter access. The Institute of Medicine recommended that contraception be treated as a preventive service because women with unintended pregnancies are more likely to engage in behaviors dangerous to themselves and their unborn children. Moreover, studies show unintended pregnancies pose a higher risk of pre-term or low-birth-weight babies, increasing the likelihood of subsequent health problems. To HHS, covering contraception is a public-health issue, not merely a matter of reproductive choice.

Given the purpose of the law, different exemptions for different types of religious institutions make sense. For example, one group of "religious employers" was completely exempt from the mandate. The first versions of the regulations required those employers to meet four criteria: (1) their purpose is the inculcation of religious values; (2) they primarily employ persons who share their religious faith; (3) they primarily serve persons who share that faith; and (4) they are structured as nonprofit, tax-exempt charitable corporations. Employees in such institutions receive no contraception benefit at all.

At the same time, the HHS regulations must balance the religious-liberty interests of all employers against the legitimate expectations of employees and the government's public health goals. In organizations that have been completely exempted from the mandate—such as parishes and dioceses—employees are more likely to share, or at least accept, the moral views of their employers. Consequently, it will not seem unfair to deny access to treatments that are inconsistent with an employer's religious views. Nor will it greatly affect the public health objectives of the law, assuming this class of beneficiaries is less likely to use contraception even if it were freely available.

But many Catholic institutions, such as hospitals and colleges, employ and serve non-Catholics. Initially, these institutions did not qualify for any exemption. But in response to criticism from the bishops and others, HHS created a second category of exemption, "to accommodate non-exempt, nonprofit religious organizations."

According to HHS, the proposed accommodation had two objectives. First, it would ensure that employees can obtain no-cost contraception. Second, it would protect certain religious organizations from "having to contract, arrange, or pay for contraceptive coverage." Insurers and third-party administrators would take over these tasks.

Doesn't this sort of accommodation make sense in our pluralistic society? HHS emphasizes that the different treatment accorded these religious organizations does not imply that the second group is less religious than the first. Instead, HHS recognizes that the employees in the second group likely have different needs and different values than those in the first group. The vast majority of Americans (including most Catholics) think the use of contraception can be a way of fulfilling their moral obligations, not betraying them.

The bishops rightly note that faith-based employers have a religious liberty interest at stake in the mandate. They sometimes forget, however, that the *employees* of these institutions also have religious liberty interests. In *United States v. Lee* (1982), the Supreme Court stated that granting an exemption to Amish employers who voiced religious objections to the payment of Social Security taxes "operates to impose the employer's religious faith on the employees."

Of course, the proposed accommodation is not the only way to balance the competing interests. The Catholic Health Association and others have suggested broadening the total exemption category to include religiously sponsored hospitals and universities, while providing contraceptives under another government program. This approach is simple, straightforward, and attractive.

But as we debate these options, let's reject the canard that the proposal initially on the table was a cynical attack on religious institutions. I don't think that's the case.

Sources

Institute of Medicine. "Recommendations for Preventive Services for Women That Should Be Considered by HHS." Institute of Medicine. July 11, 2011. Available at http://www.iom.edu/Reports/2011/Clinical-Preventive-Services -for-Women-Closing-the-Gaps/Recommendations.aspx.

United States Conference of Catholic Bishops. "Our First, Most Cherished Liberty." March 2012. Available at http://www.usccb.org/issues-and-action /religious-liberty/our-first-most-cherished-liberty.cfm.

United States v. Lee, 455 U.S. 252 (1982).

Defining Exemptions Does Not Equal Defining Religion
A Category Mistake

The U.S. Catholic bishops have voiced two distinct sets of concerns about the regulation of the Department of Health and Human Services generally mandating contraceptive coverage in employer health plans. First and most obviously, they have been worried that it will make Catholic institutions cover contraception. But the bishops have also expressed a second and deeper worry, which pertains to Catholic identity. The bishops, in other words, were deeply concerned about what the mandate says the Catholic Church *is*.

The original regulations implementing the contraception mandate exempted a narrow class of religious institutions (such as parishes and dioceses), but did not exempt Catholic universities and hospitals. So the bishops—and many other Catholics—felt insulted and misunderstood. They sensed that the government was defining religion in too narrow a way, and not appreciating the key fact that Catholic universities and hospitals are also imbued with a religious mission—the very same Catholic mission as parishes and dioceses.

But they missed a key aspect of the situation: the government wasn't *defining* religion. It was defining an *exemption* to a particular law that applies to some but not all religious institutions. This is a crucial point. Only very rarely does the government say that a particular party is religious or not religious. (When it does happen, the case generally involves an obvious scam, say a group of prisoners who feel called to start the Church of Beer, Pizza, and Football, for example.) In the vast majority of cases, the government accepts an institution's word that it *is* religious. This is a wise decision on its part, because getting into the business of certifying certain individuals or groups as sufficiently religious would arguably run afoul of the First Amendment prohibition of the government establishing religion. The government accepts an institution's religiosity, and then goes on to apply the other criteria at issue *in addition* to religiosity in order to say whether the institution is exempt from a particular law.

Some people have said, "why not use the tax code definition of religion to define the exemption from the HHS mandate?" But the answer here is that *the tax code doesn't define religion either*. In this situation too, it defines an *exemption* to taxation applicable to some but not all religious institutions. The government generally accepts an organization's claim to be religious, but goes on to apply other criteria for exemption from taxation. So, for example, a group can be as religious as it wants, but if it's not organized as a not-for-profit charitable corporation, it won't be exempt from taxation—it will still have to pay taxes! Catholic schools and hospitals are exempt from taxation not simply because they are religious, but because they also meet the other characteristics necessary for tax exemption—they are not-for-profit charities. One could imagine a for-profit Catholic facility (say, a rehab center) that wouldn't get tax-exempt status. The rehabbing patients could be personally blessed and supervised by the pope, but if the center isn't organized as a not-for-profit entity, it's just not going to get tax-exempt status.

So the question that has to be asked is why the criteria for determining whether a religious institution is tax exempt are appropriate for determining whether it is exempt from other laws? Surely, we wouldn't say that the criteria for tax exemption should determine whether a Catholic institution was exempt from health and safety laws, or mandated reporter laws. The scope of any exemption has to depend upon the purpose of the law to which it attaches. A church-sponsored day-care institution, for example, might be exempt from taxation—but it should not be exempt from fire codes, despite the fact that the historic church building itself would be. And no one would say the day care center should be exempt! The same approach applies in determining the nature of the exemption from the contraception mandate. We need to ask what the scope of a religious exemption to a mandate to provide preventive services as part of a basic benefit package should be—which is not at all the same question of what the scope of exemption to taxation should be.

Now, the original, narrow exemption generated a political, moral, and religious firestorm. It was a bad idea. But motives matter.

Procedure matters. HHS did not pull the narrow original exemption out of thin air. Sensibly, it looked around, not just at religious exemptions in general, but at religious exemptions to contraceptive mandates. Twenty-eight states have contraception mandates. Some have religious exemptions, others have none; some have broader exemptions, others have narrower ones. Federal anti-discrimination law requires coverage of contraception. So does the Medicaid program federal-state partnership. HHS modeled its exemption on the language already in place in California and New York. This was not a legally rash move. That language had been tested in two populous states, and more importantly, had already been challenged on religious freedom grounds and *upheld* by the highest courts in those states. So the language was at least somewhat road-tested for a religious exemption to a comprehensive contraceptive mandate, not for an exemption to something else. If you're a lawyer looking for statutory or regulatory language, it's generally a good idea to turn to provisions that have been litigated and upheld. It's very true that the road test wasn't perfect; the Religious Freedom Restoration Act (RFRA) doesn't apply to the states, and does apply to HHS regulations. But it wasn't just a shot in the dark either.

I understand the objections of the USCCB and others that the original exemption was too narrow. I strongly agree with the objection that it was politically unwise—in fact, it was clearly almost disastrous. But as a lawyer, I just can't go along with those who say that the original exemption was some sort of half-baked, new-fangled, anti-religious plot. And I think that matters. It is very important to me that President Obama and HHS are *not* anti-religious, given the enormous role that faith-based health care has played and will continue to play in this country. Parties of good will can fix political mistakes, but anti-religious bias can't be fixed.

Sources

Catholic Charities of the Diocese of Albany v. Serio, 7 N.Y. 3d 510 (2006).
Catholic Charities of Sacramento, Inc. v Superior Court, 32 Cal. 4th 527 (Cal. 2004).
Guttmacher Institute. "State Policies in Brief: Insurance Coverage of Contraceptives." June 1, 2014. Available at https://www.guttmacher.org/pubs/spib_ICC .pdf.

National Conference of State Legislatures. "Insurance Coverage for Contraception Laws." 2012. Available at http://www.ncsl.org/research/health/insurance-coverage-for-contraception-state-laws.aspx.

Wolters Kluwer Law & Business. "State Mandates for Insurance Coverage of Contraception before and after Health Reform." October 2013. Available at http://webcache.googleusercontent.com/search?q=cache:RnRdR0l16acJ:hr.cch.com/hld/LB_Briefing_Contraception-Coverage_10-01_final.pdf+&cd=1&hl=en&ct=clnk&gl=us

An Evolving Accommodation
Religious Minorities and the Common Good

How should religiously infused moral judgments enter into the process of lawmaking? This is a fundamental question at the heart of the debate about the objection to the contraception mandate that was voiced by the United States Conference of Catholic Bishops.

We can begin by acknowledging that official Roman Catholic teaching holds that the moral act described as contracepting is always wrong because it separates the unitive and procreative goods meant to be joined together in a sexual act. The church teaches that contraception is wrong as a matter of natural law, which means that it is wrong for all human beings to do, whether they are Catholic or not. What if they don't agree? The church teaches that they are wrong. The church also teaches that she herself is an expert in humanity and is in a privileged position to interpret the natural law.

How should Catholic moral teaching about contraception be translated into the law in an American pluralistic democracy? The church has always acknowledged that morality and law do not entirely coincide. Moreover, John Courtney Murray, S.J., and others argued long ago that contraception should not be illegal. But they also thought that it should not be encouraged. From the perspective of today's bishops, therefore, the problem with the contraceptive mandate is that it is *encouraging contraception*. It is one thing *to fail to prohibit* contraception; it is another thing entirely *to require it to be included in a basic benefit package*. From the vantage of official Catholic teaching, then, there are two problems with the contraception mandate: 1) it wrongly teaches that contraception is morally acceptable; and 2) it makes it widely available.

So the first thing to note is that the bishops opposed the contraceptive mandate, *tout court*, because they thought that it encourages a practice that will harm individuals and the common good. This opposition is a perfectly legitimate use of political freedom in the United States. Like other citizens, the bishops are free to make their case about the immorality of contraception in the public square and to argue against any form of mandate based on that argument. And they did just that. But they *lost* that case: most people in the United States do not think that contraception is intrinsically immoral. In fact, they think it can be a useful way to fulfill their moral responsibilities to their children and themselves. Moreover, unlike the bishops, most people (and their duly elected representatives) judge that the widespread availability of contraception contributes to the common good. This common judgment is important, because it reflects the moral consensus of the community, which is accurately reflected in our democratic process of lawmaking. The bishops could and did argue that the mandate is unacceptable because it goes against the common good. On my view, however, they could not plausibly argue that the mandate as a general requirement is invalid law because it violates their religious freedom. No one's religious freedom can be so expansive that it allows them to dictate what the law will require for the entire community by circumventing the democratic process.

In a representative democracy, the majority is going to make the law—and law is coercive. So a pacifist cannot plausibly argue that the country can't go to war at all because going to war violates his religious freedom. A Christian Scientist cannot plausibly argue that the country ought not to invest in medicine because it goes against her religious beliefs. And the bishops could not plausibly argue that the Affordable Care Act must not include a contraceptive mandate as part of a basic benefit package because it violates Catholic teaching. Otherwise, one person's claim of religious liberty would act as a veto against any act of lawmaking. I can think of no law-and-religion scholar who would say that the First Amendment entails such a sweeping right to invalidate federal legislation. In fact, requiring the general law never to conflict with Catholic moral teaching would not be protecting religious freedom of Catholics; it would be enshrining Roman Catholicism as the established religion. The church can say that its Magisterium is the privileged interpreter of natural law binding upon all persons simply as persons. But the state simply cannot accede to such a claim in the American constitutional framework.

What the bishops could legitimately do, however, is argue is that our nation's constitutionally inscribed respect for religious liberty compels the government to grant an *exception* to the general mandate in their case. So how do we go about thinking about exemptions based on religious-liberty claims? It is worth reviewing in some detail the history of the mandate and its evolving framework for religious exemptions.

In August 2011, the Department of Health and Human Services (HHS) issued an interim final rule setting forth a series of preventive health services for women that would be included without cost-sharing in mandated basic benefit package. One of those mandated services was FDA-approved contraception and contraceptive services. The August 2011 rule allowed a narrow exemption from the mandate for religious institutions that: 1) are mainly concerned with passing down the faith; 2) mainly *employ* their co-religionists, 3) mainly *serve* their co-religionists, and (4) are not-for-profit charitable corporations. Not only would such employers not have to cover contraception, their employees wouldn't get it covered by anyone. Despite objections by religious groups, in winter 2012, HHS Secretary Kathleen Sebelius announced that the August 2011 rule would be finalized without change.

After absorbing an immediate firestorm of protest, the Obama administration promised a revised accommodation that would insure that Catholic hospitals and colleges wouldn't have to pay for, provide, or refer for such services, but that employees of these entities would still have first-dollar contraceptive coverage. An Advance Notice of Proposed Rulemaking issued in March 2012 sketched a rough outline of the administration's broader approach: it provided a temporary enforcement safe harbor so that Catholic colleges, hospitals, and other not-for-profit entities with objections to contraception would not run afoul of the law before a new arrangement could be worked out. In addition, the administration pledged to work with interested groups to develop final regulations that would achieve two objectives: "accommodating non-exempt, non-profit religious organizations' religious objections to covering contraceptive services and assuring that participants and beneficiaries covered under such organizations' plans receive contraceptive coverage without cost sharing."

That general plan was developed in more detail in proposed rules issued in early 2013. The proposed rules did two things: First, they simplified and clarified the qualifications for the completely exempt entities, by eliminating the first three requirements, and leaving only the requirement that the entity be a religious employer under the Tax Code. Second, it set the requirements for "accommodated" entities. If an employer self-certifies that it opposes providing coverage for some or all contraceptive services, it is organized and operated as a nonprofit entity, and it holds itself out as a religious organization, it will not be required to cover those services. Unlike completely exempt organizations, the employees of "accommodated" entities will still receive no-cost contraceptive coverage. The regulations place the burden on the insurer or third party administrator to reach out to employees and inform them of the availability of those services. Issued several months later, the final rules continued this approach, while attempting further to simplify administration of the policy.

This approach quelled but did not extinguish the objections. While the Catholic Health Association found the accommodation acceptable, the U.S. Conference of Catholic Bishops continued to protest. They claimed that certifying their objection to contraceptive services constituted objectionable cooperation in the provision of such services. Relatedly, they and others argued that *for-profit* corporations whose owners objected to the services should have the same sorts of rights.

Absent Supreme Court intervention, this is where things stand. Is it the right place to be? In order to answer this question, we have to recognize that claims of religious liberty are never treated as absolute. The government (in the first instance) and the courts (in the final instance) need to look not only at the religious-liberty claims, but also at the purposes advanced by the law in question. Moreover, the court cannot defer to the religious-liberty claimant's assessment of the purposes and effects of the law in question. For example, some religious commentators have attempted to frame the RFRA (Religious Freedom Restoration Act) analysis in this way: "The mandate interferes with religious liberty. Moreover, it does not serve a compelling state interest because contraception (in our view) actually harms women and children. Therefore the mandate should be struck down."

But that sort of analysis cannot simply be applied by the courts. The church cannot put both thumbs on the judicial scale, so to speak. The *church* can talk about the nature and extent of the invasion of its own religious liberty; provided it is sincere in its claims, the courts will defer to their account of the burden. But the *government* gets to make its own case for the purposes and effects of the law; that case is not filtered through the moral framework of the religious-liberty claimant. In my view, the government's case is quite substantial given that a National Institute of Medicine Report argues that no-cost access to contraception significantly promotes the health of women and children.

Now, what about the appropriateness of the accommodation considered in itself? I think that the accommodation as finalized in the HHS rules gives very significant protection to Catholic hospitals and universities insofar as it states that they won't have to provide, arrange, or pay for contraceptive services. It repeatedly and explicitly honors the religious mission of these institutions. But it is also trying to make sure that the governmental aims of the mandate are fulfilled, by ensuring that employees of these institutions get access to contraceptives. Is this an adequate resolution of the competing interests and claims involved?

As we look at this question, I think we need to separate two sub-issues: (1) does the accommodation sufficiently protect the religious liberty of Catholic institutions; and (2) is it clear, clean, simple, and workable? In my view, the accommodation does adequately protect the religious liberty of Catholic institutions. Its workability is another matter. The four-part test for completely exempt institutions (whose employees do not get contraception coverage from anyone) in earlier versions of the regulations was unwieldy and objectionable. The latest final regulations do a great deal to remedy the situation, by substituting a single test. The requirements for "accommodated" institutions, whose employees do get coverage, is fairly straightforward, involving a process of self-certification. Yet the process by which the insurers and third-party administrators pick up and pay for that obligation borders on Byzantine.

So I would ask critics of the finalized rule to consider: Does not the rule take pains to acknowledge the religious motives of, say, Catholic universities as well as Catholic parishes? Does it not bend over backwards to try to find a solution to the moral objections on the part of places like Notre Dame, while still protecting access for employees? Some might object that the accounting procedures for the accommodation are cumbersome and too complicated. All that may be true. At the same time, it's important to keep in mind that religious liberty claimants don't have a right to avoid all contact with cumbersome and complicated regulations. Clarion calls for religious freedom are unhelpful. We need to get into the weeds and discuss the strengths and weaknesses of the different legal options on the table to protect religious freedom while the government promotes access to contraception.

Sources

Catechism of the Catholic Church, §§2366-2372. 2nd ed. Washington, DC: USCCB Publishing, 2000.

Murray S.J., John Courtney. "Memo to Cardinal Cushing on Contraception Legislation." Woodstock Theological Center. 1965. Available at http://wood stock.georgetown.edu/library/murray/1965f.htm.

Noonan, John T., Jr. *Contraception: A History of Its Treatment by the Catholic Theologians and Canonists*. Enl. Ed. Cambridge, MA: Belknap Press of Harvard University Press, 1986.

Patient Protection and Affordable Care Act (2010), Pub. L. No. 111-148, 124 Stat. 119 –124 Stat. 1025.

Pope Paul VI. *Humanae vitae* (1968).

Tentler, Leslie Woodcock. *Catholics and Contraception: An American History*. Ithaca, NY: Cornell University Press, 2004.

Regulations in chronological order:

"Group Health Plans and Health Insurance Issuers Relating to Coverage of Preventive Services under the Patient Protection and Affordable Care Act" (interim final rules with request for comments). 76 Fed. Reg. 46621 (Aug. 3, 2011).

"Group Health Plans and Health Insurance Issuers Relating to Coverage of Preventive Services under the Patient Protection and Affordable Care Act" (final rules). 77 Fed. Reg. 8725 (February 15, 2012).

"Certain Preventive Services under the Affordable Care Act" (advance notice of proposed rulemaking). 77 Fed. Reg. 16501 (March 21, 2012).

"Coverage of Certain Preventive Services under the Affordable Care Act" (proposed rules), 78 Fed. Reg. 8456 (February 6, 2013).

"Coverage of Certain Preventive Services under the Affordable Care Act" (final rules), 78 Fed. Reg. 39870 (July 2, 2013).

Employment Division v. Smith
The Eye of the Storm

In April, 2012, the Ad Hoc Committee for Religious Liberty of the United States Conference of Catholic Bishops issued "Our First, Most Cherished Liberty: A Statement on Religious Liberty." The statement was written in the context of the Conference's political skirmishes with the Obama administration, which had included contraceptive services on the list of preventive services for women that must be covered without co-payment requirements as part of the basic benefit package required by the Affordable Care Act. The bishops objected, in the first instance, to the inclusion of contraceptive services on that list. Moreover, they protested the lack of broad opt-outs for all employers (for-profit and not-for-profit) who have religiously based moral objections to subsidizing contraception as part of the health insurance coverage they provide to employees. Finally, the bishops objected to the exemptions that the Administration made available to church groups and religiously affiliated organizations such as colleges and universities. They did not think the exemptions, as drafted, adequately recognized the centrality of social services, education, and health care as an essential aspect of Catholic faith and life.

The bishops' call for respect for religious freedom is rhetorically adamant. Consider, for example, a representative paragraph:

> What is at stake is whether America will continue to have a free, creative, and robust civil society—or whether the state alone will determine who gets to contribute to the common good, and how they get to do it. Religious believers are part of American civil society, which includes neighbors helping each other, community associations, fraternal service clubs, sports leagues, and youth groups. All these Americans make their contribution to our common life, and they do not need the permission of the

government to do so. Restrictions on religious liberty are an attack on civil society and the American genius for voluntary associations.

As the foregoing passage indicates, however, the Bishops' statement is not legally specific. While it talks about seventeenth century Maryland settlers, the Civil Rights Movement, and contemporary martyrs around the globe, it does not situate itself in the context of the relevant court opinions interpreting the Free Exercise Clause of the Constitution. Here, of course, the key case is *Employment Division v. Smith*, which radically revised Supreme Court free exercise jurisprudence in 1990—over twenty years ago. In a nutshell, *Smith* states that valid, generally applicable (criminal) laws do not run afoul of the Free Exercise Clause of the Constitution, even if they hamper some religious practices. So, the free exercise clause of the First Amendment does not prohibit the state of Oregon from enacting a generally applicable criminal provision against the use of drugs without granting an exemption to Native Americans using peyote in the course of a religious ceremony. The *Smith* case would apply as well to a law enacting a generally applicable criminal provision against the use of alcohol without granting an exemption to Catholics for Mass.

The most significant thing about *Smith*, however, is not that the case upheld the prohibition, but that it changed the applicable test established by *Sherbert v. Verner* and *Wisconsin v. Yoder*. Rather than applying "strict scrutiny," which would have required a compelling state interest and a narrowly tailored law designed to impinge upon religious liberty as little as possible, *Smith* said that a rational basis test was enough, provided that the purpose of the law was not to target the affected religious group. This rational basis is much more lenient than strict scrutiny; it asks only whether the law in question is a reasonable means to a legitimate government end.

Why haven't many Catholic thinkers vigorously criticized the reasoning in S*mith*? I suspect it is because *Smith* is actually a fruit of the jurisprudential approach that they hope will one day result in overturning *Roe v. Wade*. Without saying so, activists on behalf of a broad view of religious liberty seem to be making an argument based on the spirit of the First Amendment, upon the rights found in its penumbras, upon the "spirit" of the First Amendment, not its "letter." They emphasize the expanding constitutional protections given to religious minorities such as the Amish in the 20th century. But too firm a commitment to an organically developing view of the Constitution could get them into trouble when it comes to other issues that matter to them. It is precisely this "living constitution" argument that was used to justify the development of a constitutional right to privacy, which in turn was used to confer constitutional protection upon the use of contraception and access to abortion.

In reaction to *Roe*, many (but not all) prolife legal scholars have advocated an "originalist" approach to constitutional interpretation. In defining and interpreting constitutional rights, this approach gives great weight to the text of the Constitution and the intent of the framers. That approach would undermine *Roe*, because no one enacting the Constitution, the Bill of Rights, or even the 14th Amendment thought their work impeded state laws against abortion. But this "originalist" approach would also support *Smith*, because (as Justice Scalia argues in his opinion for the Court) the framers of the First Amendment did not believe that freedom of religion entailed broad rights of exemption from neutral laws of general applicability.

Jurisprudential commitments do not always map neatly onto political and religious commitments. For many years, a significant segment of the prolife movement placed their hopes in Republican presidential candidates, who have in turn promised to appoint "originalist" judges rather than activist judges to the bench, with the aim of overturning *Roe v. Wade*. The judicial hero and hope of this segment of the prolife movement is Associate Justice Antonin Scalia, whose criticism of *Roe* over the years has been consistent and blistering. Yet his views on the constitutional protection of religious freedom are doubtless less congenial to many of the same people. Here is a key quote from Scalia's opinion in *Smith*:

> The government's ability to enforce generally applicable prohibitions of socially harmful conduct, like its ability to carry out other aspects of public policy, cannot depend on measuring the effects of a governmental action on a religious objector's spiritual development. To make an individual's obligation to obey such a law contingent upon the law's coincidence with his religious beliefs, except where the State's interest is compelling—permitting

him, by virtue of his beliefs, to become a law unto himself, contradicts both constitutional tradition and common sense (citations omitted).

Politics and constitutional interpretation make strange bedfellows: I suspect that many of those Catholics who are sharply critical of Associate Justice Harry Blackmun's majority opinion in *Roe* would applaud his dissent from Scalia's majority opinion in *Smith*:

> This [the majority's] distorted view of our precedents leads the majority to conclude that strict scrutiny of a state law burdening the free exercise of religion is a luxury that a well-ordered society cannot afford, and that the repression of minority religions is an unavoidable consequence of democratic government. I do not believe the Founders thought their dearly bought freedom from religious persecution a luxury, but an essential element of liberty—and they could not have thought religious intolerance unavoidable, for they drafted the Religion Clauses precisely in order to avoid that intolerance (citations omitted).

In their attempt to advance their political program, many activists on behalf of religious liberty as presented in this case by the USCCB have not squarely addressed the enormous change in religious liberty jurisprudence worked by *Smith*. The political discussions by advocates of religious liberty tend to unfold according to a circular four-step rhetorical dance:

1) Advocates (such as the U.S. Conference of Catholic Bishops in their annual "Fortnight for Freedom") attempt to focus their audience's attention on religious freedom as fundamental and sweeping constitutional right;

2) Their interlocutors raise the matter of *Smith*, which gives far more deference to the government's constitutional power to make law without accommodating religious beliefs. The advocates of religious liberty respond, "Well, look at the exceptions to *Smith*."

3) Their interlocutors in turn reply, "Well, actually, deciding whether an exception applies requires a careful balancing test,

taking into account the interests of the government in passing the law, not only the interest of religious liberty."

4) The advocates of religious liberty respond, "The right to religious freedom is basic and absolute."

Is there a way to escape this circular pattern of strategic, political assertion and objection? Yes, but it will take a great deal of work. First, we need to have a straightforward discussion about *Smith*—and the underlying theory of jurisprudence it embodies. We need to move beyond political strategy to principled commitment to a view of constitutional interpretation. Second, given the fact that *Smith* is the law of the land, we need to consider the contraception mandate within its framework. We need, in short, to start discussing not only religious liberty, but the contraception mandate included in the Affordable Care Act. Here are the threshold questions: Is it a "neutral law of general applicability?" Is it supported by a legitimate government interest? It is only if the answers to those questions are "no" that we need to consider whether the exceptions to *Smith* apply. And even applying the exceptions, we need to remember that the right to religious freedom is not absolute—it can always be outweighed by a narrowly tailored law and a compelling state interest.

Sources

Employment Division v. Smith, 494 U.S. 872 (1990).

Roe v. Wade, 410 U.S. 113 (1973).

United States Conference of Catholic Bishops. "Our First, Most Cherished Liberty." March 2012. Available at http://www.usccb.org/issues-and-action/religious-liberty/our-first-most-cherished-liberty.cfm.

Smith, RFRA, and the Bishops' Claims

Neutral Laws of General Applicability?

Employment Division v. Smith is the central Supreme Court opinion interpreting the First Amendment of the Constitution's protection of religious liberty. Westlaw summarizes its holding as follows:

> Although state would be prohibiting free exercise of religion in violation of free exercise clause if it sought to ban religious acts or abstentions only when they were engaged in for religious reasons, or only because of religious belief that they displayed, right of free exercise does not relieve individual of obligation to comply with valid or neutral law of general applicability on ground that law proscribes, or requires, conduct that is contrary to his religious practice, as long as law does not violate other constitutional protections.

The importance of this case for religious liberty jurisprudence is that it significantly loosened the standard for assessing most constitutional claims of religious liberty. Prior to *Smith*, government actions that substantially burden a religious practice had to be justified by a compelling state interest and narrowly tailored to affect that interest as little as possible. *Smith* significantly relaxes the government's burden: provided the government has a "rational basis" for the law in question, and is not intentionally targeting a religious group, it will not run afoul of the Free Exercise Clause of the First Amendment.

So *Smith* sets the basic framework for federal constitutional protection of religious liberty. What about the Religious Freedom Restoration Act, commonly known as RFRA? It was enacted by Congress in 1993, as part of a backlash against *Smith* and in an attempt to restore the strict scrutiny test established by *Sherbert v. Verner* and *Wisconsin v. Yoder*. As such, I honestly don't see how RFRA can be understood apart from *Smith*. In fact, as the legislative "Findings" of RFRA clearly indicate, its whole aim is to "undo" *Smith* and restore the prior test more protective of religious liberty:

The Congress finds that—

(1) the framers of the Constitution, recognizing free exercise of religion as an unalienable right, secured its protection in the First Amendment to the Constitution;
(2) laws "neutral" toward religion may burden religious exercise as surely as laws intended to interfere with religious exercise;
(3) governments should not substantially burden religious exercise without compelling justification;
(4) in *Employment Division v. Smith*, 494 U.S. 872 (1990), the Supreme Court virtually eliminated the requirement that the government justify burdens on religious exercise imposed by laws neutral toward religion; and
(5) the compelling interest test as set forth in prior federal court rulings is a workable test for striking sensible balances between religious liberty and competing prior governmental interests.

Although very short, RFRA purports to be very expansive in function—to cover all types of governmental action at every level of government. It purports, in a way, to be a super-law—almost a constitutional law. And that's part of what got it into constitutional trouble of its own. In *Boerne v. Flores* (1997), the Supreme Court declared RFRA to be partially unconstitutional; it struck down RFRA's requirements as they applied to the states. Why? The Court found that in enacting RFRA, Congress exceeded its authority under section 5 of the Fourteenth Amendment. It thereby encroached upon the legitimate power of the states. In short, Congress does not have the power to impose upon the states a stricter religious liberty test than the Constitution itself requires.

It also did not escape the Court's notice that by enacting RFRA, Congress was trying to "undo" the Court's interpretation of the Constitution in *Smith*. Congress has the power to enforce constitutional rights, but not to create or expand them. According to the *Boerne* Court:

Legislation which alters the meaning of the Free Exercise Clause cannot be said to be enforcing the Clause. Congress does not enforce a constitutional right by changing what the right is. It has been given the power to enforce, not the power to determine what constitutes a constitutional violation. Were it not so, what Congress would be enforcing would no longer be, in any meaningful sense, the provisions of [the Fourteenth Amendment].

Despite its grandiose language, RFRA is just an ordinary law—it is neither a super-statute nor a quasi-constitutional behemoth statute. Consequently, it is not likely to be the legislative savior some activists on behalf of religious liberty think it will be, especially as time goes on. It does not apply to the states—so it will provide no help against state mandates to cover contraception or other objectionable services. Protection against these mandates will require examining state constitutional protection of religious freedom as well as state RFRA laws.

RFRA *does* apply in the federal context. But even that application may not be invariably effective as time goes on. In order to understand why, it is helpful to understand RFRA's relevance in the current controversy over the contraception mandate. The Affordable Care Act does not itself mention contraception coverage; the mandate is found in the detailed regulations promulgated by the Department of Health and Human Services in order to implement the Act. There is no question that RFRA applies to those regulations; the only argument is whether the mandate survives under its requirements.

But suppose the contraception mandate were in the Affordable Care Act itself. Or suppose that Congress enacts another law on health care or any other subject that explicitly says that RFRA doesn't apply to its requirements. Here we are in a very different situation. As I just noted, RFRA is just an ordinary statute. It does not pronounce a constitutional right, although it purports to interpret the Constitution. There is no reason, therefore, that Congress cannot limit its reach, amend it, or repeal it, just as Congress can repeal any other law that it has enacted. I suspect that the protracted and unexpected battle over the contraception mandate may encourage some lawmakers to consider doing just that. After all, it would save them a lot of trouble down the road.

Sources

Boerne v. Flores, 521 U.S. 507 (1997).

Employment Division v. Smith, 494 U.S. 872 (1990).

Religious Freedom Restoration Act of 1993, Pub. L. No. 103-141, 107 Stat. 1488. (November 16, 1993), codified at 42 U.S.C. ch. 21B §2000bb et seq.

The Key Supreme Court Case for the Mandate

U.S. v. Lee

In the previous two chapters (*"Employment Division v. Smith:* The Eye of the Storm" and *"Smith,* RFRA, and the Bishops' Claims: Neutral Laws of General Applicability?"), I tried to explicate the basic framework for looking at the bishops' religious freedom claims: *Employment Division v. Smith* is the leading Supreme Court case interpreting the requirements of the Free Exercise Clause of the Constitution, and the Religious Freedom Restoration Act is the federal law that imposes additional restrictions on federal regulations in order to protect religious freedom. Lower courts and state courts may attempt to interpret and qualify those authoritative texts. But those interpretations and qualifications are not binding on the Supreme Court, whose interpretation of the U.S. Constitution and of federal law trumps that of both state courts and lower federal courts.

So is there a Supreme Court opinion that helps us consider how to evaluate the bishops' free exercise claims under both the Constitution and RFRA? I think there is: *United States v. Lee.* Here's the summary of the case taken from the syllabus to the opinion:

> Employer, a member of the Old Order Amish who employed several other Amish to work on his farm and in his carpentry shop, sued for refund of taxes, claiming that imposition of social security taxes violated his First Amendment free exercise rights and those of his Amish employees. The United States District Court for the Western District of Pennsylvania held that statutes requiring employer to pay social security and unemployment insurance taxes were unconstitutional as applied, and direct appeal was taken. The Supreme Court, Chief Justice Burger, held that: (1) exemption provided by statute for self-employed members of

religious groups who oppose social security taxes is available only to self-employed individuals and does not apply to employers or employees, and thus Amish employer and his employees were not within exemption statute; (2) because payment of taxes or receipt of benefits violated Amish religious beliefs, compulsory participation in social security system interfered with their free exercise rights; but (3) religious belief in conflict with payment of taxes affords no basis for resisting tax imposed on employers to support social security system, which must be applied uniformly to all except as Congress provides explicitly otherwise.

Why is this case so important? First, *Lee* is not interpreting the constitutional right to religious freedom under the new, laxer standard of *Smith*, but rather under the old, stricter "compelling interest" of *Sherbert v. Verner* and *Wisconsin v. Yoder*. It is this test that RFRA explicitly sought to restore. So, I think *Lee* offers a very good sense of what Congress intended to require by enacting RFRA. Second, the facts of *Lee* are more or less on point with the factual situation in the contraceptive mandate. What is at stake in both cases is the payment of money for the benefit of the welfare of employees: Amish employers are required by federal law to pay social security tax on behalf of their employees, who may or may not be Amish, while Catholic employers are required to pay to cover contraceptive insurance on behalf of their employees, who may or may not be Catholic.

So the key question about the mandate seems to me to be this: We know it is constitutionally permissible to make the Amish pay social security taxes for their employees, despite their belief that it is immoral to do so. Since this is the case, why is it constitutionally impermissible *(or* impermissible under RFRA) to make Catholic organizations pay for basic health coverage that includes contraception?

There are differences between the two cases, of course. But they do not, in my view, cut in favor of the Catholic objectors. First, the Amish appear to object to the payment of employment taxes as an evil in itself, apart from the purposes of those taxes. This objection flows from their desire to remain as separate as possible from secular life and government.

In contrast, Catholic employers do not morally object to the compelled payment of money by the government per se—or even to the general mandate to contribute to the costs of health insurance. The objection is more attenuated: they claim that they are wrongly cooperating with evil by facilitating the use of contraception by third parties. In fact, it is worth considering how attenuated the cooperation is: Together with the employee, the employer funds an entire benefit package, which is a conditional promise to provide or pay for a certain array of medical services. The access of any one covered patient to birth control medicine depends upon a very elaborate chain of causation, including 1) the decision of the covered person to seek medical attention; 2) the prescription of the physician; 3) the pharmacy's decision to fill the prescription; and 4) the covered person's decision to take the prescribed substance. Further complicating the matter is the fact that Catholic teaching does not prohibit all use of birth control medication, but only that taken with the primary purpose of preventing conception. Many women take birth control pills for other purposes, such as controlling painful menstrual cycles and ovarian cysts.

A second difference is that the matter of religious pluralism is raised more sharply in the case of Catholic employers objecting to contraception. In *Lee*, the objecting employer pointed out that his employees were Amish themselves. Moreover, the Amish had a deep and tested connection to providing for elderly or disabled workers with the resources of their own community. So the point of the Amish employers was *not* to prevent their employees from obtaining security in their old age—they provided for the same objective in a different way. (This factor proved decisive to Congress, which later chose to craft a legislative exemption for Amish employers objecting to paying social security tax for Amish employees.)

In contrast, many Catholic employers have employees who do not accept official Catholic teaching on the immorality of contraception. Some of those employees may themselves be Catholic; surveys reliably show that the overwhelming number of Catholics do not have moral objections to contraception. Moreover, many of them may actually believe they have a moral obligation to use contraception, in order to fulfill their vocational responsibilities to their spouses, families, and their other commitments. The exemption for Amish employers to pay social security tax only extended to the case of Amish employees.

Some people have objected that the government does not have a compelling interest in providing cost-free contraception, since it is readily available from other sources. I do not think this objection is persuasive, for two reasons. First, the decision to provide no-cost contraception was based on a study from the National Institute of Medicine report that maintained: 1) people access preventive services at a significantly greater rate if they are not required to make a co-payment for them; and 2) reliable contraception prevents unplanned pregnancies, which have deleterious health outcomes for both mother and child. Too closely spaced pregnancies impose a substantial drain upon the mother's own health. Moreover, a woman who is not aware that she is or may be pregnant can engage in behavior, such as consumption of alcohol, that harms her developing child.

Second, the goal of the Affordable Care Act is to provide a basic, comprehensive benefit package to all persons. There is, I believe, a significant value to its reliable comprehensiveness, both for patients and doctors. We need to ask whether a patient's right to a set array of benefits can be threatened or trumped by the employer who funds them as part of an employee's compensation package. One can easily imagine myriad objections on the part of an employer to various elements in that benefit package that come from a variety of religious and moral perspectives. What should we say about the employer who is deeply committed to zero population growth, and therefore does not want to cover maternity care? What about the Christian Scientist who believes that modern medicine is deeply misguided and immoral? Or the prolifer who is troubled by the data that prolonged breastfeeding can lead to the failure of a fertilized egg to implant in a woman's womb?

Moreover, I think the potential chaos in administering a health care benefit system that permitted employers to veto aspects of a purportedly uniform benefit plan is another point of analogy with *Lee*: In deciding that the Free Exercise Clause did not protect an individual employer's conscientious decision not to pay employment tax, the Court did not focus only on the burden in the isolated case, but upon the burden a practice of administering a potentially exception-ridden requirement would place on the system: The *Lee* Court writes:

> While there is a conflict between the Amish faith and the obligations imposed by the social security system, not all burdens on

religion are unconstitutional. The state may justify a limitation on religious liberty by showing that it is essential to accomplish an overriding governmental interest. Widespread individual voluntary coverage under social security would undermine the soundness of the social security system, and would make such system almost a contradiction in terms and difficult, if not impossible, to administer. It would be difficult to accommodate the social security system with myriad exceptions flowing from a wide variety of religious beliefs such as the Amish.

Finally, it is important not to forget that both the Amish case and the bishops' case involve the payment of money to support a governmental program. Whereas the Court has been relatively sympathetic to some types of claims of religious believers for exemptions from generally applicable laws, its sympathy has not extended to the claim to be exempt from taxation, for obvious reasons that are articulated quite powerfully in *Lee*:

> There is no principled way for purposes of this case to distinguish between general taxes and those imposed under the Social Security Act. The tax system could not function if denominations were allowed to challenge it because tax payments were spent in a manner that violates their religious belief. Because the broad public interest in maintaining a sound tax system is of such a high order, religious belief in conflict with the payment of taxes affords no basis for resisting the tax. Congress has accommodated, to the extent compatible with a comprehensive national program, the practices of those who believe it a violation of their faith to participate in the social security system. When followers of a particular sect enter into commercial activity as a matter of choice, the limits they accept on their own conduct as a matter of conscience and faith are not to be superimposed on the statutory schemes that are binding on others in that activity. Granting an exemption from social security taxes to an employer operates to impose the employer's religious faith on the employees. The tax imposed on employers to support the social security system must be uniformly applicable to all, except as Congress explicitly provides otherwise. (pp. 1056–1057)

Some have argued that the contraception mandate is not a tax, and therefore the bishops' case should be distinguished from *Lee.* I do not think that argument is persuasive, for two reasons. First, in upholding the constitutionality of the Affordable Care Act in 2012, the Court treated the individual mandate as a tax. It is hard to see why the employer mandate should be framed differently. Second, the point of the health care mandate is broadly similar to the point of the social security tax: to require employers to contribute to the well-being of their employees. As the foregoing passage from the Court's opinion in *Lee* indicates, granting the employer an exemption from the law does not merely confer a benefit upon the employer; it also imposes a burden upon the employees; the Court states that the burden "operates to impose" the employer's religion upon them.

Those opposing the contraception mandate place much of their hope in RFRA. That hope may be misplaced. RFRA was never meant to be an expansive promotion of religious liberty; it simply reinstated the stricter test articulated in *Sherbert v. Verner.* As *Lee* shows, religious liberty does not always trump the state's interest, even under the stricter test.

Sources

Employment Division v. Smith, 494 U.S. 872 (1990).
Patient Protection and Affordable Care Act (2010), Pub. L. No. 111-148, 124
    Stat. 119 –124 Stat. 1025.
Religious Freedom Restoration Act of 1993, Pub. L. No. 103-141, 107 Stat. 1488.
    (November 16, 1993), codified at 42 U.S.C. ch. 21B §2000bb et seq.
Sherbert v. Verner, 374 U.S. 398 (1963).
United States v. Lee, 455 U.S. 252 (1982).

Reading the Tea Leaves
Why the Supreme Court Is Unlikely to Block the Contraception Mandate

Many of the groups challenging the contraception mandate in the Affordable Care Act on religious liberty grounds have placed their hopes in the Religious Freedom Restoration Act (RFRA) and the only case involving RFRA to have come before the High Court thus far: *Gonzales v. O Centro Espirita Beneficente Uniao do Vegetal* (2005).

The superficial attraction of *O Centro* is obvious. As mandated by RFRA, the Court applied the "strict scrutiny" test, and the religious claimants won. The Court decided that the federal government had not proved a compelling state interest in stopping a tiny religious sect from using hoasca, a sacramental tea made from a hallucinogen banned under federal law.

Congress passed RFRA in 1993. It was a direct response to *Employment Division v. Smith* (1990), in which the Supreme Court held that the Free Exercise Clause did not require the state of Oregon to exempt Native Americans using peyote in their worship services from antidrug laws, which were neutral laws of general applicability. RFRA attempted to restore the pre-*Smith* "strict scrutiny" test established by *Sherbert v. Verner* and *Wisconsin v. Yoder* in order to broaden exemptions for religious groups to otherwise generally applicable laws.

In light of this history, *O Centro* was an uncommonly straightforward RFRA case. Noting that Congress had long exempted Native American ceremonies from federal drug laws, the Court pointed out the incongruity of prohibiting the religious use of hoasca. In short, if RFRA didn't apply in this case, it's hard to see when it would apply.

But the Court also recognized that not all religious-liberty cases can be resolved in the same way. The justices emphasized that the claimants were a small sect asking for a narrowly defined and contained exemption to a general legal prohibition. That exemption would apply only in limited circumstances—to members of the sect in question and only in the particular context of their worship services. It would not permit members to use the hallucinogenic tea outside that setting. Moreover, the scope of the exemption was highly limited—the Court stressed that only thirty people belonged to the sect in the United States. Finally, it was clear that no third parties would be directly affected, much less harmed, by granting this carefully delineated exemption.

By contrast, the exemption being sought from the contraception mandate by the U.S. Conference of Catholic Bishops and others would be far broader in both scope and effect, particularly on third parties. It is not an exemption from a negative prohibition, but an exemption from a positive requirement, which is designed to secure an array of health benefits for the general population—benefits that affect their entire lives, not merely their work lives. According to the National Institute of Medicine, first-dollar coverage of contraceptives as part of a preventive-service program improves the overall health of women and their unborn children.

Furthermore, *O Centro* dealt with a clearly defined object of the exemption: sacramental tea containing a particular hallucinogen. In contrast, the same arguments used to justify the objection to the contraception mandate can immediately apply to other services in the health-care benefit package. What if an employer refuses to cover HPV vaccinations for girls and young women because they might encourage sexual immorality in young people? What if an employer decides not to cover breastfeeding supplies because she has read literature documenting their abortifacient effects?

Moreover, unlike the sect protected in *O Centro*, the number of people affected by an exception to the mandate is not negligible. Hundreds of thousands of people are employed by Catholic institutions across the country. Ironically enough, the spate of religious-liberty cases now being brought by Catholic and other groups actually undermines their argument by showing the administrative unwieldiness of the exemption they claim. In American law, facts matter, not merely legal principles. And the facts of the contraceptive mandate are very different from those in *O Centro*.

In response to objections by the bishops and others, the Obama administration proffered a reconfigured exemption to the mandate, which broadened the protection for not-for-profit employers. Is this exemption, or one even broader to cover for-profit employers, required under RFRA, according to the framework set out in *O Centro*? I doubt it. In fact, I suspect the original, narrow exemption would have survived litigation. Maybe it's time for the bishops to take yes for an answer.

Sources

Employment Division v. Smith, 494 U.S. 872 (1990).
Gonzales v. O Centro Espirita Beneficente Uniao do Vegetal, 546 U.S. 418 (2006).
Religious Freedom Restoration Act of 1993, Pub. L. No. 103-141, 107 Stat. 1488. (November 16, 1993), codified at 42 U.S.C. ch. 21B §2000bb et seq.

A Minefield

The Troubling Implications of the
Hobby Lobby Decision

The Supreme Court's 5–4 decision in *Burwell v. Hobby Lobby Stores,* where religious exemptions to the contraception mandate in the Affordable Care Act were extended to a private for-profit company, has produced disparate reactions: jubilation among those who regarded the mandate as a grave threat to religious liberty and consternation from those who think access to no-cost contraception should be a fundamental component of health care for women. Critics complain that in extending the accommodation to Hobby Lobby, the court has misinterpreted the Religious Freedom and Restoration Act of 1993 in order to take the unprecedented step of recognizing the religious rights of certain for-profit corporations. The likely result will be an endless stream of similar religious claims from other businesses. Anticipating that criticism, the majority opinion, written by Justice Samuel Alito, asserts that the case was decided on narrow grounds, and argues that worries about exemptions being granted to religious groups opposed to vaccinations, for example, are unfounded. Writing for the four dissenting justices, Justice Ruth Bader Ginsburg questioned such assurances, arguing that the Court "has ventured into a minefield." "Approving some religious claims while deeming others unworthy of accommodation could be 'perceived as favoring one religion over another,' the very 'risk the [Constitution's] Establishment Clause was designed to preclude.'"

In granting the accommodation to Hobby Lobby, the majority ruling further contended that the administrative mechanism used to accommodate religious entities could easily be extended to commercial enterprises. Three days after issuing the *Hobby Lobby* ruling, however, the Court granted an emergency injunction to Wheaton College, temporarily allowing the Evangelical institution to avoid complying with even the minimal administrative paperwork required by the government in order to receive an exemption. Wheaton, like some Catholic groups, maintains that filling out the form that notifies the government and its insurer that it desires an exemption will still facilitate access to contraceptive methods it opposes on religious grounds. All three of the Court's women justices vociferously objected, and Justice Sonia Sotomayor went so far as to tacitly charge the majority with sophistry:

> Those who are bound by our decisions usually believe they can take us at our word. Not so today. After expressly relying on the availability of the religious-nonprofit accommodation to hold that the contraceptive coverage requirement violates RFRA as applied to closely held for-profit corporations, the Court now, as the dissent in *Hobby Lobby* feared it might . . . retreats from that position.

So at this early date, it very much remains to be seen whether the Court has issued a narrow or sweeping decision with regard to the scope of religious exemptions from laws such as the Affordable Care Act. Supreme Court cases, however, are not only or primarily about the named plaintiffs. Their purpose is to set the normative framework that governs the decisions of countless other unnamed persons (both natural and corporate), who may never have the opportunity to see the inside of the courtroom. It is the future course of cases that makes me worry about the majority opinion—not the outcome in this particular case. For what the Court has done in the *Hobby Lobby* case is transform the Religious Freedom and Restoration Act—a statute enacted by Congress to counteract a bad Supreme Court decision that harmed powerless religious minorities—into a tool for *powerful* minorities to resist what they believe to be dangerous social and political change. For example, it is not hard to see how the religious exemptions justified in the *Hobby Lobby* decision could also be applied to businesses that objected to dealing with same-sex couples. This issue arose, of course, with respect to a state RFRA in Indiana.

As "the findings and purposes" of the law itself make clear, Congress enacted RFRA for a very specific reason. In *Employment Division v. Smith* (1990), the Supreme Court had significantly relaxed the test used to evaluate the government's case in religious liberty

cases that had been previously established. In short, religious exemptions from otherwise generally applicable laws became much harder
to come by. In response to protests from both sides of the political
aisle, Congress passed RFRA, which was intended, as the Act itself
says, "to restore the compelling interest test as set forth in *Sherbert
v. Verner* (1963) and *Wisconsin v. Yoder* (1972)." The government, in
other words, had to demonstrate a compelling state interest—such as
maintaining a system of taxation or protecting public health against
infectious disease—if it wanted to burden religious exercise. Moreover, the government needed to show that it promoted that interest by
a law tailored to impinge as little as possible on religious exercise. In
practice, however, the government has nearly always won such cases.
Yet while RFRA clearly came down on the side of religious expression, it did not appreciably *expand* the religious liberty protections
available to claimants before the *Smith* decision. Very few cases have
appeared under federal RFRA in the past twenty years; most have involved members of small religions claiming an exemption from general laws that burden them without conferring any discernible benefit
on third parties. A good example is *Gonzales v. O Centro Espirita Beneficente Uniao do Vegetal* (2006), in which the Supreme Court held
that RFRA protected the right of a tiny New Mexican sect of a Bra-
zilian church to import a particular type of tea for sacramental use,
despite its hallucinogenic properties that put it in the crosshairs of
federal drug laws.

Justice Alito's opinion in *Hobby Lobby*, however, has worked a
powerful mutation on the statute. Ignoring the purposes of the legislation, not to mention its legislative history and subsequent application, Alito argues that "nothing in the text of RFRA . . .was meant to
be tied to this Court's pre-Smith interpretation of the Amendment."
That is a highly selective, if not deceptive interpretation of the statute.
Alito virtually ignores the Court's own earlier interpretation of RFRA
in *Boerne v. Flores*, which recognized that the law "purported to cod-
ify" the pre-*Smith* religious freedom jurisprudence. He further claims
that the Religious Land Use and Institutionalized Person Act of 2000
requires the Court interpret RFRA to protect "religious exercise to the
maximum extent."

The land-use act did amend RFRA's definition of religious exercise to clarify that it included non-central as well as central practices

of faith. But this amendment did not widen RFRA's purpose beyond restoring pre-*Smith* jurisprudence. Nor did it require a "broad interpretation" of the earlier statute. And the land use act, which is focused narrowly on the use of land by religious entities and the free exercise of rights of institutionalized persons, says nothing whatsoever about how to interpret RFRA. In short, Alito wants it both ways. Looking at the text of RFRA, he focuses only on the letter of the statutory mandate, ignoring even the congressional purpose. Looking at the text of RLUIPA, he expansively interprets its spirit, extending it so far as to reframe the scope and reach of RFRA in ways that are beyond both the provisions and congressional intent of either law.

What groups should be exempt from the Affordable Care Act's contraceptive mandate is a difficult issue. On the one hand, from the perspective of many religions, political questions are also moral questions—on every level. And for most people, moral questions invariably have a religious dimension. On the other hand, living in a pluralistic representative democracy, we are inevitably subject to laws and policies that we believe to be unjust. Except in the most extreme cases, however, we cannot expect to be exempted from laws that otherwise apply to everyone else. Here, of course, facts matter. If the contraception methods Hobby Lobby claims act as abortifacients do not in fact cause abortion the case for exemption is seriously weakened.

In a pluralistic society, the religious freedom of one party needs to be balanced against the rights and the legitimate expectations of others. In this case, the consciences of some religious people must be weighed against the health-care concerns of women more generally, as judged by the people's legitimately elected representatives. Yet as Ginsburg emphasizes in her dissent, Alito's opinion gives us precious little guidance on what principles of law we should use when balancing those conflicting concerns. For example, while the ruling recognizes that corporations have free exercise rights, it identifies those rights solely with the owners of the corporation. The legitimate interests of other corporate stakeholders, particularly the employees, who may not share their employer's religious views, evidently have no standing. In this instance, it seems that more money buys you more religious freedom—and more freedom to infringe on the choices of others.

Second, the opinion provides virtually no way to evaluate the strength of a plaintiff's religious-liberty claim. Although RFRA's text speaks of "substantial" burdens on a claimant's exercise of religious liberty, the ruling pulls the teeth of this requirement. According to Alito and the majority, a burden is "substantial" as long as a claimant sincerely says it is. But as Ginsburg noted, this is an invitation to run through a minefield, not a way out of one.

The injunction granted to Wheaton College reveals the problem. If it is a substantial burden for a religious institution merely to sign a paper notifying the insurance company of its objections to contraception, then why isn't it a substantial burden for a pacifist to sign a similar paper for the government conscientiously objecting to military service? But if we go down that road, how will we tell the difference between a conscientious objector and a deserter or draft dodger?

At a minimum, we can assess the substantiality of a burden by looking at whether it requires direct *participation* in an activity or merely indirect *facilitation*. We need to acknowledge the difference between, for example, fighting in an unjust war and paying taxes that help support an unjust war. In my opinion, the former is a substantial burden; the latter is not. We need to acknowledge as well, I think, that it cannot be a substantial burden on one's free exercise merely to inform the government of one's objection to a law. So too, I believe, it is one thing to be asked to provide contraception oneself, another to contribute to a benefit plan that covers contraception, and still another to be asked to inform the government of one's religious and moral objections to contraception. The first is a substantial burden, in my view. The second and third are not.

Jurists like Justice Alito (and the Republican politicians who appointed them) have long crusaded against "judicial activism," especially "legislating from the bench." Their main object of ire, of course, is *Roe v. Wade* (1973), which not only found a right to abortion in the penumbras of the Constitution, but also required the Court to delve into the messy business of evaluating various schemes for regulating abortion.

In what may be the chief irony of *Hobby Lobby*, the majority opinion puts the Court in much the same position with respect to religious liberty. Alito accepted without scrutiny the plaintiff's claim that the contraception mandate substantially burdened its exercise of religion. For the purposes of this decision, he assumed (albeit grudgingly) that the government had a compelling interest in making no-cost contraception available. In the end, the case turned on the third prong of the RFRA test: Did the government adopt the least restrictive means to achieve its end? He pointedly did not rule out the possibility that accommodating religious objections could require the government to adopt new programs—which would be supervised and second-guessed by the Court. That outcome now seems more likely after the injunction granted to Wheaton College. How is this not legislating from the bench? The conservative majority has, I would argue, become what it has so long hated.

The test proffered in the majority opinion in *Hobby Lobby* amounts to little more than judicial intuitionism. Does the government have a compelling state interest, say, in combatting racism? In the majority opinion, Alito suggests the answer is yes—but we're not sure on what grounds. What about combatting discrimination on the grounds of gender or sexual orientation? My guess is that he would say no, but there's no way to know. The logic of the *Hobby Lobby* decision is, I fear, as arbitrary as it is partisan.

Sources

Boerne v. Flores, 521 U.S. 507 (1997).

Burwell v. Hobby Lobby Stores, Inc., 573 U.S. ___ . 134 S. Ct. 2751 (2014).

Employment Division v. Smith, 494 U.S. 872 (1990).

Gonzales v. O Centro Espirita Beneficente Uniao do Vegetal, 546 U.S. 418 (2006).

Liebelson, Dana. "The 8 Best Lines from Ginsburg's Dissent on the Hobby Lobby Contraception Decision." *Mother Jones*. June 30, 2014. Available at http://www.motherjones.com/politics/2014/06/best-lines-hobby-lobby-decision.

Religious Freedom Restoration Act of 1993 (RFRA), Pub. L. No. 103-141, 107 Stat. 1488 (November 16, 1993), codified at 42 U.S.C. ch. 21B §2000bb et seq.

Religious Land Use and Institutionalized Persons Act (RLUIPA), Pub L. 106–274, codified as 42 U.S.C. § 2000cc et seq.

Roe v. Wade, 410 U.S. 113 (1973).

U.S. Department of Health and Human Services. "Women's Preventive Services Guidelines," n.d. Available at http://www.hrsa.gov/womensguidelines/#footnote2

Part 3

Conversations about Culture

For the past two decades or so, the role of religion in the public square has been dominated by the frame provided by the so-called culture wars. The theme running through the chapters in this part is that a culture war framework is not going to allow us to have the kind of nuanced, careful conversation about law, religion, and morality in a pluralistic society that we sorely need. A culture war mindset divides people into two camps: good v. evil, righteous v. damned, us v. them. Like actual warfare, it encourages people to pick sides. Loyalty is prized; those who raise questions or suggest points of consonance with political or cultural opponents are seen as traitors. Moreover, like actual warfare, cultural warfare encourages those on both sides to believe the worst about their opponents—the exact opposite of St. Ignatius Loyola's call in the *Spiritual Exercises* to presume the best intentions of one another (#22). It also erodes opportunities for cooperation about supposedly noncontroversial matters. A culture war mindset encourages us to attach clear moral labels to all the people we encounter: they are either morally worthy friends or morally reprobate foes. A liberal Democrat captured by the culture war mentality may view a legislator who opposes contraceptive coverage as an "oppressor of women." In contrast, a conservative Republican might label a prochoice legislator as a "baby killer." For different reasons, the culture war mindset leads persons on each side to treat those on the other side as moral monsters. Needless to say, most people shrink from cooperating with moral monsters—even to advance other, indisputably worthy projects.

The culture war framework has had deleterious effects upon the well-being of our political communities. Statistics show that the level of bipartisan cooperation in Congress has reached historic lows.[1] The two major parties do not try to work together; they try to undermine

119

any possible accomplishment that can be claimed by the other side. The looming example of this strategy, of course, is the battle over the budget: the Republicans were willing to let the United States default upon its loans rather than approve a budget that advanced policy aims proposed by a Democratic president.[2] This level of political rancor is not simply rough-and-tumble business as usual in the nation's capital; in fact, it threatened to send our country, still struggling out of a deep recession, into another financial crisis. It is no wonder that the approval rating for Congress is abysmally low.[3] Nor is it surprising that this level of acrimonious dysfunction has prompted many young people to turn away from politics in disgust.[4]

The political polarization over the past fifty years has manifested a significant religious dimension. Whereas the 1960s saw religious figures like Martin Luther King, Jr., Daniel and Phillip Berrigan, Abraham Joshua Heschel, and William Sloane Coffin involved in politically progressive causes such as the civil rights and anti-war movements, the 1990s and 2000s have witnessed a resurgence of politically conservative religious activism, galvanizing voters against abortion, same-sex marriage, and affirmative action. Despite the best attempts of religious leaders to rally the next generation to their cause, recent culture war activities have been counterproductive. Perceiving religious people to be disrespectful of women, intolerant of gay people, and generally acrimonious, younger people are leaving organized religion in droves.[5]

The culture wars have done more harm than good to both our political communities and our religious communities. The overarching purpose of the essays in this part is to encourage people to move beyond a culture war mentality. What does such a move involve? In my view, it has several components.

First, we need to distinguish between sociological accounts of the culture wars and normative accounts. In 1991, the sociologist James Davidson Hunter wrote *Culture Wars: The Struggle to Define America*, which sketched the growing divide between what we now call "Red States" and "Blue States." The divisions focused on politically and morally controversial issues such as abortion, homosexual rights, separation of church and state, privacy, and the morality of owning guns.[6] Hunter was describing and analyzing sociological divisions, not endorsing them; his goal was to provide a fuller picture of the social, religious, and political contexts that generated our nation's political divisions.

Yet Hunter's language of "culture wars" was seized upon by politicians, especially conservative politicians, and given a normative and religious spin. It became important, politicians and pundits said, to be on the right side of the culture wars. Four years after Hunter's book was published, the goal to give culture war language a prescriptive force received some help from an unlikely source: Pope John Paul II. In 1995, he published his encyclical *Evangelium vitae*, which was a vigorous condemnation of contraception, abortion, and euthanasia. Appalled by the fact that the legal systems of many Western liberal democracies were endorsing such practices, he framed the current situation as a terrible struggle between a "culture of life" that protects and nurtures even the most vulnerable and least socially useful human beings, and a "culture of death" that only values human persons for their capacity to produce (or consume) goods and services.[7]

Despite the similarities of language, Pope John Paul II's categories do not map perfectly upon the American sociopolitical battles as Hunter outlined them; even a moment's reflection suggests that the late pontiff would not likely be a strong proponent of Second Amendment gun rights. More profoundly, the categories of *Evangelium vitae* were not designed to describe opposing political platforms vying for the commitment of American citizens. Instead, the categories were meant to analyze the broad social movements in which individuals made their choices for or against abortion, euthanasia, and contraception. John Paul recognized, in other words, that it was not sufficient to analyze the acts of euthanasia and abortion in isolation from the broader cultural currents that either support or undermine vulnerable human beings. He wanted to call attention to the pedagogical nature of law and culture.

Pope John Paul II's categories also did not correlate neatly with the political platforms of either the Republicans or the Democrats. Like the Republicans, he advocated the legal prohibition of such practices as abortion and euthanasia. Like the Democrats, however, he recognized that the legal prohibitions were not sufficient to protect vulnerable human beings from violent harm; they also require positive social support and protection. Nonetheless, Republican strategists and religious conservatives enthusiastically adopted the Pope's language and vision in order to equate "the culture of life" with a vote for pro-life Republicans and the "culture of death" with a vote for prochoice Democrats.[8] That language not only served as a political rallying cry, however; it also effectively authorized religious conservatives to demonize their co-religionists who did not view the slate of candidates in the same way that they did. They could be dismissed as minions of "the culture of death." This is not to say that religious liberals did not demonize their more conservative fellow believers as well. They did. In the past twenty years, however, vocal religious conservatives have boldly deployed the culture war language to achieve ascendency in the public square.

Second, we need to recognize that culture war language has deep resonances in American religious and political culture; in fact, it goes back to the Puritans. As Perry Miller, Sacvan Bercovitch, and others have demonstrated, the language of prophetic indictment has a long history in American life.[9] Social reformers of all stripes have drawn upon biblical language and imagery to prophetically decry social evils, and to demand repentance and change. While the language of prophetic indictment is powerful, it also has significant drawbacks. Like an actual legal indictment, it does not invite conversation; it demands compliance. It fosters hostilities—those who employ the language of prophetic indictment are easily tempted to view those who disagree with them on any matters, ones of policy as well as ones of principle, as fundamentally corrupt.

Third, we need to retrieve a more nuanced and variegated way of assessing other people and their positions. In my view, we would all do well to balance the rhetoric of the prophets with an insight from St. Augustine (d. 430), who is also a key influence on Western thought. Augustine contended that human beings do not seek or do evil as such, but rather under the aspect of the good "*sub specie boni.*" Moreover, people pursue what they perceive to be goods; in most cases the problem is a disordered sense of priorities.[10] It seems to me that these Augustinian insights provide a more fruitful basis for conversations about morality, law, and public policy in our pluralistic society. They allow for more nuanced judgments about other people and the situations they face; they permit appreciation of the goods other people seek, as well as critique of their priorities and methods in pursuing those goods.

Those who have long been uneasy about the culture war mentality and its casualties in both the Catholic Church and American civil life have found new hope in the era of Pope Francis. In one of the first comprehensive interviews given during his papacy, Pope Francis flatly rejected the culture war mindset, saying that "We cannot insist only on issues related to abortion, gay marriage and the use of contraceptive methods. This is not possible. I have not spoken much about these things, and I was reprimanded for that. But when we speak about these issues, we have to talk about them in a context."[11]

It is not, of course, that Pope Francis dismisses Catholic teaching on these issues. Yet in calling for more "context," he is shifting the conversation in two important ways. First, he is situating the church's stance on key culture war issues in the broader frame of Catholic social teaching, which is concerned with the fate of vulnerable persons across the board, whether they are threatened by abortion, loss of income, or geographic catastrophe due to climate change.

Second, he is recalibrating the political and moral conversation, by insisting that all participants be treated with respect. "We must always consider the person. Here we enter into the mystery of the human being. In life, God accompanies persons, and we must accompany them, starting from their situation. It is necessary to accompany them with mercy."[12] For Francis, "accompaniment" does not entail endorsement of wrongdoing, but rather consists in seeing the value of the person doing the particular "wrong" in question. He refuses to reduce men and women in situations that the church considers morally compromised to the sins they have committed. Instead, he takes a gradualist approach toward moral reformation that is deeply foreign to a culture war mentality. Moreover, Pope Francis refuses to reduce interlocutors to their stances on hot-button issues. He encourages us to respond to and affirm the considerable good in our interlocutors, rather than devoting all our attention to chastising their flaws. Francis's notion of "accompaniment," I think, dovetails nicely with the Augustinian insight that all persons, no matter how mistaken, act in pursuit of the good.

The chapters in this part deal with a range of topics, including how we talk to one another in the public square and how we talk about controversial issues such as abortion, gun control, mental illness, and suicide. While the topics may change, my underlying concern to resist the black-and-white moral dichotomies of the culture wars remains constant. I also try to employ an Augustinian methodology, which does not shrink from addressing the complex and mixed motivations that drive human beings in their darkest hours.

Notes

1. Christopher Hare, Keith T. Poole, and Howard Rosenthal, "Polarization in Congress Has Risen Sharply: Where Is It Going Next?," *Washington Post* (Monkey Cage), February 13, 2014. Available at http://www.washingtonpost .com/blogs/monkey-cage/wp/2014/02/13/polarization-in-congress-has-risen -sharply-where-is-it-going-next/.

2. Jonathan Martin, Jim Rutenberg, and Jeremy W. Peters, "Fiscal Crisis Sounds the Charge in G.O.P's 'Civil War,'" *New York Times*, October 19, 2013.

3. Rebecca Riftkin, "Public Faith in Congress Falls Again, Hits Historic Low," Gallup Politics, June 19, 2014, Available at http://www.gallup.com/poll/171710 /public-faith-congress-falls-again-hits-historic-low.aspx?utm_source=alert&utm _medium=email&utm_campaign=syndication&utm_content=morelink&utm _term=Politics.

4. Hunter Walker, "Harvard Poll Shows Millennials Have 'Historically Low' Levels of Trust in Government," *Business Insider*, April 29, 2014. Available at http://www.businessinsider.com/poll-millenials-have-historically-low-levels-of -trust-in-government-2014-4.

5. Pew Research Center, Religion & Public Life Project, ""Nones' on the Rise." October 9, 2012. Available at http://www.pewforum.org/2012/10/09/nones-on -the-rise/. See also Pew Research Center, Religion & Public Life Project, "Reli- gion among the Millennials." Available at http://www.pewforum.org/2010/02/17 /religion-among-the-millennials/.

6. James Davidson Hunter, *Culture Wars: The Struggle to Define America* (New York: Basic Books, 1991).

7. Pope John Paul II, *Evangelium vitae (The Gospel of Life)* (1995).

8. Damon Linker offers a fascinating account of the strategy in *The Theocons: Secular America under Siege* (New York: Anchor Books, 2007). Linker is himself a disillusioned theocon.

9. Perry Miller, *The New England Mind: From Colony to Province* (Cambridge, MA: Belknap Press of Harvard University Press, 1983); Sacvan Berkovitch, *The American Jeremiad* (Madison, WI: University of Wisconsin Press, 1978); James Darsey, *The Prophetic Tradition and Radical Rhetoric in America* (New York: New York University Press, 1997); and David Howard-Pitney, *The African-Amer- ican Jeremiad: Appeals for Justice in America*, rev. ed. (Philadelphia, PA: Temple University Press, 2005). I discuss this phenomenon with respect to the activity of Catholic bishops around recent elections in "Prophetic Discourse in the Public

Square," Santa Clara Lecture, delivered November 11, 2008. Available at http://works.bepress.com/cgi/viewcontent.cgi?article=1033&context=kaveny.

10. Augustine, *City of God*, Book XIX, Chapter 4.

11. Antonio Spadaro, S.J., "A Big Heart Open to God" (Exclusive Interview with Pope Francis, conducted on August 19, 2013), *America*, September 30, 2013.

12. Ibid.

Watch Your Mouth

Sage Advice from St. James

It wouldn't be hard to compile a "Greatest Hits" album of contemporary Catholic teaching on specific issues, some targeted specifically at American Catholics: birth control (*Humanae vitae*), human rights (*Gaudium et spes*), abortion and euthanasia (*Evangelium vitae*), just-war theory (*The Challenge of Peace*), economic justice (*Economic Justice for All*), and the role of women (*Mulieris dignitatem*). Wherever we stand on the issues, most of us are familiar with the playlist.

Maybe the band should add a new number to its repertoire. Perhaps we need a retrosound—*a really* retro sound. Take the Epistle of James. No one could accuse its author of being soft on morals; in fact, Luther called it a "right strawy epistle" because he thought it emphasized good works at the expense of faith. There's little overlap between James's playlist and ours. In fact, the topic that most agitates him is virtually invisible today: the power of the tongue. And by that he doesn't mean the farewell tour of the Rolling Stones. He means the human capacity—and propensity—to talk. Our drive to communicate is at least as powerful as our sex drive. And, according to James, it is just as dangerous.

> Consider how small a fire can set a huge forest ablaze. The tongue is also a fire. It exists among our members as a world of malice, defiling the whole body and setting the entire of our lives on fire, itself set on fire by Gehenna. For every kind of beast and bird, of reptile and sea creature, can be tamed and has been tamed by the human species, but no human being can tame the tongue. It is a restless evil, full of deadly poison. With it we bless the Lord and Father, and with it we curse human beings who are made in the likeness of God (3:5–9).

Not a comforting passage for members of the chattering classes. Blog impresarios and mavens of the print media can't escape on the technicality that their instrument is the keyboard, not the tongue— they bless and curse with the best of them. James's warning to teachers—those who make their living by talking—is explicit and dire. More broadly, though, his message is deeply disconcerting for all of us Americans who view cell phones and instant messaging as important new recreational devices.

James is not primarily concerned with abstract questions, like the tension between freedom of expression and community values. His focus is the concrete effect that certain types of speech have on the speaker and the community. First, he thinks that people who spend too much time talking about faith, holiness, and good works won't put their money where their mouth is. Second, he worries that these talkers will judge themselves by their words, and other people by their deeds, leading to self-righteousness. James writes, "There is one lawgiver and judge who is able to save and destroy. Who then are you to judge your neighbor?" Third, James is well aware that loving one's neighbors is not compatible with running them down behind their backs. More than a millennium later, Aquinas builds on James's insights. He devotes five separate questions of the *Summa Theologiae* to "injuries inflicted by words": reviling, backbiting, talebearing, derision, and cursing. Not only does Aquinas emphasize that these practices are violations of justice, he explicitly warns that they can be mortal sins.

But James's ultimate concern seems to be the fragile unity of his community. Nothing short of bullets is more destructive of communal well-being and solidarity than destructive talk—*even if it is true.* Gossip travels, feelings get hurt, and loyalties get betrayed. Sometimes lives are destroyed. Sides are formed. More energy is put into the conversation about the fractures in the community than into the healing of them.

We see this ourselves, in families, in schools, in workplaces, in the country, and in the church. Sometimes we are overwhelmed with information which is arguably more salacious than relevant. Do we need to know whether anorexia nervosa is the sole "health problem" of the rising starlet of the day, or whether it also includes addiction to cocaine, as some tabloids might claim? Is it really necessary to unseal the court records of a political candidate's messy divorce to assess his fitness to represent his constituency in the U.S. Senate? Do we need every detail? When the sexual abuse crisis struck the church, liberals and conservatives quickly blamed its root causes on each other, with no compunction against battering the already bruised body of Christ in service of their own political agendas.

What should we do now? That's a hard question, and it deserves more systematic attention. Things aren't as straightforward as in James's time. We live in a democratic republic requiring public deliberation about the common good. We know that silence can be used to conceal injustice, and that truth-telling can sometimes be a necessary liberation. What's the difference between fraternal correction and sinful reviling of another? There are delicate lines to be drawn—just as in matters of sexual morality. James's own strategy, that "everyone should be quick to hear, slow to speak, and slow to wrath," is good advice. But it is a hard sell in this culture. Everyone says that the monastic vow of perpetual chastity is the hardest for Americans to accept. I think most people would find it a piece of cake next to the vow of perpetual silence.

Sources

Aquinas, St. Thomas. *Summa Theologica*, II-II, qq. 72–76.

Letter of James.

Napolitano, Joe. "National Briefing-Midwest: Illinois: Candidate's Divorce Records Opened." *New York Times*, June 19, 2004. Available at http://www.nytimes.com/2004/06/19/us/national-briefing-midwest-illinois-candidate-s-divorce-records-opened.html.

National Conference of Catholic Bishops. *The Challenge of Peace: God's Promise and Our Response*. Washington, DC: United States Catholic Conference, 1983.

National Conference of Catholic Bishops. *Economic Justice for All*. Washington, DC: United States Catholic Conference, 1986.

Pope John Paul II, *Evangelium vitae* (1995).

Pope John Paul II, *Mulieris dignitatem* (1988).

Pope Paul VI, *Humanae vitae* (1968).

Vatican II, *Gaudium et spes* (1965).

Model Atheist
Jeffrey Stout and the Culture Wars

For years now, Christian culture warriors such as the late Richard John Neuhaus and James Dobson have been railing against the secularists who want to repress religion and eradicate the effect of religious beliefs on public morality and law. Until recently, however, they've been shadowboxing—they have had no adequate foil, no one who publicly demonizes religion the way they demonize the godless "culture of death." But a trio of bestsellers written by militant atheists has given substance to the shadows. In *The God Delusion* (2006), Richard Dawkins warns that all religion, not merely fundamentalist religion, is irrational and therefore dangerous. In *God Is Not Great* (2007), Christopher Hitchens argues on behalf of an aggressively secular society in which religious belief has no legitimate place in the public discourse. And in *The Atheist Manifesto* (2007), Michel Onfray trots out the tired canard that religion is the enemy of knowledge and learning.

Neuhaus and Dobson might be energized by the appearance of opponents who mirror their own black-and-white view of the world. But how should those of us already weary of the culture wars respond? We need, of course, to call the authors on their prejudices and inaccuracies. But another step is equally important. We shouldn't lump all atheists together, any more than atheists ought to lump all religious believers together. It's worth talking to nonbelievers who also see some shades of gray. For example, Jeffrey Stout, a philosopher of religion at Princeton, is the sort of atheist with whom believers can have a useful conversation. His award-winning book *Democracy and Tradition* (2007) offers helpful theoretical counterpoints to the arguments set forth by Dawkins, Hitchens, and Onfray.

Are religious believers essentially unreasoning and therefore dangerous to public life? No, says Stout. Stout vigorously disputes the idea that all religious believers are irrational, and he opposes any attempt to limit their voice in public discussion. He criticizes the late Harvard political philosopher John Rawls, who was much more nuanced than either Dawkins or Hitchens, for using an overly narrow conception of what counts as rational or reasonable public argument. This criticism should be welcome to many Catholics. Rawls famously opined that it was unreasonable for people to argue that first-trimester abortions should be outlawed (he later changed his mind) or that same-sex marriage should be prohibited. Stout might disagree with arguments for outlawing abortion or same-sex marriage, but he doesn't view the people making them as necessarily unreasonable. For Stout, the key to political reasonableness is the willingness to participate in the actual give-and-take of public, democratic argument. That means giving reasons for one's own position, and due consideration to the reasons put forward by others. Stout refuses to let anyone, religious or non-religious, win an argument on the cheap by declaring those who hold opposing views "irrational" or "unreasonable."

Is a secular society inevitably hostile to religious belief? Again, Stout's answer is no. Here, Stout insists on two senses of the word "secular." Our political discourse is secularized, he says, in the straightforward sense that participants cannot "take for granted that their interlocutors are making the same religious assumptions they are." But this does not entail a commitment to a secularism that demands the public denial of theological claims and the expulsion of theological perspectives from the political sphere. Stout emphasizes that believers can draw on any language or arguments they like in making their case. What they can't expect is that everyone else will share their theological perspective. Far from wanting to strip public conversation of rich theological language, Stout thinks we might benefit from more of it: he believes that our "democracy would profit if more citizens engaged in the 'lengthy, even leisurely unfolding' of their commitments." But we must have the patience to listen to others explain their commitments in response.

Are religious communities by nature opposed to knowledge and learning? Hardly, says Stout. Deeply indebted to Alasdair MacIntyre, Stout takes for granted that all intellectual inquiry takes place within a tradition that carries a community's thought, practices, and institutions forward through time. He explicitly acknowledges that religious traditions support rigorous intellectual inquiry. Then Stout turns the tables. He asks religious believers to consider the possibility that our democratic republic might carry forward a rich intellectual and moral tradition of its own, one that values equality, individual freedom, and self-expression, but also virtue, responsibility, and many other valuable communal practices. In my view, this is a reasonable request.

Moreover, Stout's later book, *Blessed Are the Organized: Grassroots Democracy in America* (2012), offers rich ethnographical snapshots of a gloriously pluralistic America in which people of different faiths work side by side to advocate for change that benefits the common good. Neither religious faith nor pluralism is going away any time soon. If you want to think about the relevant issues in conversation with a serious nonbeliever, forget about Christopher Hitchens and read Jeffrey Stout.

Sources

Dawkins, Richard. *The God Delusion*. New York: Mariner Books, 2006.

Hitchens, Christopher. *God is Not Great: How Religion Poisons Everything*. New York: Twelve-Hachette Book Group, 2007.

Marshall, David. *The Truth behind the New Atheism: Responding to the Emerging Challenges to God and Christianity*. Eugene, OR: Harvest House Publishers, 2007.

MacIntyre, Alasdair. *After Virtue*. 3rd ed. Notre Dame, IN: University of Notre Dame Press, 2007.

McCarraher, Eugene. "This Book Is Not Good." *Commonweal*, June 15, 2007.

Neuhaus, Richard John. *The Naked Public Square: Religion and Democracy in America*. 2nd ed. Grand Rapids, MI: Eerdmans, 1988.

Onfray, Michel. *Atheist Manifesto: The Case against Christianity, Judaism, and Islam*. New York: Arcade Publishing, 2007.

Stout, Jeffrey. *Blessed Are the Organized: Grassroots Democracy in America*. Princeton, NJ: Princeton University Press, 2012.

Stout, Jeffrey. *Democracy and Tradition*. Princeton, NJ: Princeton University Press, 2004.

Bishops and Politics
Lessons from Australia

While lecturing in Australia a few years ago, I was overcome by a sense of déjà vu. The Australian newspapers were dominated by a bitter controversy between a Catholic prelate and Catholic politicians regarding embryo-destroying stem-cell research. For a moment, my jet-lagged brain wondered if I was trapped in an eerie rerun of the 2004 U.S. elections, the point at which the American culture wars arguably reached their height. The 2004 battle for the American presidency pit George W. Bush, a conservative evangelical Protestant from Texas who quoted Pope John Paul II on life issues, against John F. Kerry, a liberal cradle Catholic from Massachusetts who placed more emphasis on other issues in Catholic social teaching, such as economic solidarity.

But I soon realized that this was something different. In fact, the Australian debate played itself out in a colorful and candid way that is virtually unimaginable in our more staid American context. That said, that particular fracas in the land down under might provide American Catholics with some enduring food for thought.

In early June 2007, Cardinal George Pell, the archbishop of Sydney, called a press conference to urge Catholic politicians to vote against a bill that would expand embryonic stem-cell research. He offered several reasons for opposing the research, arguing that it had not proved as successful as research on adult stem cells and that it involved the "grotesque" manipulation and deliberate destruction of human beings. And he went on to add a vague threat: "Catholic politicians who vote for this legislation must realize that their voting has consequences for their place in the life of the church."

As it turned out, the "consequences" cut both ways. Several prominent Catholic MPs publicly stated that they would not heed the cardinal's call. On the other side, a Catholic MP who opposed the bill went out of her way to emphasize that her decision had nothing to do with the cardinal's intervention, which she deplored as an "authoritarian legalistic edict." Other reactions were quite extreme. One Catholic cabinet minister compared Pell to "that serial boofhead Sheik al Hilaly," a controversial Australian Sunni Muslim leader who has denied the existence of the Holocaust and likened immodestly dressed women to "uncovered meat." Another decried the cardinal's remarks as reminiscent of the Dark Ages, a time when "people have been burned in oil in the name of God." The bill passed the Lower House of the New South Wales Parliament with an overwhelming 65-26 vote on June 7; three weeks later it passed the Upper House with a 27-13 vote. In every possible respect, Pell's statement backfired.

Clearly, the cardinal was not attempting to impose an esoteric religious belief on the population by force or terror. He judged that the law permitting expanded stem-cell research was inimical to the common good, and he offered reasons for that judgment. It was not improper for him to communicate his views on this matter, not only to his fellow Catholics, but also to his fellow Australians. In Australia, as in the United States, citizens are free to express their judgments about whether a law or policy promotes human dignity and true human flourishing, and to inform those judgments with their religious convictions. Presumably, the cardinal wanted politicians—all politicians—to vote against the bill because they were convinced by his moral and practical arguments.

So far, so good. But what if politicians aren't convinced? Here comes the problem. The cardinal appeared to be saying that only Catholic politicians who voted against the bill would remain in good standing in the church. No matter how vague, his threat of "consequences" put some Catholic politicians in a position of having to choose between their own private good and their best assessment of the common good. It is this threat that backfired on the cardinal.

No representative democracy can flourish if it does not systematically protect public officials from efforts to make them choose between their private welfare and the public good. Laws against threatening and bribing public officials are designed to do just that. Threats involving religious sanctions are far from being the greatest threat to the integrity of the political process, but they can be real nonetheless. In the United States, the First Amendment might well protect the legal right of religious officials to make such threats—or even to offer corresponding bribes (for example, offering membership in the Knights of Malta to a politician who votes the right way). But the fact that a particular course of action may be constitutionally protected does not make it morally right, or even effective.

Given the Catholic tradition's commitment to "natural law"—to the conviction that moral norms ought to make sense to all people of good will—bishops ought to place a high priority on convincing politicians to do the right thing for the right reasons, not merely out of a fear of religious sanction. At the same time, Catholic politicians have a responsibility to listen carefully and respectfully when bishops make a case concerning what course of action best furthers the common good on issues such as stem-cell research.

What can Americans learn from Cardinal Pell's misstep? The time for the bishops to act is not immediately before the election. If the bishops want to educate politicians on issues that matter to them, it is best to do so well outside the election cycle. Why not invite all Catholics in Congress to a daylong conference on stem-cell research, at which the church's position is fully and fairly presented? And why not invite a few smart people with opposing views, so that there can be dialogue and debate? That may seem hokey, but it's one way for the bishops to encourage Catholic politicians to act on the basis of reasons rather than threats.

Sources

Barich, Anthony. "It's Ok to Vote for Anti-Catholic Greens: Jesuit." *The Record*, August 18, 2010. Available at http://www.therecord.com.au/blog/its-ok-to-vote-for-anti-catholic-greens-jesuit/.

Brennan, Frank, S.J. "Has the Catholic Church in Australia Any Credibility Left?" *Eureka Street*, October 2, 2013. Available at http://www.eurekastreet.com.au/article.aspx?aeid=38288#.U6dyv_ldV8E.

Palmo, Rocco. "Likened to 'Boofhead.' Pell takes a Pelting." *Whispers in the Loggia*, June 7, 2007. Available at. http://whispersintheloggia.blogspot.com/2007/06/likened-to-boofhead-pell-takes-pelting.html.

Moving beyond the Culture Wars
Why a Bioethics Council Needs Diversity

Is there such a thing as an ethical "expert"? Some people may doubt such a person exists, or at least have serious questions about whether academic credentials have anything to do with moral wisdom. Nonetheless, in the past couple of decades, American presidents have commissioned panels to investigate and report upon key issues at the intersection of medicine, morality, and technology. Galvanized by the global furor that surrounded the appearance of "Dolly," the first cloned mammal, President Bill Clinton constituted a National Bioethics Advisory Commission, which remained in existence from 1996–2001. President George W. Bush appointed his own President's Council on Bioethics, which was active from 2001–2009. President Barack Obama dissolved Bush's Council in June 2009, and appointed his own Presidential Commission for the Study of Bioethical Issues that same year. It is safe to assume that whoever wins the presidency in 2016 will thank Obama's commission for its service and appoint a new group of people with a new charge.

Needless to say, each president put his own normative stamp on both the composition and direction of the panel he constituted. In an essay written immediately after its dissolution, the distinguished Christian ethicist Gilbert Meilaender eulogized President George W. Bush's Council on Bioethics. His assessment merits close attention, because it reveals significant issues in deciding what constitutes a sufficiently diverse high-level deliberative body for a morally and culturally pluralistic society such as our own.

Meilaender argued that the Bush council, on which he served, got two important things right. First, it addressed the proper questions—the big questions about the purpose of human existence and the nature of human dignity. Second, it brought the right voices to the table; Meilaender maintained that members of the Bush council held diverse views, and that this enabled the council to address those big questions in and for our pluralistic society.

My own assessment of the council is mixed. Its membership, largely drawn from academia, was undeniably distinguished. It produced a number of important reports on topics ranging from human cloning to the ethics of screening newborns for genetic diseases. But the council's diversity was a pugnacious diversity, mostly pitting secular liberals against religious conservatives. Its composition reflected, in short, the "culture war" mindset of Bush himself.

Meilaender worries that a council focused on "practical policy options," generally produces "lowest-common-denominator proposals, from which the deepest and most important issues have been filtered out." I don't see why that has to be the case, particularly if the group is not composed only or primarily of academics like the Clinton and Bush councils, but also includes a wide range of practitioners. Many hospital administrators, clinical bioethicists, insurance executives, and health-care lawyers have had to figure out how to get things done in a pluralistic society without sacrificing—or requiring others to sacrifice—deeply held moral or religious principles.

Sometimes practical problems can be the mother of advances in ethical reflection. A good example is the recent struggle of Catholic health-care institutions to preserve both their existence and their integrity in an era of increased corporate integration and collaboration. This challenging environment has spurred new thinking about the traditional notion of what constitutes "cooperation with evil." Developed more than two centuries ago by Catholic moralists to analyze an individual's complicity with the wrongdoing of another, the concept of "cooperation with evil" has now been creatively and analogically—and practically—extended to illuminate and evaluate institutional complicity.

What sort of diversity is desirable for an advisory body on bioethics? In my view, the purposes assigned to the council by the executive order creating it should determine the necessary scope of diversity. For example, the bioethics commission appointed by President Bill Clinton focused on questions of law and public policy; it should therefore have included diverse views on the role of law in a pluralistic society. But it didn't—instead, the Clinton commission assumed the validity of a liberal legal theory dedicated to maximizing the scope of individual freedom from government restrictions. Its work would have been enriched by the perspectives of conservative Catholic legal scholars such as Robert George or Mary Ann Glendon, who defend a more communitarian understanding of the law.

What about the Bush council, on which George and Glendon actually served? That council included secular scientists and religious believers. But many of the religious believers were very much of the same stripe. George, Glendon, Meilaender, and the late Jean Bethke Elshtain, all council members, served on the editorial board of *First Things*, the magazine founded by the late Richard John Neuhaus. Leon Kass, the council's first chair, has also been an important contributor to that magazine.

Nor did other distinguished members add to the religious diversity; Edmund Pellegrino and Paul McHugh are also conservative Catholics. Another member, William F. May, is a prominent Christian ethicist and by no means a radical liberal. Nonetheless, he argued for a more permissive stance on embryo research than Meilaender, George, and Glendon. When he left the council at the end of his first term, his expertise and perspective were not replaced.

In the ideological construct of the culture wars, religious "true believers" are socially and politically conservative and implacably pitted against secularists. Diversity is understood to be debate between two clearly defined views. But in the real world, religion and politics interact in far more complicated and interesting ways. The membership of a council whose purpose is to consider the "big questions" ought to reflect that complexity. In selecting members to represent the voices of American Christianity, why not include someone like Cornel West, a progressive African-American public intellectual? Or perhaps Karen Lebacqz, a liberal Protestant bioethicist who served as president of the Society of Christian Ethics. Even a little more diversity among Catholics would have been nice—and easy to accomplish. Why not Lisa Cahill (Boston College) or Bryan Hehir (Harvard)? Why not Daniel Callahan, a founding father of secular bioethics (and a former editor of *Commonweal*) who is also very familiar with the Catholic tradition?

The religious diversity of the United States is messy and energetic. As the last election proved, religious believers do not line up in neat ideological lines. Some support health-care reform, some oppose it.

Some support embryonic stem-cell research, some oppose it. My own belief is that presidents do better not to flee the messiness, but instead to engage the energy and commitment of a wide range of American people of faith.

Sources

Bioethics Research Library at Georgetown University. "Archived Bioethics Websites." Georgetown University. Available at https://bioethics.georgetown .edu/library-materials/open-access-resources/archived-bioethics-websites/. (Archived materials from the National Bioethics Advisory Commission (the Clinton Commission, 1996–2001) and the President's Council on Bioethics (the Bush Council, 2001–2009)).

Kaveny, M. Cathleen. "Diversity and Deliberation: Bioethics Commissions and Moral Reasoning." *Journal of Religious Ethics* 34:2 (2006): 311–337.

Meilaender, Gilbert. "End of Discussion: Why Obama Should Have Kept the Bioethics Council." *Commonweal*, August 10, 2009.

Presidential Commission for the Study of Bioethical Issues. "History of Bioethics Commissions." U.S. Department of Health & Human Services, n.d. Available at http://bioethics.gov/history.

A Flawed Analogy
Prochoice Politicians and the Third Reich

As American presidential election cycles heat up, the political and moral rhetoric about abortion tends to reach the boiling point. Some prominent prolife Catholics have compared politicians who support abortion rights to the Nazis, and intimated that Catholics who would vote for such politicians are comparable to citizens of the Third Reich who were indifferent to the plight of those condemned to the gas chambers. Is the analogy that equates the American prochoice legal regime and Nazi Germany correct? I do not think it is.

Let me begin with a disclaimer. In contemporary American political discourse, associating someone with the Nazis is usually an insult, not an invitation to serious dialogue. But as a teacher of ethics, I have encountered many prolife students who have grappled with the Nazi analogy in a sincere and even agonized manner. Precisely because they are asking a question, not hurling an insult, they deserve an answer.

One important difference between the Holocaust and the American practice of legalized abortion has to do with the intentions of the perpetrators. The Final Solution implemented the judgment that all Jews (and other targeted populations) were a blight and drain on the German *volk*. For that reason, the goal of the Third Reich was the elimination of "inferior races." No one in the United States argues that unborn children as a class are akin to social vermin—no one is aiming to eliminate or kill all unborn children. U.S. law does not force women to have abortions.

A second difference pertains to the type of classification involved. Nazi racial classifications such as "Jewish" or "Gypsy" are both exclusive and permanent. For the Nazis, some individuals are Jews, others are not. Moreover, it was impossible for an individual to move out of a disfavored category into a favored one. Once a Gypsy, always a Gypsy. In contrast, the category of "unborn" works very differently. It is not permanent: a particular human being remains in the category for at most nine months. And it is a category in which everyone has at one point belonged. So while abortion is intentional killing in many cases, it is not genocide—it does not aim to eliminate "them," a group of people who are deemed totally and permanently different from and inferior to "us."

A third difference concerns the extent of government involvement. The Third Reich directly ordered and carried out the killing of Jews, Gypsies, homosexuals, and other populations. In contrast, the U.S. government does not demand the killing of unborn children in general or of any particular unborn child. Instead, it declines to protect the unborn against one type of private killing initiated by one particular person—the mother. Importantly, it protects the unborn from other kinds of assault. No third party has an independent right to kill an unborn child. The millions of Jews killed in the Final Solution were killed as a direct result of the policy of a ruthless government. In contrast, the millions of unborn children killed since 1973 were killed because of the individual decisions made by millions of women who as a class should be considered more desperate than ruthless.

A fourth difference pertains to the options available for assisting the victims. The Nazis cracked down on anyone who agitated on behalf of the Jews or took steps to help them. In contrast, the prolife movement in the United States has a strong political voice. Ongoing efforts to convince women to carry their pregnancies to term, and to give those women assistance in doing so, are entirely legal and legitimate, and often effective. Crisis pregnancy centers are not analogous to the "secret annex" in *The Diary of Anne Frank*.

In short, those of us who believe that the unborn are full members of the human community have morally relevant reasons for distinguishing between Nazi Germany's treatment of the Jews and the treatment of the unborn under U.S. law. What follows from keeping those reasons firmly in mind?

To begin with, keeping those reasons in mind enables us to voice our commitment to the legitimacy of the U.S. government and its Constitution. I simply fail to see how those who equate the Holocaust with legalized abortion can avoid the conclusion that the U.S. government merits the same fate as the Nazi regime.

More importantly, however, if we view abortion narrowly through the lens of the Holocaust, we miss a key aspect of the problem. The relationship between women and their unborn children is not the same as the relationship between Nazis and Jews. Many women who face crisis pregnancies are themselves financially and socially vulnerable. Carrying a baby to term is not a simple matter of refraining from intentional killing; it also requires a positive investment of one's physical and emotional strength. At the end of the process comes an anguishing decision about whether to raise the child oneself or to give it up for adoption. This means that any effective response to the problem of abortion must help vulnerable women find the strength to protect unborn human beings who are even more vulnerable than they themselves are—and find the hope that they themselves can flourish in doing so.

Sources

Burke, Archbishop Raymond L. "On Our Civic Responsibility for the Common Good." *Eternal Word Television Network*, October 1, 2004. Available at http://www.ewtn.com/library/bishops/burkecom.htm.

Dyer, Justin Buckley. *Slavery, Abortion, and the Politics of Constitutional Meaning.* Cambridge, UK: Cambridge University Press, 2013.

Editorial. "Partisans Try to Narrow Catholics' Choices." *National Catholic Reporter*, October 1, 2004. Available at http://nationalcatholicreporter.org/update/bn092404.htm.

Jenky, Bishop Daniel R. "Full Text of Bishop Jenky's Homily at Men's March and Mass—April 14, 2014." *The Catholic Post*, June 22, 2014. Available at http://www.cdop.org/post/PostArticle.aspx?ID=2440.

Lifton, Robert J. *The Nazi Doctors: Medical Killing and the Psychology of Genocide.* New York: Basic Books, 1986.

Rice, Charles. "Abortion and the Catholic Vote." *The Observer* (University of Notre Dame student-run newspaper), October 14, 2008. Available at http://ndsmcobserver.com/2008/10/abortion-and-the-catholic-vote/.

Smith, Randall. "A Cautionary Tale." *The Catholic Thing*, September 21, 2012. Available at http://www.thecatholicthing.org/columns/2012/a-cautionary

Sick Minds

What Can We Do to Prevent Another Tucson?

For nearly two decades, my sister Meg Kaveny has worked with the homeless in Portland, Oregon. Many of them are mentally ill. Meg moved to the Pacific Northwest as a Holy Cross Associate, and stayed on to earn a graduate degree in social work. She has helped teach law-enforcement officers how to better serve the mentally ill homeless, including how to make more accurate on-street assessments of the risk homeless people pose to themselves and others.

In January 2011, Jared Lee Loughner deliberately shot and severely injured U.S. Representative Gabrielle Giffords at a shopping mall in Tucson, Arizona. He also killed six people, including Chief U.S. District Court Judge John Roll, as well as a nine-year-old girl, Christina-Taylor Green. In addition to Representative Giffords, his shooting spree injured fourteen other people, including one man who was hurt while attempting to disarm him. After Loughner's arrest, he was diagnosed as a paranoid schizophrenic, and judged incompetent to stand trial; the same judgment was reached in March 2012. In August 2012, however, he was judged competent to stand trial, and pleaded guilty to nineteen counts of murder and attempted murder. He was sentenced to serve seven consecutive life sentences in November 2012. He is currently incarcerated at the United States Medical Center for Federal Prisoners in Springfield, Missouri.

Prompted by this horrific incident, I asked Meg what policy lessons we might draw from homicides involving gun violence and persons who suffer from mental illness. In particular, I asked her about how society's approach to mental health might be relevant to this question. Here are her reflections.

The ultimate culpability of Jared Loughner in killing six people and injuring many others, including U.S. Representative Gabrielle Giffords, will be debated for a long time. But the responsibility for creating the environment in which mental illness goes undetected and untreated, and in which it's easier to obtain a firearm than a driver's license, lies with all of us.

The good news is we already know what works in treating serious mental illness: client-centered, recovery-oriented treatment that takes into account the biological, psychological, and spiritual needs of the person. These terrible events in Arizona are only one chapter of a long, tragic story. Young men in their twenties obtain guns in order to extract retribution from those whom they perceive as enemies. (In general, people with severe and persistent mental illness are far more likely to be the *victims* of crime than the perpetrators.) Still, if we are to have any hope of changing the conditions that likely contributed to the devastation in Tucson, we must face some difficult facts and answer some difficult questions.

Effective mental-health treatment costs money. The longer a psychotic episode goes untreated, the less likely the person will regain his or her previous level of functioning. Are we willing to fund a comprehensive mental-health treatment system that emphasizes early intervention? Are we willing to pay the people who work in this system a living wage? The evidence suggests we're not. The National Association of State Mental Health Program Directors estimates that $2.1 billion has been cut from state mental health budgets in the past three years alone. The movement to repeal "Obamacare" in order to preserve personal liberty suggests that we are not willing to make comprehensive health care, including mental-health coverage, more available to people who need it.

Individuals make terrible choices about their physical health and their medical treatment, often knowing full well the negative consequences. But when it comes to those with a psychotic illness, the decision to live under a bridge, or not to eat, or not to seek treatment that would alleviate the suffering is not merely a lifestyle choice. In their case, the organ that evaluates options for treatment, risks, benefits, and alternatives is sick. Make no mistake: A person in the midst of a psychotic episode is suffering terribly. Are we willing to reverse a twenty-five year trend in the United States in which people with severe mental illness are allowed to live on the streets, marinating in their own excrement, under the pretext of preserving their individual freedom and civil rights? In Multnomah County, Oregon, it is not unusual for a person who is floridly psychotic to be released from civil commitment court if the person is able to state the names of nearby shelters and free-meal sites, even when previous actions indicate that she is not able to meet her most basic needs.

Finally, are we willing to make it harder for people to buy guns? The Constitution guarantees the right to bear arms, but when the Constitution was written, the arms in question were muskets, not semi-automatic handguns capable of firing many rounds per minute. In order to purchase an automobile, a person has to show proof of insurance—to cover the cost of repair or replacement of the vehicle in the event of an accident, but also to compensate people for injuries or death caused by a reckless or negligent driver. Why don't we require equivalent licensing and insurance before allowing someone to purchase a weapon capable of instant and indiscriminate carnage?

If we are not willing to address these issues, we can only expect to see a repeat of the events in Tucson. A poorly funded mental-health system and lax gun laws don't cause deadly rampages like that of Jared Loughner. But better mental-health funding, more comprehensive treatment programs, and tighter gun control might help prevent them.

Sources

Giffords, Gabrielle, and Mark Kelly. *Enough: Our Fight to Keep America Safe from Gun Violence*. New York: Scribner, 2014.

Giffords, Gabrielle, and Mark Kelly. *Gabby: A Story of Courage and Hope*. New York: Scribner, 2011.

Newport, John. *The Tucson Tragedy: Lessons from the Senseless Shooting of Gabrielle Giffords*. Denver, CO: Outskirts Press, 2011.

Santos, Fernanda. "Gunman in Giffords Shooting Sentenced to 7 Life Terms." *New York Times*, November 8, 2012.

Wikipedia. "Jared Lee Loughner." May 15, 2014. Available at http://en.wikipedia.org/wiki/Jared_Lee_Loughner.

Crime or Tragedy?
Murder and Suicide at Villanova

In January 20, 2005, Villanova University dedicated a memorial to the late Professor Mine Ener, former director of the university's Center for Arab and Islamic Studies. The last six months of Mine's life, and the circumstances of her death, had shaken the campus. The year after she was married, Mine gave birth to a daughter, Raya Donagi, who suffered from Down syndrome and associated medical complications. As time went on, Raya's condition did not improve and Mine sank more deeply into postpartum depression. By the time Raya was six months old, Mine appeared to be gripped by postpartum psychosis. On the morning of August 4, 2003, she killed Raya, later telling police that she could not bear for the baby to continue in such suffering. A few weeks later, Mine Ener took her own life.

Shocked and heartbroken, the Villanova community nonetheless refused to reduce the meaning of Mine's life to the despair, psychosis, and violence that plagued her last days. After much thought, a committee decided to create a small oasis in the library that reflected Mine's love of Middle Eastern hospitality and culture. A plaque on the wall read, "In memory of Mine Ener: scholar, teacher, mentor, friend." It also noted her dates of service at Villanova (1996–2003).

The memorial was a grieving community's act of hope, and its prayer for some peace. It was not a political act. Yet it was immediately brandished as a weapon in the culture wars. A few prolife students protested that the memorial was inconsistent with church teaching on the sanctity of life. Television personality Bill O'Reilly castigated the university for "honoring" a baby killer, as did members of the blogosphere. Villanova quickly capitulated to the pressure, announcing on January 31 that the plaque would be removed, and that Mine would be memorialized by a symposium on postpartum depression and psychosis.

What, exactly, is going on here? On one level, the controversy seems unwarranted. First, according to traditional Catholic teaching, it is highly unlikely that Mine Ener was fully morally culpable for killing either her baby or herself. Despite her best efforts to seek treatment, her postpartum psychosis deprived Mine of the minimum conditions of reason and free will necessary for someone to be morally responsible for such acts. Morally speaking, she was not a "killer." Second, the plaque created little danger of "scandal"—traditionally understood to mean fostering the misapprehension that a morally illicit act is permissible. Unlike abortion, infanticide is not only illegal, it is vigorously prosecuted. There was absolutely no suggestion that baby Raya's Down syndrome meant that her life was counted less seriously by the relevant authorities. Third, the memorial was clearly designed not to "honor" Mine's tragic acts but to remind people of the overall meaning of her life.

Why, then, the firestorm? On a deeper level, I think it goes back to abortion—but not in the way articulated by those protesting the memorial. Everyone must sense, at least on an inchoate level, that Mine Ener's story makes a perfect advertisement for Planned Parenthood: A successful, newly married thirty-seven-year-old professional woman refuses to heed standard medical warnings to have amniocentesis and gives birth to a baby with Down syndrome. She is determined to give her baby the best possible life, but she can't. Because of her baby's illness, and her own, the story ends catastrophically. If Mine had simply had an abortion, she might have had another baby, a "normal" child, whose demands would not have pushed Mine's fragile psyche beyond endurance.

So how might prolifers counter this cautionary tale? There are three possible strategies. First, blame Mine for the tragedy, and treat her as if she were morally responsible for killing her baby and herself. That is the strategy of those who denounce her as a moral monster. But what if you realize that she is also a victim, trapped by her own careening hormones and destabilized psyche? The second strategy is to treat the case as a freakish outlier. This is the approach of those who don't want to consign Mine to hell, but who don't want to "honor" her either. They want to make her disappear, so people won't think about her plight too much. The trouble with this approach is that it perpetuates an illusion. We might like to think that things in this life always work out for the best if we try to do the right thing, but sometimes they don't.

The final approach is to grapple honestly with life's moral messiness and place our ultimate trust in God. In my opinion, this is the only one that will work in the long run. As Catholics, we proclaim the hope of redemption, not just from sin, but from sorrow and death. We recognize, with St. Paul, that "the whole creation has been groaning in travail together until now" (Rom 8:22); we certainly see it in this case. The biological process of giving life to Raya and caring for her cost Mine her psyche, which in turn brought death to both mother and child. Giving life should never mean causing death. In such cases, Paul tells us, "the Spirit himself intercedes for us with sighs too deep for words" (Rom 8:26). But the heart and soul of Catholic faith is a firm hope for redemption, even in the midst of grinding sorrow. It is hope without blinkers. Easter Sunday does not erase Good Friday—it transfigures it.

So what should Villanova have done? I think its leaders should have put up a new plaque, memorializing both Mine and baby Raya. The plaque should have included this passage from *Revelations of Divine Love* by the great mystic Julian of Norwich: "All shall be well, and all shall be well; all manner of things shall be well."

Sources

Blanco, Juan Ignacio. "Mine An Ener." *Murderpedia,* n.d. Available at http://murderpedia.org/female.E/e/ener-mine-an.htm.

Julian of Norwich. *Revelations of Divine Love.* Short text and long text edition. Translated by Elizabeth Spearing. New York: Penguin Books, 1999.

St. Paul, Letter to the Romans.

Dignity and the End of Life
How Not to Talk about Assisted Suicide

Physician-assisted suicide (PAS) and euthanasia have long been the redheaded stepchildren of the prolife movement. They are dutifully included in the litany of life-related issues, yet they have not attracted the sustained attention—or passion—that has characterized the struggle against abortion. That may be about to change.

In May 2011, Gallup named PAS the most divisive moral issue in American life. According to their "Values and Beliefs" poll, 45 percent of the population now think it is morally acceptable, while 48 percent believe it to be morally wrong. In June, the United States Conference of Catholic Bishops issued its first full statement on PAS, "To Live Each Day with Dignity."

Some Catholics who focus on the struggle between the "culture of life" and the "culture of death" also seem to be girding themselves for battle on end-of-life issues. In a column in *Crisis*, Catholic media commentator Barbara Nicolosi writes, "We need an emotionally winning language for this fight. The other side should not get away with christening themselves 'mercy killers'; they are 'death dealers,' 'elder abortionists,' 'needlers.'" She urges prolifers to invoke the Nazis, who started a secret euthanasia program.

While well-intentioned, Nicolosi's strategy is mistaken. The best way to promote human dignity at the end of life isn't to clone the culture war over abortion, the effectiveness of which is highly questionable. PAS raises very different questions of law and public policy. It also plays on very different human emotions, which shape our response to the legal frameworks of the two issues.

Abortion is now a constitutionally protected choice. Assisted suicide is not. In 1997, the Supreme Court held that the Constitution leaves the matter of assisted suicide to the states to decide. As of fall 2015, five states have legalized the procedure (Washington, Oregon,

Vermont, Montana, and California). On abortion, prolifers are fighting a judicially imposed status quo. In contrast, in most states, the status quo favors those opposed to PAS and euthanasia. In fact, a review of older Gallup polls shows that opposition to assisted dying has actually grown over the past decade. In this context, a scorched-earth culture-war approach may prove to be overkill, so to speak.

Abortion kills the unborn without their consent, depriving them of their entire future. It evokes in its opponents the desire to protest injustice and to protect the innocent against unwarranted harm. In contrast, to stave off suffering among the terminally ill in the last weeks or month of their lives, PAS allows them to kill themselves with medicine provided by a physician. Since the person to be killed both instigates and carries out the killing, most people do not think it is primarily a matter of justice, although it may be wrong on other grounds, such as a violation of God's law. St. Thomas Aquinas would say that this type of private killing is a usurpation of public authority to make determinations of life and death.

Prolifers have a response. Drawing on data from the Netherlands (where euthanasia has long been legal), they have argued that PAS would be just the first step down a slippery slope. PAS (in which the patient administers the legal dose) may evolve into voluntary euthanasia (in which the physician kills the patient), which in turn could evolve into non-voluntary or even involuntary euthanasia (in which patients are killed without or against their will). Involuntary euthanasia is clearly a matter of justice.

This response is important, and in my view, insightful. But it's not sufficient. Some will question whether the Netherlands can be analogized to the United States. Others will say that the data on PAS in Oregon do not support the worries. I think these responses can be successfully addressed.

But there is a deeper problem. The prolife slippery-slope argument plays to people's generalized fears about living in a brutally unjust society. Many people of a certain age have a countervailing set of fears. The anxiety created by the prospect of one's own very bad death is far more immediate and visceral than any concern that the United States might become a Nazi dystopia. People do not want to die abandoned, alone, and in pain. They do not want to bankrupt themselves arranging for around-the-clock nursing care, or to become a physical and financial burden to their already overstretched children. In the context of these fears, the legal availability of PAS can become a security blanket, an emergency exit "just in case" their worst fears are realized.

To combat these fears, it is not enough to excoriate a culture of death. We must actively build a culture of life. Universal health care, including the latest techniques for pain control, must be widely available. In-home elder care and respite care need to be easily accessible. And churches, synagogues, and mosques ought to ramp up their ministries to the sick and the homebound. As Pope John Paul II recognizes in *Evangelium vitae*, protecting human dignity at the end of life is a matter of both justice *and* the works of mercy.

Sources

Keown, John. *Euthanasia, Ethics, and Public Policy: An Argument against Legalization*. Cambridge, UK: Cambridge University Press, 2002. See especially part III, "The Dutch Experience: Controlling VAE? Condoning NVAE?"

Nicolosi, Barbara. "Exposing Euthanasia through the Arts." *Crisis*, June 3, 2011. Available at http://www.crisismagazine.com/2011/exposing-euthanasia -through-the-arts.

Pope John Paul II, *Evangelium vitae* (1995).

Roe v. Wade, 410 U.S. 113 (1973).

Saad, Lydia. "Doctor-Assisted Suicide Is Moral Issue Dividing Americans Most." *Gallup Politics*, May 31, 2011. Available at http://www.gallup.com /poll/147842/doctor-assisted-suicide-moral-issue-dividing-americans.aspx.

Shavelson, Lonny. *A Chosen Death: The Dying Confront Assisted Suicide*. New York: Simon & Schuster, 1995.

Vacco v. Quill, 521 U.S. 793 (1997).

Washington v. Glucksberg, 521 U.S. 702 (1997).

The Right Questions
Catholic Colleges and Pop Culture

Life on college campuses follows predictable rhythms. Each February, for instance, seems to bring the annual tussle about whether or not *The Vagina Monologues* ought to be performed at Catholic colleges and universities. I understand those who think the content and rhetoric of the play is inappropriate for a Catholic campus, although in the end I don't agree. The people I don't understand are those who think the play will morally corrupt students. In my view, students are routinely exposed to far more seductive and therefore more formidable entertainments, such as *Sex and the City* and *Entourage*, two series produced by HBO that were popular with college students when they first aired, and continue to enjoy attention through Netflix and other streaming services. *Sex and the City* was broadcast from 1994 to 2004; it earned fifth place on Entertainment Weekly's list of "New TV Classics." Moreover, the series generated two feature films: *Sex and the City* (2008) and *Sex and the City 2* (201), and a prequel series, *The Carrie Diaries*, which lasted for two seasons before being cancelled in May 2014. *Entourage* has similarly durable appeal. Broadcast from 2004–2011, its first feature film was released in 2015.

Sex and the City is about four single women seeking love, sex, success, and happiness in Manhattan, while *Entourage* is about four single men seeking sex (love seems secondary), money, and adventure in Hollywood. *Sex and the City*'s protagonist is Carrie Bradshaw, a sex-and-relationship columnist for a New York newspaper who bases her writing on her own experiences and those of her friends. *Entourage*'s central character is Vincent Chase, an up-and-coming movie star from New York City who brings along his lifelong friends for the ride to fame and fortune. In a sense, the two series are the same show, with one version aimed at young women, and the other at young men.

Unlike the characters dramatized in the *Monologues*, who are broken, bruised, and socially ostracized, the characters in the two HBO series are glamorous and well connected. No one in her right mind would want to go through what the characters in *The Vagina Monologues* go through. But young women at Notre Dame have been known to discuss which character on *Sex and the City* they most identify with—the ladylike Charlotte, who wants a husband, children, and a house in the country, or the ambitious Miranda, who aims to be a successful lawyer. *Entourage* is a bit simpler; my guess is most young men wanted to be Vincent Chase, but feared they have more in common with Turtle, Vincent's aptly nicknamed gofer and driver.

Unlike *The Vagina Monologues*, which makes an appearance on campuses once a year, *Sex and the City* and *Entourage* are constant enticements. Although *Sex and the City* ended its original run in 2004, has done very well in syndication. *Entourage* has also been very popular. Both shows are also widely available on DVD and streaming services. In short, a Catholic college couldn't ban them without banning cable TV, Netflix, and the Internet.

What you can't ban, however, you can engage. It's easy to highlight the fantasy aspects of the shows; for example, no one on either of the HBO series seems to spend very much time working for all that money they throw around. It's harder, however, to engage the moral vision animating the two series in a manner helpful to students. It's easy enough to point to the *Catechism*'s list of sexual sins in order to condemn the characters. But that strategy simply makes the students' eyes glaze over. They've heard it all before—or so they think.

It seems to me that the key to engaging students about popular culture is to start with appreciation, not condemnation. Why do young people find these characters so attractive? If you strip away the glitter, what you will find in each case is something that is enduring: deep and committed friendship. The main characters celebrate each other's successes and commiserate over each other's failures. They can reveal themselves to one another without fear of rejection. Moreover, if a friend's welfare is on the line, they count on one another to tell the truth, not simply to say what the other wants to hear. The women on *Sex and the City* are sisters to one another; the men on *Entourage* are brothers.

But engagement should also mean challenge. While the characters on both shows have interesting and varied sex lives, they do not, as a rule, successfully combine sexual relationships with deep friendship. Their lovers are fascinating and sometimes all-consuming, but they are not good friends. So the ultimate existential question raised is whether it is possible to combine friendship and romantic love in a lifelong partnership. Many students at Catholic colleges hope for just such a relationship. Given the high rate of divorce among their parents' generation, many young people fear it might not be possible. One reason these shows are so popular, it seems to me, is that they grapple with the right questions—including the conflict between what is necessary to be successful in the work world and to have a flourishing family life. While women have long addressed these questions, *Entourage* showed that they also arise for men.

Christian thinkers have long pondered the relationship between different sorts of love, particularly between *agape* (deep compassion and concern) and *eros* (desire). Thomas Aquinas thought that marriage was not merely meant to ratify an erotic bond, but also to create a lifelong friendship. Philosophy is fine, students might say when pointed to Aquinas, but what about reality? In response, one might turn first to fellow Americans, rather than to Catholic exhortation. In 2008, HBO produced a wonderful miniseries about the passionate friendship and enduring marriage of John and Abigail Adams, adapted from the Pulitzer Prize–winning book by David McCullough. I suspect just such a relationship is what young Catholics want for themselves. And if they do, then what do they need to do to make it possible? What sort of vision of sex, love, and commitment could sustain it? Here, at this point, is where Catholic sexual ethics might fruitfully begin to present its vision of loving, committed relationships. So constructive dialogue between Catholic sexual ethics and popular culture might be possible if we abide for a time with the questions, before we begin pointing to the answers.

Sources

Adams, Abigail, and John Adams. *My Dearest Friend: Letters of Abigail and John Adams.* Edited by Margaret A. Hogan and C. James Taylor. Cambridge, MA: Belknap Press of Harvard University Press, 2010.

Ensler, Eve. *The Vagina Monologues.* New York: Villard Books, 2007.

Hibbs, Thomas S. "Father Jenkins' 'Creative Contextualization.'" *Catholic World Report*, April 25, 2011. Available at http://www.catholicworldreport.com /Item/397/father_jenkins_creative_contextualization.aspx.

Kaveny, Cathleen. "Be Not Afraid: 'The Vagina Monologues' on Catholic Campuses." *Commonweal Magazine*, March 9, 2009.

Kaveny, Cathleen. "The Perfect Storm." *America*, May 8, 2006.

McCullough, David. *John Adams.* New York: Simon & Schuster, 2002.

Either/Or?
Catholicism Is More Complex

We Americans are attracted to dualistic views of the world. Our most popular entertainment has long featured White Hats and Black Hats. For example, the *Star Wars* saga pits Jedi knights, the Light Side of the Force, against the Sith warriors, who represent the Dark Side. Our politicians repeatedly and successfully invoke dualistic themes: In the 1980s, Ronald Reagan portrayed the United States in a battle against the "Evil Empire" of the Soviet Union, while two decades later, George W. Bush denounced Iraq, Iran, and North Korea as the "Axis of Evil."

We like our religion dualistic, too. In recent years, some American Catholics have adopted a black-and-white attitude toward the broader culture, reducing our nation's moral controversies to a battle between the "culture of life" and the "culture of death." Bill Donohue, the president of the Catholic League for Religious and Civil Rights, is always good for a caustic riposte from the front lines of the culture wars: "Hollywood likes anal sex. They like to see the public square without nativity scenes. I like families. I like children. They like abortions. I believe in traditional values and restraint. They believe in libertinism. We have nothing in common."

Many American Catholics are sympathetic with Donohue's stance, if not always with his style. The Web site of Catholic screenwriter and media expert Barbara Nicolosi prominently featured quotations describing her as "a modern-day anti-Jonah, passionately crashing the gates of today's Ninevehs—New York and Los Angeles." She wanted to use her media savvy "to encourage and help a new generation of Catholic culture warriors in their mission." Not surprisingly, then, Nicolosi's speech to the annual meeting of the Catholic Press Association in May 2005 (posted on her blog) sounded dualistic themes. Nicolosi summarized her assessment of the current state of the film industry with the reflection: "The dividing line between the life with

God and the life without him will be more and more clear in culture. It's kind of a relief."

It's not at all a relief, at least to me. No one denies there are morally problematic forces at work in American society and culture. But dualism is not the answer. Why not? First, it occludes our awareness of our own sin and shortcomings. If we see ourselves as fully committed warriors on behalf of the culture of life, we are not likely to be receptive to the scrutiny of our own agenda, motives, and means. After all, we know that we are on the side of the angels—we think that God is supplying our virtue (our strength and goodness). Even if we do have flaws, they pale in comparison to those of our enemies.

Second, a dualistic worldview inevitably corrodes charity. If those who disagree with us are the enemies of the culture of life, they are worthy of nothing but our enmity. We don't need to understand their perspective, or ask ourselves hard questions about whether and how persons acting in good faith might reach the position they have reached. By definition, they are not acting in good faith—they are minions of the culture of death.

Third, a dualistic worldview ultimately distorts our perception of reality by forcing everything we see into two diametrically opposed categories. *The Passion of the Christ* is "good" because it carries the banner for a Christian worldview, while *Million Dollar Baby* is "evil" because it threatens to undermine that worldview. But life (and art) can't always be divided up so neatly. Take *Million Dollar Baby*, which won the 2004 Academy Award for Best Picture. The controversy in a nutshell: Frank, the gruff old trainer, has come to love Maggie, the female boxer he coaches, like a daughter. After a fight leaves her paralyzed, he cares for her devotedly through her increasing tribulations, including gruesome bedsores and the amputation of a gangrenous limb. In the end, he accedes to her repeated requests to help her die, even though he fully believes that doing so will cost him his own soul.

It's easy, and safe, for Christians to dismiss *Million Dollar Baby* as propaganda for the culture of death. It's harder to ponder the challenge it poses to our own worldview. These challenges aren't external salvos from anti-Christian Hollywood; they are internal tensions with which Christian thinkers have long wrestled. How should we think about situations where the demands of the moral law seem to conflict with our paramount obligation to love our neighbor? What sort of self-sacrifice do love of God and love of neighbor require? Is it selfish to protect our own moral purity rather than do what's necessary to help someone in desperate need? What constitutes authentic help to someone who is suffering? Should a good father accept eternal damnation as a consequence of relieving his daughter's suffering the only way he knows how? Should a pious mother beg God to let her take her unrepentant child's place in hell? Should a saint be willing to be damned *ad majorem Dei gloriam*? Even though I ultimately disagree with Frank's decision to facilitate Maggie's suicide, I am sympathetic with his moral struggle and see value in recognizing and engaging—rather than dismissing—his difficult questions.

Million Dollar Baby isn't opposed to Christianity *per se*; it is opposed to a sanitized version of Christianity in which there are no questions, only answers. It is ironic that so many self-described "orthodox" Catholics have adopted the culture-war mindset, since such thinking is far more at home in Protestant Christianity than in Roman Catholicism. I wonder what it will take for Catholics to begin interpreting John Paul II's descriptions of the "culture of life" and the "culture of death" less dualistically, with a view toward Augustine's categories of the "City of God" and the "City of Man." None of us can say for sure in which city we ourselves will reside, much less anyone else. The citizens of the two cities will live together intermingled until the end of time, when God will finally separate the wheat from the chaff. Until then, Augustine's hats are not black and white, but various shades of gray.

Sources

Augustine. *City of God.* Translated by Henry Bettenson. New York: Penguin Books, 2003. See especially Books 14 and 19.

Bush, George, W. "Address before a Joint Session of the Congress on the State of the Union, January 29, 2002." *Public Papers of the Presidents of the United States,* 2002, bk. 1, 129–36.

Cluchey, Jeremy. "Who Is Catholic League President Bill Donohue?," *Media Matters for America.* December 20, 2004. Available at http://mediamatters.org/research/2004/12/20/who-is-catholic-league-president-william-donohu/132482.

Matera, Angelo. "Barbara Nicolosi: A Godspy Interview." *Godspy: Faith at the Edge.* March 27, 2008. Available at http://oldarchive.godspy.com/culture/Barbara-Nicolosi-A-Godspy-Interview.cfm.html.

Nicolosi, Barbara. "Christian Imagination and the Media." *Church of the Masses.* May 24, 2005. Available at http://www.patheos.com/blogs/churchofthe masses/2005/05/718/

Pope John Paul II, *Evangelium vitae* (1995).

Reagan, Ronald. "Remarks at the Annual Convention of the National Association of Evangelicals, March 8, 1983." *Public Papers of the Presidents of the United States*, 359–64.

Part 4

Conversations about Belief

This part focuses on conversations between and among persons who are members of the same faith community as well as the same political community—American Roman Catholics. Those conversations are marred by the same divisions that scar the political discussion in the United States. They encompass many of the same political-moral issues, such as the appropriate legal response to abortion or same-sex marriage. Yet they also include issues that are largely controversial only within Roman Catholic communities, such as the leadership roles appropriate to women, and the role of Catholic theologians vis-à-vis the magisterium. The wounds of division, I think, are experienced as far more searing when they rend the Catholic community than when they rip at the political community at large. The Roman Catholic Church has long understood itself as the body of Christ; cleavages within that body are often perceived as having a far more profound impact than the quotidian divides over matters of law, morality, and public policy in a liberal democracy.

The tensions between the culture of openness, prominent after the Second Vatican Council, and the culture of identity, prominent among "JP II Catholics" who embrace the late pontiff's often dualistic moral categories, take center stage in this chapter. As the label suggests, proponents of the culture of identity have reacted against the excesses of "aggiornamento"—or openness to the broader culture practiced by those who lived through Vatican II. Instead, they have prioritized maintaining a distinct Catholic identity, shaping religious practices and moral beliefs, in the face of an overwhelming secular culture. In this framework, the beliefs and practices that set Catholicism apart—that constitute its distinctness—are seen as precious, because they contribute to the voluntary formation of a solid Catholic identity among people who are no longer confined by the intimacy of a Catholic ghetto, but overwhelmed by the fast-paced anonymity of modern life.

Some proponents of the culture of identity, for example, stress the importance of unquestioning obedience to Catholic teaching against contraception; they treat it as a communal identity marker. I find this approach rather ironic, since the tradition itself has framed its moral teachings, even on controversial matters such as contraception, as a matter of reasonable belief, not tribal loyalty. Indeed, as Pope Francis said in his highly publicized interview with Jesuit media, "We should not even think, therefore, that 'thinking with the church' means only thinking with the hierarchy of the church."[1] As such, I explore this tension between obedience to and disagreement with the Catholic hierarchy in a couple of essays dealing with contraception and the church.

Without denying the truth of Catholic teaching, Pope Francis has repeatedly expressed strong concerns about the moral dangers associated with the culture of identity. In one of his first messages as Pope, he pointed to the temptation for the church to lose itself in narcissistic and self-referential concerns. "A Church that does not go out of itself, sooner or later, sickens from the stale air of closed rooms."[2] He acknowledged, of course, that going out risks an accident. But he claimed to "prefer a thousand times over a Church of accidents than a sick Church." Two years later, in a sermon he delivered at a mass with newly created cardinals, he cautioned the new leaders about excessive focus on the church's own purity: "There are two ways of thinking and of having faith: we can fear to lose the saved and we can want to save the lost. Even today it can happen that we stand at the crossroads of these two ways of thinking. The thinking of the doctors of the law, which would remove the danger by casting out the diseased person, and the thinking of God, who in his mercy embraces and accepts by reinstating him and turning evil into good, condemnation into salvation and exclusion into proclamation."[3]

But there is a deeper question: who, in fact, is a diseased person? What, in fact, is a morally dangerous point of view? The Roman Catholic approach to moral thought has not, traditionally, walled itself off from the moral perceptions of all people of goodwill. Ironically, a certain universal scope and reference is a key part of Catholic identity; as the Second Vatican Council acknowledged, "The Church herself knows how richly she has profited by the history and development of humanity."[4] Its characteristic "natural law" methodology is controversial and often misunderstood and misapplied. The basic presupposition of this methodology, however, is that the fundamental precepts of morality must be both applicable and accessible in principle to persons who do not share the faith. Moreover the "natural law" tradition, at least at its best, sees itself as able to incorporate the moral wisdom found in other traditions as well. The roots of these twin convictions are theological; a Catholic sensibility places great stress on the doctrine of creation as well as that of redemption, even after the fall. The Creator of the world and its Redeemer are one and the same.

It is understandable, of course, that proponents of the culture of identity experience themselves as under siege in the broader culture, particularly on sexual issues. It can be tempting to batten down the hatches, and to ensure that Catholic institutions present and pass down Catholic teaching in a completely unambiguous manner. At the same time, it can be counterproductive to reduce Catholic teaching to a moral "tax code"—especially when the code that is put forth selectively includes only parts of the church's teaching. For example, firing Catholic teachers who do not conform to Catholic sexual morality can raise other issues of social justice, as I discuss in the chapter about the decision of a Catholic school to fire a pregnant teacher.

A second difficulty I have with the culture of identity is that it is ill-equipped to grapple with the thorny questions involving development of doctrine. Consideration of how and why church teaching has changed in the past, and what might justify changes now and in the future, can be very destabilizing to those whose primary concern is to protect the Catholic tradition against erosion or dilution from outside forces. So they deflect or ignore explicit questions of development of doctrine on today's controversial issues, fearing that it would be nothing more than capitulation to the broader culture. Here, too, the culture of identity risks a type of incoherence. The Catholic theological and moral tradition has always developed in dialogue with and in partial debt to other systems of thought. The structures settled upon for church authority, for example, heavily borrowed from the institutional framework in the Roman Empire. Similarly, the shape of Catholic moral teaching is deeply indebted to Greek philosophy. Catholic beliefs, judgments, and sensibilities did not grow from a "distinctly Catholic" acorn, but prospered and expanded by a complex engagement with the cultures in which Catholic believers were immersed.

As the Second Vatican Council explicitly recognizes, the *sensus fidelium*—the considered and steady judgment of the Catholic faithful—is a key element in the development of doctrine. Consequently, one important role for theologians is to mediate and translate between the hierarchy and the Catholic faithful. I have been increasingly worried that this mediation is too rare a phenomenon in recent years. Many younger theologians are "JP II Catholics" who often support the culture of identity, espouse dualistic thinking, and see themselves as servants of the bishops' evangelization and catechization. As a general rule, therefore, they do not see themselves as articulating the position of the faithful in order to press for doctrinal development. Ironically, one reason for this phenomenon might be the fact that an increasing number of theologians are lay men and women. In previous years, many moralists were priests who had the burden and privilege of hearing confessions. Having seen how Catholic teaching on contraception deeply affected, and sometimes deeply harmed, devout Catholic men and women, they could draw upon this experience in arguing for development in moral teaching on matters such as contraception.

As I indicate in several chapters in this part, I find it deeply striking that so many Catholics in the pews consider the moral acceptability of contraception to be a settled issue, while so few Catholic moralists and public intellectuals go on to consider what a virtuous family life would look like if that was the case. Most members of the Catholic commentariat who write about marriage and family life take care to articulate their opposition to contraception and to pledge their support of Pope John Paul II's Theology of the Body. Their contributions to the discussion are commendable; they will doubtless be very useful to some lay Catholics. Statistics suggest, however, that they speak for a small minority. Who, I wonder, is helping the vast majority of churchgoing Catholics think through the moral and practical issues they see themselves as facing in raising families in our time?

Some proponents of the culture of identity will doubtless say that the problem is one of catechesis and evangelization. If only the vast majority of Catholics could truly see the beauty of the Theology of the Body, they would rethink their practices and reform their family lives. I do not think this approach is likely to succeed, in large part because central to Pope John Paul's approach is a very fixed conception of gender roles. While it proclaims the fundamental equality of women and men, it does not easily accommodate leadership roles for women. Consequently, it is not likely to be attractive in our era and time, in which women are doctors, lawyers, military leaders, Supreme Court justices, and heads of state.

The most significant challenges to the plans for a new evangelization, however, are of the church's own making. The clergy sex abuse crisis, which broke in Boston, Massachusetts, in 2002, has since spread to all areas of the globe. The crisis has touched bastions of European Catholicism such as Germany and Ireland, whose church rolls are hemorrhaging.[5] The accounts of the victims are so harrowing that the narratives of anti-Catholic fictional tracts such as *Awful Disclosures of Maria Monk, or, The Hidden Secrets of a Nun's Life in a Convent Exposed* (1836) pale in comparison.[6]

For many Catholics, however, the major challenge to their faith is not the fact that some priests abused children—most people recognize that priests are human beings, and that all human beings can be terrible sinners. It was the response of the hierarchy when such misdeeds were discovered that shocked and appalled nearly everyone. Rather than standing with the victims, many bishops protected the perpetrators, often moving them from parish to parish to give them second, third, and even fourth chances to make good.[7] While the church has made great strides in recent years, ongoing scandals show that the problem has not been entirely conquered. Some bishops continue to prioritize the well-being of clergy over the well-being of children.[8]

The clergy sex abuse crisis not only eroded the loyalty of lay Catholics to the church. It also undermined the church's moral authority. Most people, in my view, are virtue theorists, whether they know it or not. They recognize, in other words, that the best people to ask about difficult questions are the ones who have proven themselves sound and reliable in answering easier ones. The converse is also true. We do not ask someone who demonstrably cannot add or subtract for help with a college algebra problem. We do not ask someone with multiple bankruptcies for help with constructing the family budget. Similarly, it is difficult to give credence to teaching on difficult matters of sexual morality given by a group of people who did not recognize that the sexual abuse of children was a serious wrong. I explore these and other implications of the sex abuse crisis in several essays in this part.

Notes

1. Pope Francis, "A Big Heart Open to God," *America,* September 30, 2014.

2. "Pope: Mission, the Best Cure for the Church," Vatican Radio, April 18, 2013. Available at http://en.radiovaticana.va/storico/2013/04/18/pope_mission, _the_best_cure_for_the_church/en1-683985.

3. Pope Francis, Homily at the Holy Mass with the New Cardinals, February 15, 2015. Available at http://w2.vatican.va/content/francesco/en/homilies/2015 /documents/papa-francesco_20150215_omelia-nuovi-cardinali.html.

4. Vatican II, *Gaudium et spes* (1965), no. 44.

5. Juergen Baetz, "Germans Quit Church during 2010 Sex Scandal," Associated Press, July 29, 2011. Available at http://news.yahoo.com/germans-quit-church -during-2010-sex-scandal-152602181.html; Diarmuid Martin, "A Post-Catholic Ireland?," *America,* May 20, 2013.

6. Gerald Renner and Jason Berry, "Head of Worldwide Catholic Order Accused of History of Abuse," *The Courant,* February 23, 1997. Available at http:// www.courant.com/news/connecticut/hc-marcial-maciel-02-1997,0,7176951 .story?page=1.

7. John Jay College of Criminal Justice, *The Nature and Scope of Sexual Abuse of Minors by Catholic Priests and Deacons in the United States 1950–2002* (Washington, DC: United States Conference of Catholic Bishops, 2004). Available at http://webcache.googleusercontent.com/search?q=cache:XSpfp0bkBSwJ:www .bishop-accountability.org/reports/2004_02_27_JohnJay_revised/2004_02_27 _John_Jay_Main_Report_Optimized.pdf+&cd=3&hl=en&ct=clnk&gl=us.

8. A.G. Sulzberger and Laurie Goodstein, "Bishop Indicted; Charter Is Failing to Report Abuse." *New York Times,* October 14, 2011, A1.

Family Feuds
What's Keeping Catholics Apart?

More and more American Catholics have been bemoaning the polarization in the church, but no one seems to have any idea how to address it. I would like to suggest that we take another look at the framework for dialogue provided by the Catholic Common Ground Initiative. Founded in 1996 as part of "an effort to lesson polarities and divisions that weaken the Church," the Initiative was spearheaded by Cardinal Joseph Bernardin of Chicago and the indefatigable Msgr. Philip Murnion, a priest of the Archdiocese of New York. While both men have since gone to their eternal reward, the framework they modeled for dialogue is a lasting gift to American Catholics.

The Initiative is now housed at the Bernardin Center at Chicago's Catholic Theological Union. While it continues its work, it is fair to say that the Initative has taken a lower profile in recent years. When I mentioned Common Ground in a recent conversation with colleagues, I got a puzzled look, and a query: "Oh, is that still around? What does Common Ground do, anyway?" I have long struggled to give a pithy answer to this question. I finally found what I was looking for in the tenth anniversary Mass homily given by Cincinnati Archbishop Daniel Pilarczyk, who chairs the Initiative's steering committee: "The Catholic Common Ground Initiative," he said, "is committed to keeping the members of the church, all of them, of whatever ecclesial stripe they may be, on speaking terms with one another."

As Pilarczyk emphasized, "Called to Be Catholic," the foundational document of the Initiative, provides an outline agenda for civilized Christian conversation. The Initiative's "efforts to get people back on speaking terms are not the efforts of outsiders trying to mediate a family fight," the archbishop said, "but of members of the family of Christ trying to ameliorate the quality of the ongoing family conversation." The celebration of the Eucharist is at the heart of every Common

Ground event. The grace of the sacrament supports and perfects nature: from a psychological perspective, it's just a lot harder to demonize someone after you've seen them hunched over in prayer.

Common Ground did not promise miracles. At its best, it opened possibilities of conversation; it can't compel conversations to take place. I remember a panel on religious life at Common Ground's 2002 annual conference dedicated to "Participation in the Church." Two of the panelists were strong and insightful religious women: Sr. Doris Gottemoeller, RSM, former president of the Sisters of Mercy of the Americas, and Mother Mary McGreevey, RSM, a founding member of the Sisters of Mercy of Alma, Michigan, which broke away from the Sisters of Mercy of the Americas in the 1970s. Sr. Doris was the former president of the Leadership Conference of Women Religious, which embraced the reexamination of religious life after the Second Vatican Council, while Mother Mary was the president of the Council of Major Superiors of Women Religious, which sought to preserve more traditional practices. Mother Mary was in full habit; Sister Doris wore a blouse and skirt and a simple crucifix. Despite their differences, they articulated similar struggles and similar aspirations for community life. Then a lay member of the audience asked the sixty-four-thousand-dollar question: "You obviously have so much in common—including a deep love for the church. Why are there two sets of Sisters of Mercy and two conferences of women religious?" No one on the panel said a word. The question hung in the air. At least it was asked.

Things have changed greatly over the past two decades, in both the church and the world. What new challenges does the Common Ground Initiative face? I see three:

1. *Changing Generations, Changing Issues.* Common Ground was put together by Catholics whose identities were forged in the tumult of the Second Vatican Council. But time marches on. What are the issues that divide Catholics in Generation X? My own sense is that there are new fissures between priests and the laity. Sociologists tell us that a small group of "JPII Catholics" see the world as a battleground between the culture of life and the culture of death; that group is likely to supply most of the priests. But the majority of Gen-X Catholics seem to be negotiating a

less confrontational relationship between the culture and the church, placing less emphasis on a pure and distinct Catholic identity. The Millennial generation is more removed from religion in general.

2. *Common Ground in the Blogosphere.* I have my doubts that blogs will help Catholics of different stripes remain on speaking terms. There is none of the non-verbal, face-to-face communication needed to build trust and patience. Blogging doesn't place a premium on nuance, tact, or reflective judgment. It's a shoot-from-the hip kind of medium.

3. *The Emergence of Ideological Enclaves.* Pilarczyk noted that one thing the Initiative has learned is that "some people are simply not interested in conversation with persons who have differing opinions." An increasing number of people tend to watch only CNN or Fox News, EWTN or the *Daily Show*, to read only the *New York Times* or the *Wall Street Journal*. If you don't encounter people you disagree with, you don't have to deal with them.

In the end, though, if we are going to be Catholic, we have to be catholic—we need to find ways of communicating with one another as members of the same Body of Christ, despite our differences. The practical strategies developed over the past decade by the Common Ground Initiative are only sustained by the deep theological conviction that there is but "one body and one Spirit" (Eph 4:4).

Sources

Bernardin, Joseph. *Catholic Common Ground Initiative: Foundational Documents.* Eugene, OR: Wipf & Stock, 2002.

Bishop, Bill. *The Big Sort: Why the Clustering of Like-Minded America Is Tearing Us Apart.* New York: Houghton Mifflin, 2008.

Catholic Common Ground Initiative. "Shaping Parish Life: Ongoing Influences of Vatican II and the Catholic Common Ground Initiative—Address by Katarina Schuth, Response by Kevin Ahern." 2013. Available at http://www.youtube.com/watch?v=-4YEXP-OiKk.

Cross, Mary. *Bloggerati, Twitterati: How Blogs and Twitter Are Transforming Popular Culture.* Santa Barbara, CA: Praeger, 2011.

Johnson, Mary, S.N.D. de N., Patricia Wittberg, S.C., and Mary L. Gautier. *New Generations of Catholic Sisters: The Challenge of Diversity.* New York: Oxford University Press, 2014.

The Martyrdom of John Roberts
Catholic Squabbling, Then and Now

John Roberts came from a socially prominent and financially comfortable family. He attended what many considered the most prestigious university in the country before going to law school. An expert advocate, he engaged in vigorous debate about legal matters with the chief justice of the highest court in the land.

But this John Roberts was never nominated to serve on the U.S. Supreme Court. Instead, he was hanged, drawn, and quartered on December 10, 1610, convicted of the capital offense of being a Catholic priest. He was the son of a gentleman, not of a steel plant manager. He studied at Oxford and the London Inns of Court, not Harvard. And the legal debate he conducted with Lord Chief Justice Edward Coke was in Newgate Prison, where Roberts was on trial for his faith, and for his life. He admitted to being a priest and a Benedictine monk, but denied the charge that he had deceived the English people.

In 1970, John Roberts was canonized by Pope Paul VI as one of the Catholic martyrs of England and Wales. Superficial impressions suggest that Supreme Court Chief Justice John Roberts is anything but a candidate for martyrdom. Instead, some people, including some on the Religious Right, suspect he is an ambitious careerist. This suspicion is fueled by the impression that he has been remarkably reticent about his jurisprudential convictions. By all accounts, his legal work has been careful and measured. His colleagues maintain that his professional temperament is, well, judicious: he is open to hearing both sides of an argument, and opposed to crude "us vs. them" characterizations of legal controversies. But this worries some "movement conservatives," including some Catholics. If you're nuanced, you're wishy-washy and can't possibly believe that anything is worth dying for.

But the martyrdom of John Roberts casts doubt on the charge that nuance and a certain open-minded flexibility are incompatible with deep conviction. The politically active "movement Catholics" of Roberts's day believed that true commitment to the Catholic faith included a willingness to depose a Protestant sovereign in order to return a Catholic to the throne. Roberts, in contrast, seems not to have been much inclined toward revolutionary plotting; instead, he spent much of his time ministering to plague victims. Politically, Roberts was sympathetic with the group that proposed something like the doctrine of separation of church and state: a good Catholic can be a loyal subject of a Protestant sovereign in matters temporal and political. But a good Catholic priest will never renounce his faith or consent to deprive his flock of the sacraments.

Still, people on all sides of the political spectrum, including Catholics, were worried about Supreme Court nominee John Roberts, largely because he hadn't forthrightly revealed his basic jurisprudential commitments. Despite the differences, the worry is the same: no one wants to be duped. Liberals worried that Roberts is a stealth Antonin Scalia. Conservatives worried that he is a stealth David Souter. The fear of being duped is hardened into ineluctable opposition by bitterness against perceived past injustices. Democrats thought that the Republicans stole the 2000 presidential election, and by all rights shouldn't have been in a position to appoint anyone to the Supreme Court. Republicans thought that the Democrats tried to deprive them of just that opportunity in the late 1980s and the early 1990s, by their treatment of Robert Bork and Clarence Thomas. In this climate, who could blame Roberts for his taciturnity?

The more fundamental question, of course, is how to restore a climate of relative trust, the urgency of which is sharpened by recalling the social and political circumstances in which St. John Roberts found himself. Political divisions, both in the general population and among Catholics, were rife. Catholics were bitter at Henry VIII for rejecting and suppressing their faith, and they blamed Elizabeth I for obtaining the throne by feigning sympathy for it. They resented the severely repressive measures taken late in her reign and in the reign of James I, who had promised tolerance for Catholics. On their part, Protestants bitterly remembered the repressive policies of Queen Mary Tudor, under whom nearly three hundred of their number were burned to death in less than four years. The repressive policies adopted by both Catholic and Protestant rulers were rooted in political insecurity, which was in turn exacerbated by a political climate permeated with deception. Catholics accused Protestants of lying outright; Protestants accused Catholics—particularly Jesuits—of resorting to equivocation, even under oath. The Spanish Armadas of 1588, 1596, and 1597, and the Gunpowder Plot of 1605 left Elizabeth, and then James, feeling assailed by an enemy both fierce and nebulous. They could not fully trust anyone.

That cycle of deception, betrayal, and violence had a long-lasting effect on the political climate in England. But what seem most chillingly relevant to me now are the bitter divisions that existed then among the beleaguered English Catholics themselves. The political divisions, which seemed so important at the time, weakened the Catholic Church in England for centuries. Would the English martyrs, looking at things from the perspective of eternity, say the divisions were worth it? I doubt it.

Sources

Brown, Nancy Pollard. "Southwell, Robert [St Robert Southwell] (1561–1595)." Nancy Pollard Brown In *Oxford Dictionary of National Biography*, edited by H. C. G. Matthew and Brian Harrison. Oxford, UK: Oxford University Press, 2004. Online ed., edited by Lawrence Goldman, January 2008. Available at http://www.oxforddnb.com/view/article/26064.

Carlyle, E. I. "Roberts, John [St John Roberts] (1576–1610)." Rev. Dominic Aidan Bellenger. In *Oxford Dictionary of National Biography*, edited by H. C. G. Matthew and Brian Harrison. Oxford: Oxford University Press, 2004. Online ed., edited by Lawrence Goldman, January 2008. Available at http://www.oxforddnb.com/view/article/23758.

Devlin, Christopher. *The Life of Robert Southwell: Poet and Martyr*. New York: Farrar, Straus and Cudahy, 1956.

Duffy, Eamon. *Saints, Sacrilege and Sedition: Religion and Conflict in the Tudor Reformations*. London: Bloomsbury, 2012.

Pollen, John Hungerford. *Acts of English Martyrs Hitherto Unpublished*. London: Burns and Oates, 1891.

No Academic Question
Should the CTSA Seek "Conservative" Views?

The 2014 gathering of the Catholic Theological Society of America (CTSA) took place in sunny San Diego, but there were storm clouds gathering around the meeting's agenda. In particular, Duke Professor Paul Griffiths gave a plenary address that criticized what he perceives to be theologically liberal tendencies of both the Society and many members. The address followed the May 2013 report from the Society's Ad Hoc Committee on Religious Diversity and the subsequent October 2013 response letter from then–CTSA President Richard Gaillardetz.

As I pondered Professor Griffiths's plenary address to the society, Rex Harrison in *My Fair Lady* persistently popped into my head—and not just because of Griffiths's charming English accent. Harrison's Dr. Henry Higgins famously asked, "Why Can't a Woman Be More Like a Man?" In the end, I think Griffiths's talk amounted to the question, "Why Can't the CTSA be more like the Academy of Catholic Theology (ACT)?" The answer to that question, I think, properly shapes the response to another, more pressing matter that has occupied the CTSA in recent years: what can or should the organization do to be more welcoming to "conservative" theologians? To the extent that advanced theological education helps to shape the larger debates within American Catholicism, this is not merely an academic question.

What would it mean, concretely, for the CTSA to be more like ACT? Griffiths suggested that the task would have both positive and negative aspects. He argued that certain theological topics should be nurtured and supported by the CTSA but others actively "discouraged." My worry here is that this narrowing of focus is actually inconsistent with the mission of CTSA, which seeks to encourage a more free-wheeling discussion then does ACT. In fact, if you look at their respective membership rosters, mission statements, and conference programs, it is clear that the two groups operate with different understandings not only of what theology is, but also of the purposes of their own meetings.

Over thirteen hundred scholars and teachers belong to the CTSA, which was founded in 1946. More than four hundred members normally attend the annual meetings, which include wide-ranging plenary addresses as well as more specialized sessions on disparate topics. Themes are generally broad, meant to spark discussion in a wide range of sub-disciplines, from moral theology to systematics to sacramental theology. For example, the 2014 theme was "Identity and Difference: Unity and Fragmentation." The theme for 2015 was "The Sensus Fidelum." Most significantly, the CTSA's official mission is capacious: "Our purpose, within the context of the Roman Catholic tradition, is to promote studies and research in theology, to relate theological science to current problems, and to foster a more effective theological education, by providing a forum for an exchange of views among theologians and with scholars in other disciplines." Despite the claims of some, there is no ideological test for membership: anyone can join who possesses the appropriate academic qualifications, normally a doctorate in theology or related studies.

In contrast, ACT is a much smaller and narrowly focused organization. Founded in 2007, it has about a hundred members. ACT conferences tend to take up very specific themes, such as "Catholic Thought in the Wake of the Enlightenment" (2013); "Faith Theologically and Philosophically Considered" (2011); and "Blessed Is She Who Believed: The Role of Mary in Catholic Faith" (2008). Membership is closely regulated; prospective members are nominated for election by current members, who vote (in a closed ballot) at the annual meeting. The tight control over membership reflects the mission of the organization: "The Academy of Catholic Theology's principal purpose is to foster theological work of the highest intellectual standard that is faithful in the Spirit to the Revelation of God in Christ, as that Revelation has been handed on in Scripture and Tradition, and authoritatively interpreted by the Magisterium." While the larger Catholic tradition in fact provides a nuanced account of magisterial authority, and endorses certain forms of theological critique, the members of ACT seem to place a high value on avoiding any sort of conflict with the magisterium.

A special evening session in San Diego was devoted to theological diversity at the CTSA—and specifically to the question of what the CTSA could do to make conservatives, many of whom belong to ACT, feel welcome. As the foregoing comparison of mission and culture reveals, the question is really this: what should a group that has a broader and more free-wheeling account of its purpose do to accommodate others who have a more focused and arguably narrower view of the task at hand?

My own view is this: The CTSA should be open, *positively*, to considering topics, questions, and positions that "conservatives" believe have been neglected. More discussion about topics often deemed "theologically conservative" is good—of Mariology, of traditional devotions, of metaphysics, of *obsequium* to the magisterium. Yet the CTSA must not acquiesce to *negative* pressure to narrow its discussions and deliberations to fit the parameters of ACT. To do so would be to abandon its own mission. This is especially important when it comes to how the CTSA is governed. The society's Ad Hoc Committee on Theological Diversity noted that some "conservatives" have complained that they aren't elected to officer and board positions in the CTSA. But an official leadership position is not simply an honorific; it triggers a fiduciary duty to fulfill the basic mission of the organization. So the question to be asked of *all* candidates for CTSA offices is whether they are committed to that mission. I would not vote for anyone—"liberal" or "conservative"—who disdained the broad forum to which the CTSA is institutionally committed.

Griffiths's critique of the CTSA raised another question for me. Why, actually, do "conservatives" want greater participation in the CTSA, given the fundamental nature of their disagreement with its goals? Griffiths sketched a view of the nature and purpose of theology that is sharply divergent from that held by many in the CTSA. If the disagreement about first principles between CTSA and ACT is as fundamental as Griffiths suggests, why isn't the best course of action for each group to wish each other well in the pursuit of different paths, the values of which will eventually be known by their fruitfulness?

Yet many distinguished members of the CTSA leadership are deeply committed to broadening participation by conservatives. For some, it is a question of ecclesiology: they believe it is somehow not "Catholic" to have various groups pursuing theological inquiry independently of one another. They believe we all need to stay together to instantiate our Catholic identity. My view is somewhat different. I think the CTSA's purpose requires it to accommodate as wide as possible a range of theological opinion. All members should be treated with respect. No one's views should be ridiculed. At the same time, I do not think the CTSA should constrict its discussion in order to keep this or any group from leaving because they find some aspects of the discussion uncomfortable.

The CTSA runs an academic conference—and an academic conference is not the Body of Christ, after all. To put it another way, leaving the CTSA isn't leaving the church. This means that it is not a breach of ecclesial communion if one group decides it can do better work within a more narrowly defined theological context—liberal or conservative. Within the church, there has always been ample room for different groups to pursue their calling in parallel, inconsistent, and sometimes contesting ways. Jesuits aren't Franciscans, who in turn definitely aren't Benedictines.

If the members of ACT think they can do better work in a less pluralistic academic setting, God bless them. CTSA members can and will read their work, and find other settings in which to engage them. What the CTSA should not do is compromise its distinctive mission of fostering a more open conversation between the Catholic theological tradition broadly construed and other areas of human learning. It would indeed be a sad irony if the CTSA acquiesced to pressure to constrict its conversations about neuralgic topics in the name of promoting inclusiveness.

Sources

Academy of Catholic Theology. "Mission Statement" Academy of Catholic
    Theology. n.d. Available at http://www.academyofcatholictheology.org/.
Catholic Theological Society of America. "What is the CTSA?" Catholic Theological Society of America. 2014. Available at http://www.ctsa-online.org
    /about_us.html.
Griffiths, Paul J. "Theological Disagreement: What It Is and How to Do It."
    Plenary Address before the Catholic Theological Society of America. Proceedings of the Catholic Theological Society of America 69 (2014): 23–36.

The "New" Feminism?
John Paul II and the 1912 Encyclopedia

2013 marks the twenty-fifth anniversary of *Mulieris dignitatem*, Pope John Paul II's apostolic letter on the dignity of women and a lynchpin of his effort to formulate a "new feminism." Reaction to the pope's proposals has been mixed. Among lay women, his reflections seem to be received more enthusiastically by a minority that dedicate themselves to traditional full-time motherhood—which increasingly includes home schooling—than it is by the majority of Catholic women who are called, by vocation or necessity, to work outside the home. And yet John Paul II never explicitly condemns working women, or even working mothers. In fact, both he and Pope Benedict XVI have made statements calling for social support of women with dual vocations, including flexible, family-friendly employment policies.

Why the wariness about the new papal "feminism"? Can it be dismissed as anti-Catholic prejudice or the fruits of so-called radical feminism? I don't think so. That wariness is rooted in the history of ideas and arguments, not in bigotry or ideology. In his apostolic letter, John Paul makes claims about the nature of women that were in fact used in the last century to argue for what most of us would consider to be unjust political, economic, and social subjugation, including denying women the right to vote. While the pope does not endorse such subjugation himself, he also fails to explain why the premises of his argument do not compel him to do so. So his "new feminism" doesn't raise red flags only for radical feminists.

The easiest way to see the problem is to compare *Mulieris dignitatem* with the article "Woman" from the 1912 *Catholic Encyclopedia* (available online at www.newadvent.org). The similarities are striking—and troubling. On the positive side, both documents emphasize the equal dignity of women and men. Both underscore the importance of Christianity in bringing new insight and commitment to the transcendent value of women's lives. Both present the Virgin Mary as the ideal woman. Both emphasize the importance of maternal virtues for all women, not merely physical mothers. Both strongly defend a divinely ordained difference and complementarity between men and women. Consequently, both are worried about the baleful effects of blurred gender roles. The encyclopedia admonishes: "Just as it is not permissible to take one sex as the standard of the other, so from the social point of view it is not allowable to confuse the vocational activities of both." John Paul sounds the same theme: "In the name of liberation from male 'domination,' women must not appropriate to themselves male characteristics contrary to their own feminine originality."

But what exactly constitutes the wrongful appropriation of male characteristics? John Paul doesn't say. The 1912 encyclopedia, however, is not nearly as reticent. Any systematic acceptance of women as political or social leaders is unacceptable, because "man is called by the Creator to this position of leader, as is shown by his entire bodily and intellectual make-up." The encyclopedia maintains that society must first recognize that the primary vocation of women is to be wives and mothers—and therefore refuse to admit women to jobs that interfere with their primary vocation.

Second, societies should direct the education of women toward their roles as wives and mothers. The encyclopedia hastens to observe that "the Catholic Church places here no barriers that have not already been established by nature." While a few women might go on to earn higher degrees, "the sexes can never be on an equality as regards studies pursued at a university."

Third, the best hope for the multitudes of immigrant women exploited by ruthless capitalists is not the promotion of an individualistic conception of human rights that applies to men and women alike, but a return to a more organic conception of society organized in accordance with Catholic teaching. In such a society, women ought to influence political life indirectly, not directly, because from the perspective of the encyclopedia "it is difficult to unite the direct participation of woman in the political and parliamentary life of the present time with her predominate duty as a mother." Consequently, concludes the encyclopedia, "the opposition expressed by many women to the introduction of women's suffrage . . . should be regarded by Catholics as, at least, the voice of common sense."

So, in 1912, the *Catholic Encyclopedia* proclaimed that in seeking the right to vote, women were not rightly promoting their own dignity, but wrongly interfering with God's plan for sexual complementarity. We know that Pope John Paul didn't endorse such a view. We just don't know why he didn't. We know only that the premises of his anthropological argument are virtually identical to those in the encyclopedia. In other words, the pope's position can easily be used again to promote a worldview that undermines the ability of women and men to work together in the political, economic, and social spheres.

Does it matter? I believe it does. A proper anthropology takes into account both the differences and the commonalities between the sexes. For years, the Vatican has been worried primarily about the erosion of difference. With the global rise of religious fundamentalism, however, it will be equally important to emphasize the common gifts and abilities of men and women—including a common right and duty to participate in the political life of the nation.

Sources

Catholic Encyclopedia. New York: Robert Appleton Company, 1912, s.v. "Woman."
Pope John Paul II. *Mulieris dignitatem* (1988).

Catholic Kosher
Is the Ban on Contraception Just an Identity Marker?

Testifying before Congress about religious liberty in February 2012, William Lori, archbishop of Baltimore, proffered an analogy. The government would not force a kosher deli to serve ham sandwiches, Lori observed; so why force Catholic hospitals to provide their employees with contraception coverage?

I was surprised that a bishop would make this comparison—and certain that Aquinas, who helped define the Catholic natural law tradition, would have been shocked. Catholics traditionally have seen the prohibition against contraception as a moral norm binding on all human beings, like prohibitions against murder, theft, and lying; by contrast, the laws of kashrut are cultic precepts that bind only Jews. But then I began to wonder whether Lori was on to something. From a sociological perspective, the prohibition against contraception does seem to be morphing from a universally applicable moral norm into a cultic norm that marks and defines Catholic identity—one strict form of it, anyway—within a broader pluralistic culture.

Traditionally, Catholics don't build religious identity around adherence to absolute negative moral norms, but rather view those norms as the foundation of an acceptable moral identity. Yet many Orthodox Jews (especially those living in pluralistic societies) do build their identity around the laws of kosher, measuring their religious and communal commitment through their recognition of ritual laws of purity and contamination.

Those who treat the prohibition against contraception as the linchpin of a faithful Catholic life are transforming the prohibition into a religious identity marker. If their blogs are any indication, Catholics who publicize their commitment to this church teaching tend to see those who don't follow it as inauthentic Catholics. That is more akin to a cultic judgment than a moral one. Significantly, no one talks about the prohibitions against stealing, lying, or murdering this way. Someone who commits murder would be labeled a sinner or a bad Catholic—not an inauthentic one.

The similarities go further. Conformity to cultic norms generally takes a great deal of thought and vigilance, and Natural Family Planning demands ongoing vigilance in ways analogous to keeping kosher. Just as there are competing rabbinical schools, there exist NFP experts, as well as study groups and manuals, to address technical questions. Not surprisingly, enterprising adherents to both Jewish dietary prohibitions and the Catholic ban on contraception have invented smartphone apps to make conformity easier.

In contrast, I'm not aware of an app for "not killing"—or "not stealing," for that matter. That's because most people don't spend too much time thinking about whether and how to conform to basic moral prohibitions. In fact, the more fundamental the moral prohibition, the less time we ought to think about it. We would worry greatly about someone who said, "I want a promotion. I could kill my boss and take her job . . . but that would be wrong." Killing the boss is or should be unthinkable.

A critic might object by noting that some Catholics forgo both birth control and NFP, "leaving room" for God to plan their family. But this approach is also strikingly inconsistent with the way negative moral prohibitions operate in the Catholic tradition. After all, no one says, "I'm leaving room for God to plan my career, so I'm not going to steal my coworker's ideas." In the Catholic moral framework, the point of negative moral absolutes is to conform to God's law, not to leave room for divine providence to operate. Our tradition does not frame the relationship of God's will and human activity in this mutually exclusive way.

Can't the norm against contraception be both a universal moral norm and a cultic Catholic one? From a sociological perspective, pulling this off would be tricky. General moral norms are meant to gather all people together into the same moral community, highlighting commonality. (Think, for example, of the *Universal Declaration on Human Rights*.) Cultic norms, by contrast, emphasize differences among subcommunities, focusing on what sets them apart.

A hundred years from now, no one will remember these political skirmishes around religious liberty. But some future historians of

Catholic moral theology might point to Bishop Lori's testimony as a turning point, marking the moment when the church's official teachers began to concede that the prohibition against contraception could plausibly be defended no longer as a matter of a universal moral law, but only as a cultic precept binding on Catholics. Four decades after *Humanae vitae*, that prohibition looks increasingly like a form of Catholic kashrut.

Sources

Aquinas, Thomas. *Summa Theologica*, I-II, q. 103.

Maccoby, Hyam. *Ritual and Morality: The Ritual Purity System and its Place in Judaism*. Cambridge, UK: Cambridge University Press, 1999.

Pope Paul VI, *Humanae vitae* (1968).

United Nations (General Assembly), Universal Declaration of Human Rights (1948).

United States Conference of Catholic Bishops. "Bishop Lori Tells Parable of the Kosher Deli and the Pork Mandate in Congressional Testimony." February 16, 2012. Available at http://www.usccb.org/news/2012/12-030.cfm.

West, Christopher. *Theology of the Body for Beginners: A Basic Introduction to Pope John Paul II's Sexual Revolution*. Rev. ed. West Chester, PA: Ascension Press, 2009.

The Big Chill

Humanae Vitae Dissenters Need to Find a Voice

Over the past quarter-century, Catholics who support *Humanae vitae* have done a superb job articulating the ways their adherence to church teaching against contraception fits into their view of family life. For example, Helen Alvaré, professor at George Mason Law and former spokeswoman for the U.S. Catholic bishops, edited a volume titled *Breaking Through: Catholic Women Speak for Themselves*. The book showcases ten accomplished women who fully accept church teaching on sexual morality, situating their lives and vocations within a larger context of religious belief.

Are we likely to see a similar volume from Catholic women who believe the responsible use of birth control is compatible with their faith and their vocations as wives any time soon? I doubt it. This large cohort of Catholic women is largely silent. And who could blame them?

The ecclesiastical climate has chilled considerably in the forty years since Pope Paul VI issued *Humanae vitae*. At the time the encyclical was published, the use of contraception by married couples was still seen by most prelates as a matter on which people of good faith could disagree. That began to change under John Paul II, who treated contraception as the doorway to the "culture of death." Proponents of his "Theology of the Body" maintain that spouses who use contraception are lying to one another with their bodies and withholding themselves from one another in the sexual act. This hardly encourages respectful conversation with Catholic couples who find contraception morally acceptable.

The theological climate has shifted too. Many of today's emerging Catholic moralists were drawn to their field by the examples of Pope John Paul II and Pope Benedict XVI. They accept and defend the teaching against contraception. And those who don't accept it do well to maintain a prudent silence. The ecclesiastical actions taken against

Charles Curran, Elizabeth Johnson, and Margaret Farley have had a chilling effect on academic discussion of sexual morality.

In short, over the past twenty years, Catholic bishops have largely squelched open debate among their people about the morality of contraception. Many have worked to thwart frank discussion about what Catholic parents owe their marriages, their children, and other vocational commitments they have apart from family. If the price of admission to this crucial conversation is adherence to *Humanae vitae*, then nine out of ten Catholic couples aren't qualified to say a word.

Obviously, those who dissent from *Humanae vtae* have cause to lament this state of affairs. But those who support church teaching also have reason to be worried, because it encourages a type of compartmentalization that is fundamentally foreign to the Catholic tradition. If people are not encouraged to reflect on their normative commitments in a holistic manner, they tend to segregate them from one another. They put the church in one box, marriage and family life in another. Catholics who compartmentalize their moral commitments risk isolating themselves from the considerable wisdom of the tradition on matters of sex, love, and embodiment. A church that encourages such compartmentalization is hardly catholic. How can that kind of church interpret the complexities of our world? How can it avoid being seen as one more commitment among many others, just something to do for an hour on Sundays?

So instead of ignoring ordinary Catholics who use contraception, it would be better for the church to encourage them to articulate how their views can be seen as consistent with the deepest insights of the tradition. Encourage them to read *Humanae vitae*. But also encourage them to read the Majority Report of the Birth Control Commission—convened by Paul VI—which tried to show that church teaching on contraception could be authentically developed.

Most progressive Catholics hope the Majority Report position will eventually win the day, just as Vatican II's defense of religious liberty superseded the condemnation of that freedom in the Syllabus of Errors. But winning the day takes work. John Courtney Murray, SJ, worked to show how religious liberty was consistent with the Catholic tradition. John Noonan's magisterial volume *Contraception* (1968) did much the same thing for birth control. As that book approaches its fiftieth anniversary, it's time to reread it.

Progressive Catholics need to make sure that the next generation can situate their argument within the Catholic moral tradition, rather than presenting it in a purely secular manner. Does that mean a lot of conservatives—including "John Paul II" bishops—are going to welcome such arguments with open arms? Of course not. They'll still call those Catholics dissenters. But at least they will be dissenters engaged in the tradition, not cordoned off from it.

Sources

Alvaré, Helen M., ed. *Breaking Through: Catholic Women Speak for Themselves.* Huntington, IN: Our Sunday Visitor, 2012.

McClory, Robert. *Turning Point: The Inside Story of the Papal Birth Control Commission, & How* Humanae Vitae *Changed the Life of Patty Crowley and the Future of the Church.* New York: Crossroad, 1995.

Murray S.J., John Courtney. *We Hold These Truths: Catholic Reflections on the American Proposition.* New York: Sheed & Ward, 2005.

Newport, Frank. "Americans, Including Catholics, Say Birth Control Is Morally OK: Birth Control Has the Broadest Acceptance among 18 Behaviors." *Gallup Politics,* May 22, 2012. Available at. http://www.gallup.com/poll/154799 /americans-including-catholics-say-birth-control-morally.aspx.

Noonan, John T., Jr.. *A Church That Can and Cannot Change: The Development of Catholic Moral Teaching.* Notre Dame, IN: University of Notre Dame Press, 2005.

Noonan, John T., Jr. *Contraception: A History of Its Treatment by the Catholic Theologians and Canonists.* Enl. ed. Cambridge, MA: Belknap Press of Harvard University Press, 1986.

Pope John Paul II. *Evangelium vitae* (1995).

Pope John Paul II. *Man and Woman He Created Them: A Theology of the Body.* Translated by Michael Waldstein. Boston, MA: Pauline Books & Media, 2006.

Pope Paul VI. *Humanae vitae* (1968).

Pope Pius IX. *Syllabus of Errors* (1864).

West, Christopher. *Theology of the Body for Beginners: A Basic Introduction to Pope John Paul II's Sexual Revolution.* West Chester, PA: Ascension Press, 2009.

How About NOT Firing Her?
Moral Norms and Catholic School Teachers

In the 1950s, Catholic schools could take for granted that the common morality endorsed by American culture more or less accorded with Catholic morality. That is not the case anymore, as emerging controversies in parochial schools demonstrate. For example, in December 2013, a vice principal at a Catholic high school in the state of Washington was terminated from his position when it became known that he had entered into a same-sex marriage. A few months later, he fired a lawsuit against the archdiocese for wrongful termination, violation of Washington's anti-discrimination laws, and violation of public policy. Around the same time, an unmarried teacher at a Roman Catholic middle school in Montana was fired after getting pregnant. Both cases generated a tremendous amount of bad publicity.

So what should the church do? One possibility is to treat it as a media problem to be managed as expertly as possible. Soon after news of the Montana case broke, the popular blogger Deacon Greg Kandra developed a public relations strategy on how to fire a pregnant unwed teacher at a Catholic school in a kinder, gentler way, so as to avoid bad publicity for the Catholic Church.

But I have another suggestion: you could just *not* fire her. The school has the option of not enforcing the morality clause as a contractual term in this particular case. It should consider exercising that option.

Everyone knows that St. Thomas Aquinas says that an unjust law is no law at all, but rather an act of violence (actually, Aquinas's reasoning is much more subtle on this question, but that is for another day). But he also says something that gets far less attention: a law that imposes a burden unequally upon members of the community is also an act of violence—even if it furthers the common good.

Contract law is private law, not public law, but I think that Thomas's insights are applicable by analogy here. The pregnant, unwed mother is no guiltier than the father—who cannot be as easily identified as she can. Nor is she more morally culpable than other people who have premarital sex (a number estimated at greater than 90 percent), most of whom don't get "caught" by getting pregnant, and some of whom might also be members of that school community. In fact, if statistics are correct, we are in a situation in which there is massive disregard for the principle that all sexual intimacy outside of marriage is seriously wrong. She is also more vulnerable than other people, since getting another job while dealing with the stress of a pregnancy, much less an unplanned pregnancy, is significant. So the burden of the moral law against fornication is applied unequally. Moreover, the church should consider that it is arguably against the common good, since it will likely encourage people, not to refrain from premarital sex, but to obtain an abortion if they get pregnant.

My guess is that the contractual provision at issue is a general morals clause—saying that the teacher is obliged to conduct herself in accordance with Catholic moral teaching. Aquinas tells us that prudence is required in the interpretation and application of general laws. It's one thing to fire the Spanish and the French teacher, each married to other people, caught canoodling in the broom closet at school. It's another thing entirely to fire a single teacher, who presumably did not behave inappropriately at school, and whose only evidence of sexual impropriety is her pregnancy—which in our culture, should also be seen as evidence of moral courage. Rather than obtaining an abortion, which would have allowed her to keep her job by hiding evidence of sexual activity, she is going through with the pregnancy.

Some would say that the firing is necessary for pedagogical reasons: to "teach" the importance of Catholic teaching on sexual morality. But it would be good to ask: 1) is this the most effective way to communicate this message to young people; and 2) is this line of action communicating other lessons that are inconsistent with other aspects of a Catholic worldview? My own view is this: in a world in which Catholic teaching on sexual matters is so widely dismissed, even by Catholics, this kind of necessarily selective enforcement is going to make Catholic teaching seem arbitrary and cruel. I appreciate Kandra's attempts to blunt the effects, but I still think they are there.

My second point is a bit more difficult to state. Catholic schools say they exist to support a total Catholic worldview. Well, Catholicism is a religion of "being," not a religion of "willing." Membership in the community depends upon, in most cases, baptism as an infant. The sacramental framework talks about ontological changes. You are part of the Catholic family—no matter what. That is the most deeply countercultural message the church can convey in American culture, which has a deeply voluntarist strain—you say something wrong, you do something wrong, you're out of the club: we choose to exclude you or you choose to exclude yourself. (That's also why I'm so worried about the spread of evangelical Catholicism, which I think tends to turn Catholicism into one more American Christian sect.)

I think the message that firing this teacher conveys to the students is that they, too, are subject to being "fired" from the Catholic community if they misbehave in any way. After all, the little school is probably the main Catholic community they've known. For all the talk of love and understanding and forgiveness, in the end, it is a hard and abstract contractual provision—a sign of willing, not being–that counts the most. For all the talk of a rich and humble inner life, it is a wholesome appearance that matters most. (And they all know—we all know—people who appear beautiful and holy who are in fact deeply corrupt. The prime example of this phenomenon, of course, is the pervasive corruption in the Legion of Christ.)

And I would think that many students, and even many parents, might exercise their own wills and walk away from all this—not necessarily the morality, but the perceived meanness. A similar issue is raised in cases involving the firing of same-sex partners at Catholic schools. It's probably not lost on the students or parents that sexual issues are the only issues that are enforced under the morals clause. Now, I am not saying that you should fire a teacher for driving a climate-changing Hummer or purchasing luxury goods that are knowingly—or at least likely—made in sweat shops. But part of the message that the firings may be communicating is that sexual morality is important (a firing offense) and everything else, well, not so much. Is that really the message that these dioceses wish to convey?

I don't think the future of Catholic schools in the United States can be considered apart from broader questions about how evangelization operates in today's culture, in which many Catholics know and sympathize with people who are gay, and women who get pregnant out of wedlock. We are no longer living in the 1950s.

Sources

Berry, Jason. "Father Marcial Maciel and the Popes He Stained." *Newsweek*, March 1, 2013. Available at http://www.newsweek.com/father-marcial -maciel-and-popes-he-stained-62811.

Berry, Jason. "The Legion of Christ and the Vatican Meltdown." *National Catholic Reporter*, June 21, 2012. Available at http://ncronline.org/news/vatican /legion-christ-and-vatican-meltdown.

Kandra, Greg. "How Do You Fire a Pregnant Unwed Teacher from a Catholic School? Here's a Suggestion." *The Deacon's Bench*, February 4, 2014. Available at http://web.archive.org/web/20140822011800/http://www.patheos.com /blogs/deaconsbench/2014/02/how-do-you-fire-a-pregnant-unwed-teacher -from-a-catholic-school-heres-a-suggestion/.

Morris-Young, Dan. "Court Greenlights Fired Gay Teacher's Lawsuit against Catholic School." *National Catholic Reporter*, May 23, 2014. available at http://ncronline.org/news/faith-parish/court-green-lights-fired-gay-teachers -law-suit-against-catholic-school.

Truth or Consequences
In Ireland, Straying Far from the Mental Reservation

The clergy sexual abuse scandal ripped apart the Catholic Archdiocese of Dublin, Ireland, at the turn of the twenty-first century, just as it devastated so many other Catholic communities throughout the world around the same time. Although the Irish Constitution no longer confers a "special position" upon the Roman Catholic Church, the ties between the church and the Republic remained close, given the fact that over eighty percent of the population identified as Catholic.

So in response to media reports of clergy sexual abuse in the 1990s, the Irish government constituted a commission to investigate the sexual abuse of children by clergy in the Archdiocese of Dublin, which was chaired by Circuit Court Judge Yvonne Murphy. Due to the sheer volume of evidence, the commission took nearly a decade to complete its work. On May 20, 2009, the commission released a 2600-page report, which chronicled pervasive abuse of children in the orphanages and schools run by the Catholic Church in Ireland.

Needless to say, the abuse itself is deeply disturbing. But an even greater cause of consternation is the pattern of avoidance and denial engaged in by so many Irish prelates who were in a position to protect the children. Some Irish prelates invoked the concept of "mental reservation" to justify misleading others about the abuse situation. For example, Cardinal Desmond Connell, the archbishop of Dublin from 1988 to 2004, told a victim that he did not lie to the media in order to cover up the use of diocesan funds to settle the victim's case. The cardinal emphasized that "he had reported that diocesan funds are not used for such a purpose; that he had not said that diocesan funds were not used for such a purpose." According to the victim, "Cardinal Connell considered that there was an enormous difference between the two."

If Blaise Pascal, the seventeenth-century mathematician and Jansenist philosopher, could read the Murphy Report on clergy sexual abuse in Dublin, he would doubtless say, "I told you so." In his *Provincial Letters*, Pascal mercilessly satirized the whole idea of mental reservation, particularly as defended by Jesuit moralists. In the process, he gave Catholic casuistry a bad reputation that endures to this day. If you look up "casuistry" on Dictionary.com, the first definition you get is "specious, deceptive, or oversubtle moral reasoning, esp. in questions of morality."

After reading the Murphy Report, it is tempting to say Pascal was right. In my view, however, giving in to that temptation would be a mistake. Any moral framework is subject to abuse. But when applied in good faith, it is able to pinpoint the underlying problem with the Irish deception—something that Pascal's critique, for all its cleverness, simply cannot do.

Lying, defined as "speaking a falsehood with intent of deceiving," is viewed by the church as an intrinsically evil act. Consequently, it is never right to lie, no matter what the consequences. Nonetheless, it is sometimes permissible to give an ambiguous answer—not a falsehood—in the hope that the questioner will take it the "wrong" way and act accordingly. By articulating this concept of permissible equivocation, sometimes called "mental reservation," Catholic moralists tried to do justice to our complicated reality. They recognized that the integrity of human communication depends on the practice of speaking the truth, while acknowledging that others will press us for information they have no right to know, sometimes to harm innocent people. The balance between these two values is difficult to strike. The Holy See condemned the more extreme "strict mental reservation" in 1679 because it allowed a speaker to deceive others by saying part of a true sentence out loud, and reserving the other part in one's own mind.

The Elizabethan Jesuits were no strangers to the hazards of truth-telling. Henry Garnet, SJ, and Robert Southwell, SJ, both wrote treatises on the topic—which was of far more than academic interest to them. Both risked their lives bringing the sacraments to recusant Catholics, because saying or attending Mass was a punishable offense. When caught, tortured, and interrogated, they practiced mental reservation—not to save themselves, but to protect their fellow believers. Convicted of treason, both Southwell and Garnet were hanged, drawn, and quartered.

It is the courage and sacrifice of Southwell and Garnet that reveal why the use of mental reservation was so problematic in the Irish sexual abuse situation. Pascal's approach suggests the root problem is that prelates such as Cardinal Connell were culpable for lying—because to Pascal, mental reservation always amounts to lying. But that suggestion is incorrect. Suppose one altar boy—a victim of abuse—attempted to protect another potential victim cowering in the closet by saying to the abuser, "He is not here—he is not feeling well." That's a mental reservation if there ever was one. But it's not a lie. And in this case, every Catholic moralist would say it is completely justified.

Mental reservations, *pace* Pascal, are not always wrong. But they are wrong in some circumstances. In his treatise on the topic, Garnet took pains to argue that no form of mental reservation was justified, and might even be a mortal sin, if it would run contrary to the requirements of faith, charity, or justice.

What were the circumstances under which the Irish prelates practiced mental reservation? According to the Murphy Report:

> The Dublin Archdiocese's preoccupations in dealing with cases of child sexual abuse, at least until the mid-1990s, were the maintenance of secrecy, the avoidance of scandal, the protection of the reputation of the church, and the preservation of its assets. All other considerations, including the welfare of children and justice for victims, were subordinated to these priorities. The archdiocese did not implement its own canon-law rules and did its best to avoid any application of the law of the state.

The truths of faith are illuminated by the lives of the martyrs. Southwell and Garnet practiced mental reservation to save innocent victims while sacrificing themselves. The Irish prelates practiced mental reservation to save themselves while sacrificing innocent victims. And that makes all the difference.

Sources

Dailey, Alice. *The English Martyr from Reformation to Revolution*. Notre Dame, IN: University of Notre Dame Press, 2012.

Department of Justice and Equality, Republic of Ireland. "Report by Commission of Investigation into Catholic Archdiocese of Dublin (Murphy Report)." November 29, 2009. Available at http://www.justice.ie/en/JELR/Pages/PB09000504

Gregory, Brad. *Salvation at Stake: Christian Martyrdom in Early Modern Europe*. Cambridge, MA: Harvard University Press, 2001.

McCoog Thomas M., S.J. *The Society of Jesus in Ireland, Scotland, and England, 1589–1597*. Farnham, UK: Ashgate, 2012. See especially Chap. 3, "'Lurking Papists': Treasons, Plots, Conspiracies, and Martyrdoms, 1594–1595."

Pascal, Blaise. *Provincial Letters* (1656–57).

Unspeakable Sins
Why We Need to Talk about Them

During his tenure as cardinal archbishop of Boston, Bernard Law vigorously defended the position of the Catholic Church on abortion, which is sometimes described as an "unspeakable" act in authoritative church teaching. All the while, it turns out, the cardinal was turning a blind eye to another act that most people consider "unspeakable"—the sexual abuse of children or adolescents by Catholic priests within his archdiocese.

The label "unspeakable" hits us at a primal level, implying that the act in question is not only beyond all justification, but also that it cannot be discussed without sending shudders up the spine of anyone with an ounce of moral sensitivity. In this political and ecclesiastical context, when our bishops continue to "make the papers" both for their stand on prochoice politicians and for their involvement in sexual abuse cases, it may be worth considering the consequences that the invocation of this label may have for our common moral reflection.

First, the language of "unspeakableness" makes a radical demand, forcing those who hear it to focus all their attention and concern on the victims. In some contexts, its use is perceived as an essential rhetorical tool. Many prolife activists may view it as necessary to combat the invisibility of unborn life to the ruling elites of the United States, particularly the courts. And many lay Catholics may well see it as essential to counter the invisibility of abused children to the ruling elites of the church, particularly the American hierarchy.

Second, the language of unspeakableness suggests that perpetrators are akin to monsters, thereby outside the realm of human concern. It is easy to do this if you don't know the perpetrators personally—you can demonize them, you can reduce their whole lives to a terribly wrong choice or series of choices. But it is not so easy to do if you do know the perpetrators. You may see the good they have done, or sense the almost unbearable pressures that brought them to make the wrong choice, or know how they were broken and abused in ways that led them to break and abuse others. In certain cases, you may even doubt the continuing validity of the label itself. For example, many people with gay friends or relatives have come to question the stigma and shame associated with consensual homosexual acts between adults, long considered "unspeakable" in societies influenced by Christianity. Even if they view such acts as morally problematic, they would resist labeling them "unspeakable."

Third, it is all too easy to think of the "unspeakable" as the "unforgivable." For Christians, this is a very dangerous move. We believe there is no sin that God cannot forgive, if it is repented by its doer. Christ came to save us from sin and death—full stop. Once we start drawing a line between "garden variety" forgivable sins and "unspeakable" unforgivable sins, tacitly or informally, we cast doubt on the depths of God's mercy and the sufficiency of God's grace. The only unforgivable sin mentioned in Scripture, the sin against the Holy Spirit, is generally interpreted to refer to the unwillingness of a wrongdoer to accept the divine offer of forgiveness.

What about God's justice? The relationship between divine justice and mercy is strained by the witness of the past century, which has encompassed evil on an almost unimaginable scale and depth: the Holocaust, the Armenian genocide, the killing fields in Cambodia and Rwanda. We also know too much about atrocities that are rooted not in a coordinated plan of extermination, but in the depths of individual perversion: I am haunted by an article I recently read about the rape of a nine-month-old baby girl. No glib answer will suffice; no theological nicety will solve the problem. We can only stand mute at the foot of the cross.

The language of "unspeakableness" has practical and theological problems. It is polarizing; it suggests that being *for* the victim means being *against* the perpetrator, and conversely implies that human compassion for the perpetrator means downplaying the harm suffered by the victim. And so some members of the Catholic hierarchy were comfortable calling abortion an "unspeakable act"—they empathized primarily with the victims. But their conduct suggests that they did not consider clergy sexual abuse similarly "unspeakable";

they empathized primarily with the perpetrators. The trouble with the polarization caused by the language of "unspeakableness" is that it suggests there is no way for the community *rightly* to be *for* both the victims and the perpetrators, to the ultimate detriment of all concerned.

To try to overcome the polarization, we need speech, not silence— the very speech that is not encouraged by the language of "unspeakableness," which is more comfortable with denying the existence of a problem than with addressing it forthrightly. But we have all seen how the church's teaching on abortion has become more credible as it has expanded its concern for the women involved, striving to alleviate the pressures leading them to seek abortions, and to offer forgiveness and support to those who have had them. Most Catholics now know we need to speak and to hear the hard truths about what abortions do to unborn life *and* about what leads women to seek abortions.

In the case of clergy sexual abuse, we also need to be rightly *for* both the victim and the perpetrator, by speaking and hearing hard truths. Victims' groups have done a good job informing us about the ways in which sexual abuse can harm children and adolescents. We need to learn more from them about what they need now, both from the institutional church and from their fellow Catholics in the pews. But hard as it sounds, we also need to learn from the perpetrators. How much do we know about what makes someone a sexual abuser? How can we identify and stop people at risk of such behavior before they start? Catholic treatment facilities need to become expert in the boundaries between sickness and sin, which may be far more porous than we would like to think. In so doing, they might help solve the broader problem of sexual abuse of minors, which extends far beyond the borders of the Catholic Church.

There has been much scholarly writing recently on "truth and reconciliation commissions," and the program of restorative justice they attempt to promote in societies scarred by gross injustices, such as apartheid or political kidnapping, intimidation, and torture. Human forgiveness works on a different plane than divine forgiveness. No one can forgive on behalf of the victims. No one can usurp the right of victims to forgive—or not to forgive—their tormentors, even if their tormentors repent. Nonetheless, truth-and-reconciliation commissions have tried to create social conditions under which repentance and forgiveness may take root and grow in human hearts. Perhaps the church, which sees itself as an "expert in humanity," not just in matters narrowly religious, may find these commissions' way of proceeding illuminating as we all continue to deal with the fallout of the "unspeakable" sins of our time.

Sources

Phelps, Teresa Godwin. *Shattered Voices: Language, Violence and the Work of Truth Commissions.* Philadelphia, PA: University of Pennsylvania Press, 2004.

Plante, Thomas G. and Kathleen L. McChesney, eds. *Sexual Abuse in the Catholic Church: A Decade of Crisis, 2002–2012.* Santa Barbara, CA: Praegaer, 2011.

43

A Darkening
Why a Church Scandal Does More Harm Than the New Atheism

When I was teaching at Notre Dame, I had the opportunity to witness some spectacular events. For example, in October 2001, I was overwhelmed by the experience of attending a U2 performance at the Joyce Center on campus. But not every event delivers the fireworks one might anticipate. On the Wednesday after Easter in 2010, nine hundred Notre Dame students serenely walked into the DeBartolo Performing Arts Center to see a debate between Christopher Hitchens and Dinesh D'Souza. "Is Religion the Problem?" was the question. About two hours later, they serenely walked out, their faith intact. No dorm rector lost sleep dealing with the death of God that night. Why not? Thinking about this question gave me a new perspective on the latest wave of revelations about the history of sexual abuse in the church.

Did the believer D'Souza trounce the atheist Hitchens? Alas, no. I talked to a diverse group of faculty members who agreed that Hitchens was the more agile debater. It was the way the debate itself was framed that failed to grab the crowd. Advertised as a contest about the role of religion, the event turned out to be a debate about the existence of God. And the God whose existence was in question was the God of the philosophers—Aristotle's unmoved mover, Kant's guarantor of morality, the deists' supreme architect. Hitchens argued that the big bang theory and evolution better explain the universe, while D'Souza maintained that intelligent design offers a more coherent explanation.

None of this touched the religious core of the largely Catholic student body. Why not? Because the God of the philosophers is a sketchy abstraction to them. He bears about as much relationship to the triune God they worship as a completed census form does to one's actual family members. Moreover, neither debater seemed particularly aware that the theory of evolution is largely a problem for evangelical Protestants, not for Catholics.

So how do you pry Catholics loose from their faith? Well, you could call into question the reliability of the community that mediates the identity of God—the church. If your computer network crashes, it doesn't take the Internet with it. Yet when the church crashes, many Catholics find that access to God has been permanently impaired. Most Catholics do not encounter God as solitary individuals, but in the context of families, parishes, and the larger church. God is vividly and immediately present to us, especially in the readings and Eucharist of Sunday Mass. God's identity is enmeshed in a rich texture of rituals and relationships mediated to us by our two-thousand-year-old tradition.

So I was surprised that Hitchens didn't march us through the usual litany of the church's failings, or cast even one of his famous aspersions on Mother Teresa. Even more surprisingly, however, he didn't bring up the sexual abuse crisis—or his plan to have Pope Benedict XVI arrested when he visits England later this year. I found myself wondering whether Hitchens was pulling his punches. But maybe he felt that the newspapers were doing his work for him.

Many Catholics who survived the first wave of the crisis (which was actually the second) are now floundering. But why? On a purely intellectual level, nothing has changed. On an affective level, however, it's all becoming too much. The breadth and pervasiveness of the crisis darken our religious imaginations, and seep into our worship and prayer. The Gospel story of the Good Shepherd who searches for the lost sheep drives home the fact that some bishops threw the littlest members of their flock to the wolves. It doesn't help to point out that the vast majority of priests aren't abusers, and that all people, including priests and bishops, are redeemed sinners. The challenge posed here isn't at the level of logical analysis, but at the level of imaginative association and affective identification. That's why the evident involvement of the bishops in the transfer of priest-abusers hits many people so hard.

Traditionally, theologians attempted to safeguard believers against scandal by distinguishing between the church's mystical identity as the spotless bride of Christ, on the one hand, and the acts committed by sinful human beings acting in its name, on the other. Yet we live in a relentlessly anti-metaphysical era, where such distinctions come across as nothing more than a cop-out, an attempt to preserve power while evading responsibility. When churchmen try to explain such teachings, it only exacerbates the alienation.

So an effective response to the crisis will take more than truth commissions to find out what happened in the past and policy committees to protect children in the future. It will also take the development of new ways of enabling believers to identify imaginatively and affectively with the church. We will need the contributions of artists and novelists, not merely those of lawyers and psychologists.

In the final analysis, the debate between Hitchens and D'Souza was theater. No one's Catholic faith was really on the line. The sexual abuse scandal, however, was and is reality. In real life, losing one's faith is less like losing an argument than like losing a source of light. It's like sitting in a chapel at sunset, dully watching the vivid harmony of color bleed out of the stained-glass windows, leaving nothing but a flat, leaden monochrome in its place.

Sources

Doyle, Thomas P., A.W. Richard Sipe, and Patrick J. Wall. *Sex, Priests, and Secret Codes: The Catholic Church's 2000 Year Paper Trail of Sexual Abuse.* Los Angeles, CA: Volt Press, 2006.

D'Souza, Dinesh. *What's So Great about Christianity.* Washington, DC: Regnery Publishing, 2007.

Hitchens, Christopher. *God Is Not Great: How Religion Poisons Everything.* New York: Twelve—Hachette Book Group, 2009.

Hitchens, Christopher. *The Missionary Position: Mother Teresa in Theory and Practice.* New York: Twelve—Hachette Book Group, 2012.

Pidd, Helen. "Richard Dawkins Calls for Pope to Be Put on Trial: Critics Including Christopher Hitchens Are Exploring Legal Options for Pope Benedict to Face Trial in UK." *Guardian,* April 11, 2010. Available at http://www .theguardian.com/world/2010/apr/11/critics-trial-pope-benedict-xvi.

Scicluna, Charles J., Hans Zollner, and David John Ayotte. *Gregorian Symposium on Sexual Abuse of Minors.* Mahwah, NJ: Paulist Press, 2012.

The Long Goodbye
Why Some Devout Catholics Are Leaving the Church

Several Catholics I know and respect have chosen to worship in other Christian churches as a matter of conscience. Their decision was painful and a long time coming. Pope Benedict XVI did not move heaven and earth to accommodate their concerns, as he has done for the Society of St. Pius X and traditionalist Anglicans. Still, I think he and other members of the hierarchy ought to be worried.

The Catholics I have in mind aren't teenagers or sexual libertines. They stand among society's caretakers; two are legal professionals whose vocation requires them to articulate or enforce basic norms of justice. If a conservative is defined as someone dedicated to preserving a society's basic values, they are staunch conservatives.

Thirty years ago, devout Catholics like these friends of mine would have stayed in the church to fight or to suffer, or maybe both. What has changed? Why are they and others like them leaving? After talking with a number of people in their situation, here's what I see.

Leaving the Catholic Church is possible for these cradle Catholics in a way that it wasn't for their grandparents and parents. They have been taught and believe that God's saving grace is everywhere, not merely within the structure of the Roman Catholic Church. They emphasize the generosity of a loving God, who would not refuse anyone whose knee bends at the name of God's Son. So they believe that they will remain within Christ's church, even as they loosen their ties with the Catholic communion.

They worry that, in important ways, the Catholic Church is not acting like Christ's church now. Like many Catholics, they have long doubted the wisdom of elements of church teaching on matters of sexual morality (contraception and gay marriage, for example) or gender roles (the all-male priesthood). But for two reasons they were content to wait, praying and hoping for change. First, they trusted in the basic good sense and good faith of the church leadership. Second, they were confident in the general trajectory of the post–Vatican II church, which they assumed was solidly based in the teaching of the council, especially the council's statements on ecumenism, episcopal collegiality, and the role and spiritual dignity of the laity.

Needless to say, their faith in church leadership has also been badly shaken by the sexual abuse crisis.

For some, frustration boiled over after the Vatican released a statement that seemed ineptly to equate as sacramental crimes the sexual abuse of minors and any attempt to ordain women. For the women I spoke with this supposed PR gaffe raised once again the deep suspicion that among those at the highest levels of the church hierarchy there remains a deep, visceral, and seemingly inexpungable disrespect for—and even fear of—women.

These Catholics see no hope of institutional reform. They think the Curia largely views the sexual abuse crisis as a problem of individual sinfulness, not of broader flaws in church teaching and practices. Vatican II is fast becoming a ceiling for reform, not a floor for reform, as the emphasis increasingly falls on interpreting it in continuity with the Council of Trent in the liturgical, political, and moral realms. As we saw in the fracas over the health-care reform bill, key members of the U.S. hierarchy are calling for loyal deference to ecclesiastical authority even on matters Vatican II recognized to be within the competence of the laity, such as the technical meaning of a complicated piece of legislation.

In the end, most people are what some ethicists call evidence-based virtue theorists. They think that if you cannot get the answer to a basic moral problem right, your advice on more complicated issues will not be reliable. The inability of the hierarchy to grasp immediately the basic injustice of clergy sexual abuse undermines their claim to wisdom on difficult and divisive issues of sexual ethics. To some people, the conjoining of women's ordination and sexual abuse showed that the hierarchy was not merely bumbling in its approach to these issues, but twisted in its ultimate presuppositions about what the real threats facing the church today are.

From the perspective of these Catholics, doctrine and practice are not developing but withering. But why not stay and fight? First, because they think remaining appears to involve complicity in evil;

second, because fighting appears to be futile; and, third, because they don't like what fighting is doing to them. The fight is diminishing their ability to hear the gospel and proclaim that good news. The fight is depriving them of the peace of Christ.

The challenge to American Catholics, then, is coming now from two sides. We have long been in conversation with other Catholics in the pews. But what do we say to Catholics who have abandoned the pews as a matter of conscience?

Sources

Byron, William J., and Charles Zech, "Why They Left: Exit Interviews Shed Light on Empty Pews." *America*, April 30, 2012.

D'Antonio, Michael. *Mortal Sins: Sex, Crime, and the Era of Catholic Scandal.* New York: Thomas Dunne Books, 2013.

Dreher, Rod. "I'm Still Not Going Back to the Catholic Church: Pope Francis Only Confirms My Decision to Leave." *Time*, September 29, 2013.

McDonough, Peter. *The Catholic Labyrinth: Power, Apathy, and a Passion for Reform in the American Church.* New York: Oxford University Press, 2013.

O'Brien, Sheila. "Excommunicate Me, Please." *Chicago Tribune*, August 4, 2010.

The Pew Forum on Religion and Public Life. "U.S. Religious Landscape Survey— Religious Affiliation: Diverse and Dynamic." February 2008. Available at http://www.pewforum.org/files/2008/06/report2-religious-landscape-study -full.pdf.

Reese, Thomas. "The Hidden Exodus: Catholics Becoming Protestants." *National Catholic Reporter*, April 18, 2011. Available at http://ncronline.org /news/faith-parish/hidden-exodus-catholics-becoming-protestants.

That '70s Church
What It Got Right

Unpacking some boxes after a recent move from South Bend, Indiana, to Chestnut Hill, Massachusetts, I came across my confirmation stole, which I made in the spring of 1978. The members of my class were told to personalize our stoles to reflect our unique faith journeys. Then completing my first year of Latin, I wrote the word Credo on one panel with Elmer's Glue in the best cursive I could muster, and then covered the glue with a layer of deep blue glitter. On the other panel, I traced a simple cross, using the same technique. (This was not a theological statement: a crucifix was beyond my severely limited artistic abilities.) To make a border for my stole, I attached the cornflower trim that my late, beloved grandmother had used in sewing my First Communion dress eight years earlier. That dress was Marian blue. The girls in my First Communion class were discouraged from wearing traditional white lace dresses and veils, because they were expensive and impractical. We were all very disappointed at the time. Now, I am grateful. My grandmother's handmade blue dress with its cornflower trim is a tangible sign of the communion of saints.

I do not remember much about the confirmation ceremony itself. I am pretty sure we sang "On Eagle's Wings." Don't judge—it was the '70s! I also remember feeling a mixture of accomplishment, relief, and release. We had just completed a demanding two-year program, fulfilling requirements that included weekly classes, multiple service projects, and periodic weekend retreats. Being confirmed meant that we were finally adult Catholics. We continued to go to Mass. But for most of us, that was the end of any formal instruction in the faith. Like other adult Catholics, we learned to juggle secular and sacred responsibilities. As time went on, the former began to crowd out the latter. My generation's connection with the church became more and more attenuated. For many people I know, the connection was finally broken by the revelations about the sexual abuse of minors by priests and the way bishops covered up those crimes.

So, I belong to what many Catholics now dismiss as one of the church's lost, post–Vatican II generations. Catholic prelates and internet pundits regularly scorn the fifteen years following the Second Vatican Council as the "silly season," the era in which catechesis was evacuated of all substantive content in favor of supposedly trivial activities such as sharing, caring, and constructing felt banners. The catechesis of the 1970s became a cautionary tale, the model of what *not* to do in passing on the faith.

For many years, I was sympathetic to that analysis. But I am increasingly uneasy with the wholesale dismissal of the catechetical programs of my youth. First, the stock caricature of the period is unfair. The programs had far more content then they are given credit for. Second, the criticism only reinforces polarization within the church. Scapegoating 1970s religious-education programs fosters the illusion that the church's problems can be fixed by going backward, by inoculating children with something like the simple question-and-answer method and content of the Baltimore Catechism. But the root problem facing the church, then and now, is not catechesis. The root problem is that Catholics didn't have—and still don't have—a way of dealing constructively with the substantial and irreversible changes in both the church and the culture. Those changes began before the council and only accelerated in its immediate aftermath. They show no sign of abating today, much less of being reversed. Among those developments were the suburbanization of the Catholic population, the astonishing affluence and high levels of education among post–World War II Catholics, the powerful shift away from Catholic defensiveness and toward ecumenical and interreligious cooperation, and the unprecedented rates of Catholics marrying outside the fold.

How did religious instruction try to deal with these changes? My parochial elementary school used the very popular *Life, Love, Joy* series published by Silver Burdett and written by Carl Pfeifer and Janaan Manternach. My own textbooks have long gone to their eternal reward. But my mother, who taught sixth-grade CCD for many years, held on to her old teacher's handbook, which I recently perused. The content is surprisingly rich. The series proclaims itself to be "grounded in the traditional teaching and practices of the Catholic

Church, while respecting recent developments in the theological and social sciences." Among the theological developments it reflects is the emphasis on Scripture called for by Vatican II. The theme of sixth-grade religious education was "Growth in the Spirit," which is explored in units titled: "Abraham and the Mystery of Faith," "Moses and the Mystery of Freedom," "David and the Mystery of Service," and "Jeremiah and the Mystery of Hope." The series took care to emphasize that these mysteries were deepened and revealed in Christ Jesus, and passed on in their fullest form in the Catholic tradition. A final unit in the book reinforces the Christocentric understanding of the themes by reflecting on the meaning of major Catholic holy days.

Judging by this text, the content of the series was both rich and deep. So what was the problem? Some Catholics have claimed that students were not sufficiently drilled with objective, impersonal, timeless propositions and rules. It is true that the emphasis in my program was on fostering personal and conscientious appropriation of a Catholic worldview, rather than on inculcating a set of prefabricated questions and answers. As I recently learned, the reason for this new approach was historical. Catholics were appalled by the carnage of the Second World War and the unimaginable evil of the Holocaust, and they were horrified by the possibility of a nuclear confrontation with the Soviet Union. Questions about the moral presumptions of the modern state, including the United States, had to be asked. Catechism-trained Catholics had participated in the Nazi horrors, often with blind obedience to authority. The goal of post–Vatican II Catholic catechesis was not to foster obedience, but instead to cultivate responsible men and women who were shaped by the Catholic Christian vision, sensitive to our debt to the Jewish people, and independent enough to stand up to injustice, even if sanctioned by church or state.

So the pedagogical strategy of *Life, Love, Joy* made sense in itself. It was overcome, however, by a wave of superseding events. My overwhelming impression of the church in which I grew up was instability. In first grade, the nuns at my parochial school wore long habits; in second grade, they wore short habits; and in third grade, they wore no habits. When I was a fourth-grader, the parochial school closed, and I went to public school from then on. First Communion was originally administered in first grade, and then it was administered in second grade. First confession was held before First Communion, then it was after First Communion, and then it was off on its own, in fifth grade. Parish music and décor changed radically with each pastor. The votive candles mysteriously disappeared one day and the tabernacle seemed to be on walkabout in the front of the church.

The culture was changing rapidly as well. Women were joining— and remaining in—the workforce in great numbers. Marriages were breaking up. Even the country seemed to be breaking up, as the battles over Vietnam were succeeded by the scandals of Watergate, which dominated television and newspapers.

My generation was not lost because of religious miseducation. It was lost because of the changes in the culture. No CCD program, no matter how rich and nuanced, could overcome the challenges created by the simultaneous breakdown and reconfiguration of the institutional Catholic world and the American social world.

Many influential prelates and lay Catholics now say that it is better to create a bulwark against the chaos, by presenting Catholic teaching and moral rules in a classical, timeless manner. The new Catechism seems to encourage just that. It abstracts doctrinal propositions not only from the context in which they were formulated, but also from the documents in which they were promulgated. This obscures the various levels of authority attributed to the various doctrines. It presents Catholic belief in the manner of a tax code.

I don't think this will work. More important, if the vast numbers of young Catholics who continue to leave the church is any indication, it is not working. In fact, the glaring disjunction between an ahistorical presentation of Catholic teaching and the rapid pace of ecclesial and social change is likely to prompt even more skepticism and cynicism. I think that in the long run, the only solution is to teach young people how to think and pray within the context of a tradition that is not exempt from historical development and change.

The Roman Catholic tradition does not need to be afraid of history; its central claim is that God became a man who fully experienced the contingencies of life in a certain time and place. The relationship between eternity and history has always been porous. In order to articulate eternal aspects of relationships within the Godhead, for example, early Christian theologians drew upon concepts deeply tied to particular times, places, and philosophical schools. We are not God. We cannot escape the historically conditioned aspects of our tradition.

Guided by the Holy Spirit, our community can come to a deeper understanding of the mysteries of our faith as it moves through time. God willing, it can even correct its mistakes—such as its acceptance of slavery and its absolute prohibition of lending money at interest.

Growing up Catholic in the 1970s gave me the sense that the church was unstable, even fickle. It also, however, gave me some wonderful role models for trusting in God's fidelity in tumultuous times. Our CCD teachers were young wives and mothers who had grown up with the Baltimore Catechism. Unlike their own children, most of them had gone to parochial schools. No one had taken the time to explain to them the continuities between the pre–Vatican II era and the post–Vatican II era. They had to figure it out for themselves. And they did figure it out, because handing on their faith to their children was important to them. They were not nostalgic about their own religious education, because they had an intuitive sense of its limitations. At times uncomfortable about the scope and nature of the change, they put their trust in God's providence.

I admire these women tremendously. Their example prepared me for life as an adult in a changing church much better than any amount of memorization ever could have. And I thank God for the communion of saints, those among the living as well as those in paradise.

Sources

Kinkead, Thomas L. *Baltimore Catechism Set - Vol. 1–4*. TAN Books: Charlotte, North Carolina, 2010.

Pfeifer, C. J., and J. Manternach, J. *Growth in Spirit* (Teacher's Edition). Morristown, NJ: Silver Burdett Company, 1977.

Pfeifer, C. J., and J. Manternach, J. *Life, Love, Joy: Grades 1–6*. Morristown, NJ: Silver Burdett Company, 1968.

Pfeifer, C. J., and J. Manternach, J. *Silver Burdett Religious Education Program: Grades 1–8*. Morristown, NJ: Silver Burdett Company, 1977.

Part 5

Cases and Controversies

The essays in this section deal with difficult or controversial cases. They are arranged in a manner designed to accomplish two purposes: to show how difficult cases can sharpen moral reflection, and to demonstrate that controversial cases can foster the development of tradition.

Lawyers and judges have a saying: "Hard cases make bad law." In my view, that is usually if not always true. A moment's reflection shows that a community's laws are typically designed to deal with the majority of situations, not with anomalous events. Suppose the speed limit on a city street is 40 miles per hour; that speed limit regulates day-to-day behavior and inculcates a habit (e.g., prudent travel) specific to that street, in most weather conditions and most circumstances. It is not meant to apply at rush hour in a blizzard; nor is it designed to limit the progress of an ambulance driving a heart attack victim to the hospital. Conversely, those two outlying examples ought not to be the focus of lawmakers' concerns when they are deliberating what the speed limit ought to be on a particular street.

In most cases, then, law needs to set norms for action that apply generally and for the most part in order to achieve its proper regulatory and pedagogical functions. At the same time, thinking about hard cases can be a useful exercise, for both lawyers and moralists. Cases can be hard in several different ways, and reflection upon each sense of difficulty can sharpen our overall moral reflection. First, some cases are hard because they force us to consider how well our abstract moral and legal categories interact with the messiness and ambiguity we encounter in the world. It is one thing, for example, to say that one is absolutely opposed to the death penalty. It is another thing to hold that position in the face of the vivid details of a monstrous act. In one of the essays in this part, I test my own categorical opposition to the death penalty by considering a horrific home invasion and murder in Connecticut.

Other cases are hard because we have not yet developed the appropriate way to understand them. We need to find them a place within our moral universe, by identifying and highlighting their morally salient features. New technological developments raise these sorts of challenges, which arise in fields ranging from war (e.g., the morality of drones) to biotechnology (e.g., the morality of cloning) to nanotechnology (e.g., the moral status of "thinking" computers). Such challenges are also raised by new applications of established technologies, and in "Forever Young: The Trouble with the 'Ashley Treatment'" I consider this particular topic in light of a 2004 Seattle case involving plastic surgery and hormone therapy performed on a mentally handicapped child.

A third set of cases is difficult because their resolution forces us to return to the well of first principles and basic commitments. Most moral problems can be resolved by the application of ordinary practical reason. Some situations, however, require us to reflexively engage our fundamental moral commitments—a process that can, in an effort to ensure a type of moral consistency, cause us to subsequently reflect on other moral positions. For example, an abortion-related question can force us to reflect on why we think abortion is wrong—because it takes an equally valuable human life, or because it takes a human life that is particularly precious due to its innocence and helplessness? Once we have answered this question, however, we may need to review our attitudes about other life issues such as euthanasia and the death penalty. All of these are topics with which I grapple in this chapter.

A fourth set of cases count as hard cases because they involve practical judgment as well as commitment to moral principle. Deliberating about whether to stage a boycott, for example, involves far more than a decision about whether the practices of the prospective target are sufficiently objectionable. One also has to consider whether the boycott is likely to succeed in attracting the attention and commitment of customers and other third parties. If not, it may be counterproductive. Equally complicated is discernment about how far to cooperate with other persons or entities engaged in morally objectionable activities. We need to consider not only the gravity of others' wrongdoing, but also the good that can be achieved by cooperating with them—particularly when that good involves saving the lives of other innocent third parties. In this chapter, I therefore consider difficult ethical cases involving both boycotts and moral cooperation.

Finally, a fifth set of cases pose difficulties because they apparently involve a clash of values. Consider, for example, the tensions within the Roman Catholic Church that developed in connection with the 2014–2015 Synod on the Family called by Pope Francis.[1] A key flash point in the discussion was the readmission to communion of persons who had been divorced and remarried without obtaining an annulment. Those who opposed the move, such as Cardinal Gerhard Müller, argued that fidelity to the divine plan for indissoluble marriage is paramount: "The Lord has become involved in a marriage between a man and a woman, and for this reason the bond exists and originates in God."[2] Those who supported the move, such as Cardinal Walter Kasper, judged that the value of mercy, which Kasper considers to be an attribute of God, was of paramount concern. "After the shipwreck of sin, not a second ship, but a lifesaving plank should be made available to the drowning person."[3]

One way to resolve such clashes is to place them in a broader context. Pope Francis himself seems sympathetic to Kasper's position, but cautions that it is not a panacea. The decisive concern is to reintegrate the divorced and remarried into parish life. Enabling them to receive communion is only a part of that endeavor.[4] Pope Francis situates both doctrines and virtues within the broader context of the life of the church, which is the Body of Christ. The transmission of the essentials of the faith—including doctrine—is his constant focus: "Why can't they [the divorced and remarried] be godfathers and godmothers? 'No, no, no, what testimony will they be giving their godson?' The testimony of a man and a woman saying 'my dear, I made a mistake, I was wrong here, but I believe our Lord loves me, I want to follow God, I was not defeated by sin, I want to move on.' Anything more Christian than that?"[5]

In addition to helping moral agents to sharpen their thinking, difficult cases can also foster the development of tradition. Deliberation about actual cases and controversies does not take place in a vacuum. It occurs in the context of a broader normative tradition that consists of a complex network of practices, as well as institutions that allow those practices to continue through time. As Alasdair MacIntyre taught us so well, a tradition includes far more than a set of moral rule books: "A living tradition then is an historically extended, socially embodied argument, and an argument precisely in part about the goods which constitute that tradition."[6]

Decisions about hard cases, in my view, engage various elements of the broader tradition in several ways: they cause us to ask what the tradition's virtues require of us; they force us to consider the implications of various maxims, such as "Do unto others as you would have them do unto you"; they invite us imaginatively to inscribe our new challenges within the framework modeled by our saints and heroes in order to extend a tradition to fit new circumstances; and they inspire us to reflect on past experiences of ourselves and of the community. When any of these dynamics is engaged, as the last essay in this part shows, members of a tradition can be pressed to overturn what has previously been considered settled teaching.

In this part, then, I consider difficult ethical cases in order to unpack and develop the reasoning of two traditions that have become intertwined in the lives of many American Catholics: the American tradition emphasizing human dignity, due process, and equal protection under the law, as well as the Roman Catholic moral tradition emphasizing the status of each human being as made in the image and likeness of God. These are hard cases; doubtless many readers will disagree with some or all of my assessments. My hopes for this part, however, do not depend upon securing agreement; they will be realized if the essays contained within it serve to stimulate robust moral reflection on pressing ethical questions.

Notes

1. For more information on the synod, see, e.g., United States Conference of Catholic Bishops, "2014–2015 Synods of Bishops on the Family." Available at http://www.usccb.org/issues-and-action/marriage-and-family/2014-2015-syn ods-of-bishops-on-the-family.cfm.

2. Gerhard Müller, *The Hope of the Family: A Dialogue with Cardinal Gerhard Müller*, ed. Carlos Granados and trans. Michael J. Miller (San Francisco, CA: Ignatius Press, 2014), 51.

3. Walter Kasper, *The Gospel of the Family* (New York: Paulist Press, 2014), 31.

4. Madeleine Teahan, "Communion Alone Is 'Not the Solution' for Divorced

and Remarried Catholics, Says Pope Francis," *Catholic Herald*, December 8, 2014. Available at http://www.catholicherald.co.uk/news/2014/12/08/communion -not-the-solution-for-divorced-and-re-married-catholics-says-pope/.

5. Ibid.

6. Alasdair MacIntyre, *After Virtue: A Study in Moral Theory*, 3rd. ed. (Notre Dame, IN: University of Notre Dame Press, 2007), 222.

The Consistent Ethic
An Ethic of "Life," Not "Purity"

First proposed by Cardinal Joseph Bernardin in a lecture at Fordham University thirty years ago, "the consistent ethic of life" challenged American Catholics involved in the prolife movement to broaden their focus beyond abortion. Bernardin asked them to engage other issues where human life and dignity were threatened, such as the ominous possibility of nuclear conflagration, the routinization of capital punishment, and the specter of legalized euthanasia. Moreover, he contended that a consistent regard for the sacredness of each and every life would not abandon vulnerable human beings after they were born. He proclaimed: "Those who defend the right to life of the weakest among us must be equally visible in support of the quality of life of the powerless among us: the old and the young, the hungry and the homeless, the undocumented immigrant and the unemployed worker."

To say that the "consistent ethic of life" did not catch on with the American hierarchy would be an understatement. Bernardin's proposal was roundly and repeatedly criticized over the years by an increasingly organized and vocal band of conservative prelates and pundits, most notably Cardinal Bernard Law, the late Richard John Neuhaus, and George Weigel. They feared that grouping abortion with other life issues would dilute its primacy as an issue of social justice. Relatedly, they suspected that the emphasis on issues of social welfare would give dodgy cover to Catholics to vote for Democratic politicians favoring a strong governmental safety net despite the fact that those politicians are prochoice.

Buttressed by a growing cadre of bishops appointed by Pope John Paul II and Pope Benedict XVI, the opponents of Bernardin's "consistent ethic of life" won their battle, at least for the short term. Consider, for example, two recent versions of "Forming Consciences for Faithful Citizenship," the voting guide issued by the U.S. Conference of Catholic Bishops in preparation for the national elections.

Abortion is not only paramount in "Faithful Citizenship," it is also pervasive, occluding other issues that Cardinal Bernardin would have seen as essential to the protection of vulnerable life. Both the 2008 and 2012 versions of the document barely engage the worst economic crisis since the Great Depression, despite the fact that it plunged many families into homelessness and many children into food insecurity. While "Faithful Citizenship" does not entirely rule out voting for a prochoice politician, it makes justifying such a choice only slightly less difficult than the task Odysseus faced in navigating his ship between Scylla and Charybdis.

But to say that "Faithful Citizenship" refuses to situate abortion within Bernardin's "consistent ethic of life" does not mean that it stands entirely alone. Abortion is not primarily grouped with other issues of life and death, but instead with two other issues that the bishops have recently made their legislative priorities: the protection of traditional marriage and the defense of religious liberty. In my view, abortion has now been situated as part of an emerging "consistent ethic of purity."

Religious liberty is not an abstract constitutional issue for the bishops; it raises the very concrete possibility that Catholic institutions will be tainted by cooperating in their employees' decision to use contraceptives —which church teaching presents as a violation of the natural law. The underlying concern for cultic purity tacitly animating the bishops' religious liberty strategy broke to the surface in Archbishop William Lori's testimony before a congressional committee, in which he claimed that forcing Catholic institutions to pay for insurance coverage for birth control is analogous to making a Kosher deli sell pork.

To many conservative Catholics, same-sex marriage is not merely a policy mistake, but an anti-sacrament, a perverse rite that has the potential to contaminate the divinely blessed institution of heterosexual marriage. Bishop Thomas Paproki of Springfield made this view explicit by recently holding an exorcism to banish the "diabolical influence of the devil" from the Illinois legislature, which had recently legalized same-sex marriage. Doubtless because of their own scandals, the bishops seem to be almost obsessed by the connection between sex, purity, and defilement. At their November meeting in Baltimore, they voted to draft a formal pastoral statement on pornography.

Needless to say, the bishops' understanding of what counts as purity and defilement can be challenged on a number of fronts. Here, however, I want to focus on a different question: what happens when abortion is framed as part of the "consistent ethic of purity" rather than the "consistent ethic of life"? It becomes nothing less than the massacre of the Holy Innocents.

Unborn life can easily be configured as in some sense superior to the lives of human beings who have already been born, because it is unsullied, innocent, and new, all of which set it one step closer to its divine origins (a popular prolife picture book for children is called *Angel in the Waters*, by Regina Doman). Unlike its mother, who after all, has had sex (perhaps under "illicit" circumstances), the potential victim of abortion is virginal and pristine. Moreover, unborn life can quickly take upon itself the character of something greater than itself, becoming a living symbol of the future of humankind. Hidden away in the womb, devoid of distinguishing features, unable to make its own idiosyncratic preferences known, an unborn life can become a veritable icon of sanctity, a living symbol of pure hope and goodness.

It is understandable that prolifers would try to combat abortion by inflating the status of its potential victims, by configuring them somehow better and purer than those who already have taken their first breath. In my view, however, this approach is a mistake. It tacitly accepts the sharp division in status between the born and the unborn advocated by many committed prochoice activists, although it assigns the mirror image values to those falling in each category. It also feeds into worrisome trends in the larger culture, which idolizes youth, beauty, and unlimited potential.

It is time to place abortion back where it belongs: not in a "consistent ethic of purity," but in a "consistent ethic of life" that recognizes the dignity of all human beings, pure and impure. Thirty years after Cardinal Bernardin began to weave it for us at Fordham, the "seamless garment" should be taken out of mothballs, so that it can be cleaned, pressed, and made ready to meet the challenges of a new era. Perhaps the era of Pope Francis, and his insistence upon the joyously transforming power of the Gospel, will provide the impetus to do just that.

Sources

Bernardin, Joseph. *Consistent Ethic of Life*. Edited by Thomas G. Fuechtmann. New York: Sheed & Ward, 1988.

Doman, Regina. *Angel in the Waters*. Illustrated by Ben Hatke. Manchester, NH: Sophia Institute Press, 2004.

Paprocki, Bishop Thomas. "Homily for Prayers of Supplication and Exorcism in Reparation for the Sin of Same-Sex Marriage." Diocese of Springfield in Illinois. November 20, 2013. Available at http://dio.org/blog/item/350 -bishop-paprocki-s-homily-for-prayers-of-supplication-and-exorcism -in-reparation-for-the-sin-of-same-sex-marriage.html#sthash.F6ZFRAPt .JzyErYUj.dpbs.

Pope Francis. *Evangelii gaudium* (2013).

United States Conference of Catholic Bishops. "Bishop Lori Tells Parable of the Kosher Deli and the Pork Mandate in Congressional Testimony." United States Conference of Catholic Bishops. February 16, 2012. Available at http:// www.usccb.org/news/2012/12-030.cfm.

United States Conference of Catholic Bishops. "Bishops Call for Pastoral Statement on Pornography." United States Conference of Catholic Bishops. November 12, 2013. Available at http://www.usccb.org/news/2013/13-205.cfm.

United States Conference of Catholic Bishops. *Forming Consciences for Faithful Citizenship*. Washington, DC: United States Conference of Catholic Bishops, 2008, with a new introductory note, 2012. Available at http://www.usccb .org/issues-and-action/faithful-citizenship/forming-consciences-for-faithful -citizenship-document.cfm.

Contraception, Again
Where Can We Find Compromise?

The Catholic Church teaches that the basic requirements of morality are accessible in principle to all human beings through the natural law. The church also teaches that Christ conferred on the church special insight into the requirements of natural law. Ideally, this two-source framework for moral insight results in a harmonious, mutually reinforcing relationship. But what happens if there is a conflict? We have a real methodological challenge on our hands.

Take the matter of contraception. In 2006, the U.S. Conference of Catholic Bishops issued a statement entitled "Married Love and the Gift of Life," which reaffirmed the church's teaching that contraception violates God's plan for married love. After the Obama administration announced its intention to include contraception in the basic benefit plan mandated by the Affordable Care Act (2010), the American bishops protested vociferously, arguing that forcing Catholic employers to subsidize contraception constituted requiring unacceptable cooperation in an intrinsically evil act.

For centuries, the Catholic Church (and most of Western Christianity) taught that it was a sin for a couple to deliberately impede the fertility of an act of marital intercourse. This sin was seen as a violation of the natural law, binding all people, not merely Catholics. In the first part of the twentieth century, the broad consensus about the immorality of contraception began to break down. Most other branches of Christianity no longer believe that contraception is always immoral. Polls show that over 80 percent of Americans, including Catholics, think it is not immoral to use contraception. More than 90 percent of women who have ever had sexual intercourse have used some type of contraception. If the law of nations (the *ius gentium*) is any clue to the natural law, it might be important to note that most Western countries have not only repealed laws banning contraception, but have also endorsed it as a legitimate form of family planning. The Vatican is not unaware that many of the faithful ignore the teaching on contraception. Pope Francis convened an extraordinary synod of bishops on the topic of "Pastoral Challenges of the Family in the Context of Evangelization" in part to address church teaching on contraception. In preparation for the synod, the pope also took the extraordinary step of asking the bishops around the world to survey the views of ordinary Catholics on family issues including birth control.

So how do we think about a situation in which many, if not all, apparently reasonable and good people (including Catholics) now hold that the use of contraception by married couples is sometimes justified, while the church continues to maintain it is always objectively immoral? There are four main ways of dealing with the tension between faith and reason in this case. One dissolves the tension, one diminishes it, one denies it, and one attempts to reframe it. People on both sides of the question employ all four ways. In my view, only the last one has any hope of moving us beyond the impasse. Even so, a quick resolution of the conflict does not seem likely.

First, you can dissolve the tension by letting go of either faith or reason. If you're a conservative, you can downplay reason and emphasize the church's role as a privileged interpreter of natural law—especially the role of the magisterium. The trouble with this view is that it essentially relinquishes the fundamental insight of a natural law approach, which is that moral norms have to "make sense" to good people of all stripes, not merely to pious Catholics. If you're a liberal, you can minimize any role for the church in interpreting natural law, especially on matters of sexual ethics. But this approach throws the baby out with the bath water. Church teaching can be wrong on occasion, but it is never irrelevant.

Second, you can diminish the tension by blunting the force of church teaching. For example, you could recast the prohibition against contraception as a matter of religious law, binding only on Catholics, or present it as an ideal for Catholics to strive for rather than a moral requirement for everyone. Both liberals and conservatives might find this approach congenial, but to do that would be to ignore the fact that the precepts of Catholic sexual morality are not meant to be analogous to arcane liturgical requirements binding only for Catholics. And presenting the teaching as an ideal begs the question of whether it is actually a good ideal for everyone.

Third, you can deny the tension, pretending that the disjunction between broadly settled moral opinion and official church teaching is just temporary; you can tell yourself that everything will work out in the end. Conservatives tell themselves that the world will come around to see that the church is right, and liberals tell themselves that the church will admit that the world is right. But many, including myself, believe that this is just wishful thinking.

The fourth approach is more radical: it attempts to eliminate the conflict by reframing the question. A successful example of this type of reframing was the Second Vatican Council's declaration on religious liberty. The church's old approach was that "error had no rights," while its new frame puts the issue in terms of people's consciences, not abstract propositions. *Dignitatis humanae*, the Second Vatican Council's *Declaration on Religious Liberty*, proclaims that a person has a right to worship God according to the dictates of his or her conscience—even if one's conscience is mistaken.

What would such reframing look like in the case of contraception? Interestingly, both liberals and conservatives have attempted to recast the question of contraception's morality by shifting the focus from each sexual act to the marriage as a whole. Some liberals maintain that it is the whole marriage that has to be open to new life, not each individual marital act—the position taken by the majority report of the birth-control commission appointed by Paul VI, but rejected in *Humanae vitae*. Some conservatives contend that marriage is a total gift of the self, including one's capacity to generate new life—a view based on John Paul II's theology of the body.

So which view of marriage is more persuasive? Only time will tell which Catholic view of marriage prevails. Reframing the question of contraception in this way, however, can allow the natural law to operate more fruitfully as the church continues its journey through time.

Sources

Guttmacher Institute. "Contraceptive Use in the United States." Guttmacher Institute. Originally published June 2014. Available at http://www.guttmacher.org/pubs/fb_contr_use.html.

Newport, Frank. "Americans, Including Catholics, Say Birth Control Is Morally
    OK." *Gallup Politics*, May 22, 2012. Available at http://www.gallup.com
    /poll/154799/americans-including-catholics-say-birth-control-morally.aspx.
Pope John Paul II. *The Theology of the Body: Human Love in the Divine Plan.*
    Boston, MA: Pauline Books & Media, 1997.
Pope Paul VI. *Humanae vitae* (1968).
United States Conference of Catholic Bishops. *Married Love and the Gift of Life.*
    Washington, DC: United States Conference of Catholic Bishops, 2007.
Vatican, Synod of Bishops, Extraordinary General Assembly. "Pastoral Chal-
    lenges to the Family in the Context of Evangelization: Preparatory Docu-
    ment." Holy See. 2013. Available at http://www.vatican.va/roman_curia
    /synod/documents/rc_synod_doc_20131105_iii-assemblea-sinodo-vescovi
    _en.html.
Vatican II. *Dignitatis humanae* (1965).
Yardley, Jim. "With Survey, Vatican Seeks Laity Comment on Family Issues."
    New York Times, November 9, 2013.

When Does Life Begin?
Two Prolife Philosophers Disagree

While I was teaching at Notre Dame, my esteemed colleague John Finnis received the third annual Paul Ramsey Award for Excellence in Bioethics from the Center for Bioethics and Culture (CBC), a conservative Christian think tank. Paul Ramsey (1913-88) was a pioneer in the field of bioethics. He was also one of my teachers at Princeton.

Looking at the CBC website, I wondered whether its leaders would consider Ramsey himself suitable for the award it issues in his name? Firmly prolife, Ramsey still considered some questions—such as the status of the early human embryo—to be legitimately debatable by committed Christians. I'm not sure the CBC feels the same way. The chair of its nominating committee, C. Ben Mitchell, has said that denying that the early embryo is a human being is analogous to denying the humanity of Jews and slaves. Would Paul Ramsey agree?

I don't think so. In fact, Ramsey had serious reservations about the position that individual human life starts at fertilization—an opinion Finnis shares with the worthy previous recipients of the Ramsey Award, Germain Grisez and Edmund Pellegrino, both Catholics. In Ramsey's classic and wide-ranging essay "Abortion: A Review Article" (1973), he engages in vigorous, detailed, and still-relevant debate with Grisez's *Abortion: The Myths, the Realities, the Arguments* (1970).

In that book, Grisez argues that individual human life begins when egg and sperm unite, creating a fertilized ovum (a zygote) with a full complement of forty-six chromosomes. That zygote then undergoes cell division, becoming an embryo. But there is a wrinkle to the argument: for about two weeks after fertilization, that embryo may split, resulting in identical twins. Less commonly, two embryos may combine, resulting in one individual. As Ramsey notes, "there is fluidity and indeterminacy in either direction during the earliest days following conception." So how do we think about the various entities involved in twinning and combination?

In the case of twinning, Grisez argues, we must think in terms of three distinct human individuals. The original embryo—let's call it A—is a human individual distinct from its parents. The twins—let's call them B and C—are human individuals distinct from each other and from the fertilized egg from which they sprang. What is the relationship among A, B, and C? Grisez explains that "we should think of the twins as the *grandchildren* of their putative parents, the individual that divided being the true offspring, and the identical twins of that offspring by atypical reproduction." In other words, A is the child of the parents, and B and C are the grandchildren. This is odd, since A neither died nor gave birth. Rather, A split through a form of asexual reproduction. Grisez likens the split to the way in which "two individual animals of many lower forms of life can develop by the division of a single, existing individual." In his article, Ramsey conjectures, with a note of incredulity, that Grisez must be talking about halved earthworms.

What about two embryos combining to form one? Grisez says this involves two individuals, A and B, combining to form C, who is a distinct new individual. He suggests this scenario is analogous to that of "a grafted plant." Ramsey's response: "With considerable astonishment we may ask whether any such 'individuality' is the life we should respect and protect from conception. In trying to prove too much, Grisez has proved too little of ethical import."

Analogies to earthworms and plants seemed implausible to Ramsey. So did Grisez's invitation to think of identical twins as the grandchildren of the woman who gave birth to them. Grisez's attempt to preserve the claim that individuated human life begins at fertilization sacrifices too much of what we know about human nature—both from a Christian perspective and a scientific one. After all, human beings reproduce sexually, not asexually. Humans are mortal; they die and their bodies disintegrate. They don't split neatly into two with no loss, cost, or remainder (as in twinning), nor do they merge fluidly into one another (as in combination).

Ramsey thought it plausible that an individuated human life does not begin until the possibility for twinning and combination has passed, a stage called restriction, about two weeks after fertilization.

Assuming Ramsey was right, what does that mean for research on human embryos that destroys them in the process? If the embryos have not reached the stage of restriction, such research would not count as homicide, because it wouldn't involve killing a human being.

If it's not homicide, is such research morally permissible? Perhaps, given its potential benefits. But not necessarily. Ramsey was deeply suspicious of the scientific imperative to manipulate human destiny in the name of progress. He was keenly aware of the slippery slope such research puts us on. Should the research prove effective, the inevitable temptation will be to use more developed embryos and even fetuses in our research to get better results. In his view, that *would* be homicide.

Paul Ramsey's powerful and fearless intellect led him to differ not only from secular liberals, but also from religious conservatives. If the CBC issues an award in his name, its leaders ought to refrain from demonizing as Nazis or slaveholders those who hold positions that Ramsey himself considered defensible.

Sources

Center for Bioethics and Culture. "The Paul Ramsey Award." Center for Bioethics and Culture. 2014. Available at http://www.cbc-network.org/paul-ramsey/.

Grisez, Germain. *Abortion: The Myths, the Realities, the Arguments*. New York: Corpus Books, 1970.

Mitchell, C. Ben. "First-Person: Clones from Newcastle." *Baptist Press*, August 12, 2004. Available at http://www.bpnews.net/18855/firstperson-clones-from-newcastle.

Ramsey, Paul. "Abortion: A Review Article." *The Thomist* 37 (1973): 174–226.

Why Prolife?
It's about People, Not Abstractions

Prolife websites regularly display the faces of adorable infants and small children. This is a savvy move. Anthropologists and psychologists say that the structure of a baby's face (a head "too large" for the body; a high forehead; large, round eyes; short, narrow features; and full cheeks) elicits a particular set of responses from adults. We are biologically programmed to nurture and protect babies; our normal impulses toward self-protection and aggression are quelled in their presence. A baby's face advertises, "I am not like an adult. I bear you no harm. Take care of me. I am innocent."

Who can be blamed for wanting to protect the blameless? Yet if it's simply the blamelessness of the unborn that motivates our desire to keep them from harm, we're missing the point of Christian anthropology. We protect the unborn not because they are perfectly innocent; we protect them because they bear the image and likeness of God—the very same image and likeness they will bear when they are no longer defenseless and cute.

St. Augustine certainly wasn't fooled by the cuteness of babies. In the *Confessions*, he memorably describes how even the tiniest, cutest members of the human species can be morally flawed. He writes, "I have myself observed a baby to be jealous, though it could not speak; it was livid as it watched another infant at the breast." Brutally unsentimental, Augustine tells us that in the sight of God, "there is none free from sin, not even the infant who has lived but a day upon this earth." Augustine's views were highly influential on official Catholic teaching. According to the *Catechism*, "Adam and Eve transmitted to their descendants human nature wounded by their own first sin and hence deprived of original holiness and justice." In order to remove this "sin with which we are all born afflicted . . . the church baptizes for the remission of sins even tiny infants who have not committed personal sin."

The doctrine of original sin fell into desuetude after Vatican II. To the extent that popular presentation of the doctrine of original sin had devolved into an unhealthy preoccupation with the eternal fate of unbaptized infants, its temporary disappearance wasn't entirely bad. But it may be time to bring it back, in a suitably nuanced form.

In their now infamous paper "The Impact of Legalized Abortion on Crime," Stanford law professor John Donohue and University of Chicago economist Steven D. Levitt made the controversial argument that legalized abortion accounts for the "large, widespread, and persistent drop in crime in the 1990s." The argument is as follows: the women who are most likely to seek abortions are teenagers, the economically disadvantaged, and the unmarried. They are also the women who are statistically most likely to give birth to children who will grow up to engage in criminal activity, since the lack of a stable and nurturing home environment "is strongly linked to future criminality."

If we assume that the argument against abortion rests on the absolute innocence of unborn life, Donohue and Levitt's argument poses a problem. We could, of course, challenge the data. But what if it is correct? Then we can be tempted to draw a distinction between the "innocent" baby in the womb (whom we protect) and the "guilty" teenage criminal (whom we condemn). Sometimes, the distinction is drawn so sharply that it obscures the fact that the baby and the teenager are one and the same. The unborn child is seen as a flawless symbol of humanity, rather than as a unique and flawed human being. The teenager is dismissed as unworthy of our concern. This is a dangerous temptation: it's easy to love humanity in general, but it's hard to love individual human beings, warts and all.

If we keep in mind the doctrine of original sin, however, we can put the Donohue/Levitt argument in proper perspective. First, it may well be correct. We shouldn't be surprised that many women who seek abortions don't have the resources to nurture their children. Neither should we be surprised that children who aren't provided with basic nurturing turn out to be prone to wrongful behavior. The doctrine of original sin affirms the essential sociality of human beings: We shape one another's character for evil and for good. The *Catechism* unblinkingly recognizes the "negative influence exerted on people by communal situations and social structures" that are the fruit of human sinfulness (408).

Second, even if it is correct, the Donohue/Levitt argument does not provide a justification for a pro-abortion social policy. We protect human beings—even human beings in the womb—not because they are entirely innocent of sin. We protect them because they are made in the image and likeness of God, despite their sinfulness. We see the very same *imago Dei* in an unborn baby and the juvenile delinquent she will become fifteen years later. The gospel of Jesus Christ is not mesmerized by cuteness.

Third, the Donohue/Levitt argument shows why we can't separate life issues from social justice issues. If an unborn child matters not because she is a symbol of humanity, but because she is a particular human being, we need to ensure that she is cared for after she is born. To do that, we must care for her mother too: a woman's educational level is one of the most powerful predictors of the welfare of her children. By caring for individual children, their mothers, and their fathers, we improve the lot of society as a whole by minimizing in the right way the factors that lead to criminal behavior. In Catholic teaching, sin— like redemption—has both a social and a personal dimension. So does redemption.

Opposition to abortion motivated solely by the perceived blamelessness of the unborn betrays Christian anthropology and fractures the Catholic social tradition. When such opposition is animated by a commitment to protect the *imago Dei* in each person, however, Catholics preserve both the church's anthropological vision and unified social teaching. Anti-abortionists would thus do well to nuance the justification of their position.

Sources

Augustine. *A Treatise on the Merits and Forgiveness of Sins and on the Baptism of Infants.* Edited by Philip Schaff. Amazon Kindle, 2011.

Catechism of the Catholic Church, §§ 385–409.

Donohue, John J., III, and Steven D. Levitt. "The Impact of Legalized Abortion on Crime." *Quarterly Journal of Economics*, 116, no. 2 (2001): 379–420.

Levitt, Steven D., and Stephen J. Dubner. *Freakonomics: A Rogue Economist Explores the Hidden Side of Everything.* New York: HarperCollins, 2005.

The ACLU Takes on the Bishops
Tragedy Leads to a Misguided Lawsuit

On November 29, 2013, the American Civil Liberties Union filed a federal lawsuit on behalf of Tamesha Means in the Eastern District of Michigan. The lawsuit demanded compensatory and punitive damages for medically negligent treatment she allegedly received in the course of her pregnancy and miscarriage at Mercy Health Partners (MHP), a Catholic health facility in Muskegan. The plaintiff suffered from a decreased volume of amniotic fluid caused by the rupture of her amniotic sac. Means claims that MHP did not inform her that this situation would be lethal for her unborn child and could be seriously harmful to her if labor likely fatal to the fetus was not induced.

Of course, medical malpractice lawsuits are not uncommon in the United States. What makes this case unusual is the identity of one of the defendants: the U.S. Conference of Catholic Bishops. The alleged negligent act: promulgating the Ethical and Religious Directives for Catholic Health Care Services.

According to the complaint, the USCCB was responsible for the harm Means suffered because it "directed the course of care Plaintiff received" from MHP. According to the plaintiff, Directive 27 does not require Catholic hospitals to disclose the option of a "previability pregnancy termination," because (she claims) the church does not see it as morally legitimate. The plaintiff also blames Directive 45, which prohibits abortion. That directive reads: "Every procedure whose sole immediate effect is the termination of pregnancy before viability is an abortion, which, in its moral context, includes the interval between conception and implantation of the embryo." The plaintiff contended that Directive 45 prevented MHP from either completing the miscarriage or referring her to a place that would do so.

But did Means identify the right defendants? Contrary to popular belief, the USCCB does not have the power to tell individual bishops—or Catholic healthcare systems—what to do and what not to do. The conference promulgated the directives as an abstract set of norms applicable to Catholic hospitals. But it lacks the power to make them operationally effective. When it comes to canon law, the local bishop has the authority to enforce and interpret the directives in his diocese. But when it comes to secular law, what makes the directives binding on the Catholic hospital is their inclusion in its bylaws—a decision made by its religious sponsor, not the USCCB or even the local bishop. So the USCCB's promulgation of the directives cannot be considered the proximate cause of any harm suffered by the plaintiff.

In any case, the directives themselves are not to blame for the harm suffered by the plaintiff. The facts as alleged suggest a combination of garden-variety medical malpractice and misinterpretation of the directives. Not informing the patient about her treatment options is clearly negligence—but it is not uniquely Catholic negligence, even if it occurs in a Catholic hospital. Nothing in the directives prevents a Catholic hospital from being fully honest with a patient about her situation and its prognosis. Directives 47 and 49 do allow a hospital to induce labor in situations like the plaintiff's under the principle of double-effect. In such a case, the death of the unborn child, who would not have survived anyway, is not intended; it is foreseen and accepted as a side effect of treating the mother's illness. Therefore, the procedure the plaintiff claims she was not offered would not count as a prohibited "abortion" under church teaching.

But the bishops do face a larger problem. In a highly publicized case that unfolded in the fall of 2009, Phoenix Bishop Thomas Olmsted excommunicated Margaret Mary McBride, RSM, for authorizing a Catholic hospital to perform a procedure necessary to save the life of a pregnant woman with severe pulmonary hypertension. Focusing mainly on the physical structure of the act, he claimed the procedure was an impermissible direct attack on unborn life. If he had had his way, the woman would have been left to die along with the baby—and the hospital would have, and should have, lost its license.

Fortunately, Catholic moral theology has moved beyond Olmsted's sort of rank physicalism in analyzing human acts. It is repudiated by John Paul II in *Veritatis splendor* and by conservative moralists such as Germain Grisez and Martin Rhonheimer, who recognize that determining the object of the act requires that one put oneself in the shoes of the acting person, in order to determine his or her immediate purpose in acting. It is not sufficient to look at the physical structure of an act from a perspective external to the agent. Nonetheless, taken out of context, a few lines in the directives could support Olmsted's mistaken view.

Properly understood, Catholic moral teaching requires Catholic hospitals to try to save both mother and unborn child, and if that is not possible, doctors must save the patient that can be saved. In early pregnancy, that's the mother. The time has come for the Bishops' Conference to revise the directives to make that crystal clear.

Sources

The Arizona Republic. "Statements from the Diocese of Phoenix and St. Joseph's." AZ Central. May 15, 2010. Available at https://accountsolution.gcion .com/redirect/?returnSessionKey=true&returnAutoLogin=true&redirectUR L=http%3A%2F%2Fwww.azcentral.com%2Fcommunity%2Fphoenix%2Farti cles%2F2010%2F05%2F14%2F20100514stjoseph0515bishop.html%3Ffrom %3D global.

Eckholm, Erik. "Bishops Sued over Anti-Abortion Policies at Catholic Hospitals." *New York Times*, December 2, 2013.

Grisez, Germain. *Living a Christian Life.* Vol. 2 of *The Way of the Lord Jesus.* Quincy, IL: Franciscan Press, 1993. See especially chap. 8, sec. D: "Is abortion always the wrongful killing of a person?"

O'Rourke, Kevin. "What Happened in Phoenix?" *America*, June 21, 2010.

Pope John Paul II. *Veritatis splendor* (1992).

Pope John Paul II. *Evangelium vitae* (1995).

Rhonheimer, Martin. *Vital Conflicts in Medical Ethics: A Virtue Approach to Crainiotomy and Tubal Pregnancies.* Edited by William F. Murphy. Washington, DC: The Catholic University of America Press, 2009.

Tamesha Means v. United States Conference of Catholic Bishops, complaint, USDC E.D. Michigan, Southern Division. Available at https://www.aclu.org /cases/tamesha-means-v-united-states-conference-catholic-bishops.

United States Conference of Catholic Bishops. *Ethical and Religious Directives for Catholic Health Care Services.* 5th ed. November 17, 2009. Available at http://www.usccb.org/about/doctrine/ethical-and-religious-directives/.

Co-Opted by Evil?
Abortion and Amnesty International

How involved can you become in someone else's wrongdoing without becoming morally tainted by it? This is a question we all face, whether we worry about giving a coworker ten dollars to buy cigarettes that will eventually kill him, or regret paying taxes that help support an unjust war and/or unjust population control policies. It is a question that the Catholic moral tradition has long analyzed under the concept of "cooperation with evil." The basic features of this moral teaching have remained the same over the centuries. But there have also been significant points of development, and new points of controversy that demonstrate the challenges the church faces in a society that is far more interdependent and pluralistic than the one in which the concept was first established.

Here are the basics. Intentionally furthering the wrongdoing of another, traditionally known as "formal cooperation," is never permitted. So you can't give your coworker cigarette money with the intention that he smoke himself to death so that your best friend can take his job. The real arguments are over "material cooperation," which involves performing a morally good or neutral action foreseeing that it may contribute to someone else's wrongdoing but not intending for it to. It is sometimes permissible, sometimes not, depending on a number of factors, including the distance between the cooperator's act and the act of the wrongdoing party. Other factors point to a cost-benefit analysis that considers the good to be gained by cooperation, the gravity of the wrongful act, and whether refusal to cooperate can prevent the wrongdoer from acting. Finally, we ask whether the potential cooperator is under duress or some sort of obligation, and whether the cooperation will cause "scandal," which means leading people into sin by making them think that morally wrong behavior might just be okay after all. So, paying taxes is generally permissible cooperation; the duress is significant, and the connection between a taxpayer's contribution and unjust governmental policies is remote. Nobody thinks taxpayers morally endorse every policy and program supported by public money, so there is little danger of scandal.

How has our understanding of the context in which cooperation creates a moral problem changed? The first and most important question is how to weigh the pervasiveness and degree of moral disagreement. Two hundred years ago, the moralists writing about cooperation with evil took for granted that respectable society would agree with their judgments about which actions were morally permitted and which were prohibited. Today's controversies involve Catholics cooperating in actions that many respectable people do not acknowledge as wrong: for example, abortion, euthanasia, surgical sterilization, same-sex marriage.

Second, the class of potential cooperators now includes institutions or corporate persons as well as individuals. Should Catholic hospitals enter into affiliations with secular hospitals that offer services prohibited by church teaching? Should Catholic Charities go out of the adoption business rather than agree to place children with homosexual couples in accordance with a state law prohibiting discrimination on the basis of sexual orientation? The stakes raised by institutional cooperation are higher here in every respect. On one side, failure to cooperate may mean going out of business, and leaving vulnerable people in the lurch. On the other, if Catholic institutions engage in close, ongoing cooperation with those engaged in practices prohibited by church teaching but widely accepted by the broader community, they may run the risk of giving scandal. People may doubt that the church is really serious about its moral objections to those practices.

Third, for some members of the church hierarchy, the emerging motivation seems to be not merely avoiding scandal but taking an active prophetic stand against a morally hostile culture. Consider the case of Amnesty International (AI), which abandoned its neutral position on abortion in 2007, in favor of a limited prochoice position (it advocates abortion rights in the case of rape, or when the life or health of the mother is in grave danger). In response, Cardinal Renato Martino of the Pontifical Council for Justice and Peace not only denounced AI, but also urged all Catholics to withdraw their support of it. In 2009, AI expanded its support for abortion access, arguing for the repeal of criminal penalties for women who seek or obtain abortions, and for those who provide information about abortion. In 2014, AI launched a major campaign in favor of sexual and reproductive rights, which included a pledge to "work with partners to consolidate public and political support for the decriminalization of abortion."

Giving to AI in order to support its many other endeavors, in my view, entails only a slight and morally acceptable material cooperation with the performance of abortions. Additionally, scandal is unlikely, especially if a Catholic makes a private donation. Even if her support of AI is made public, however, it is doubtful that anyone will necessarily interpret it as deliberate support of abortion. So continued financial support of AI is probably justified under the traditional understanding of what constitutes cooperation with evil (especially since AI is one of the most effective human rights organizations in the world; it won a Nobel Prize for its efforts in 1977).

Some people, such as Cardinal Martino, may feel called to bear prophetic witness against abortion by advocating for the total withdrawal of financial support from organizations with any sort of prochoice position. But is everyone? If everyone is a prophet against abortion in this way, who will take up the cause of the refugee, the detainee, the "disappeared," and the tortured? Christianity teaches that these other such victims are made in the image and likeness of God no less than the unborn, and AI does much—even if unknowingly—to protect the *imago Dei* in them. Thus while Catholics might feel the need to reform AI, I'm not sure that all are morally obligated to boycott the organization.

Sources

Amnesty International. "Amnesty International Defends Access to Abortion for Women at Risk." Press release, June 14, 2007. Available at http://web cache.googleusercontent.com/search?q=cache:k6_FrpL1vxQJ:https://www .amnesty.org/download/Documents/68000/pol300122007en.pdf+&cd=1&hl =en&ct=clnk&gl=us.

Amnesty International. *The Total Abortion Ban in Nicaragua: Women's Lives and Health Endangered, Medical Professionals Criminalized.* London, UK: Amnesty International Publications, 2009.

Amnesty International. "My Life, My Health, My Education, My Choice, My Future, My Body, My Rights." March 6, 2014. Available at http://webcache

.googleusercontent.com/search?q=cache:kHpxJfPeSYoJ:https://www.amnesty
.org/en/documents/ACT35/001/2014/ar/+&cd=1&hl=en&ct=clnk&gl=us.

Amnesty International. "Sexual and Reproductive Rights under Threat Worldwide." Press Release, March 6, 2014. Available at http://webcache.googleuser
content.com/search?q=cache:gUmA4FGwE5YJ:https://www.amnesty.org
/en/articles/news/2014/03/sexual-and-reproductive-rights-under-threat
-worldwide/+&cd=1&hl=en&ct=clnk&gl=us.

Fisher, Anthony, O.P. "Co-Operation in Evil," *Catholic Medical Quarterly* 44,
no. 3 (1994): 15–22.

Kaveny, M. Cathleen. "Appropriation of Evil: Cooperation's Mirror Image,"
Theological Studies (2001): 280–313.

Keenan, James, S.J. "Prophylactics, Toleration, and Cooperation: Contemporary
Problems and Traditional Principles," *International Philosophical Quarterly*
29 (1989): 206–20.

McFeely, Tom. "No Amnesty for the Unborn." *National Catholic Register*, June
12, 2007. Available at http://www.ncregister.com/site/article/2904.

Boycotts in a Pluralistic Society
How and Where Do We Draw Moral Lines?

How do we signal our moral objection to certain practices or activities in a pluralistic, capitalistic society? One way is to mount a boycott—to make our objections clear to businesses by hitting them where it hurts: in the cash register.

The most famous boycott in the past century, of course, was the Montgomery Bus Boycott (1955–56) organized by Martin Luther King, Jr. in order to protest the bus company's practices of segregation. In the late 1970's and early 1980's, many people in the United States and Europe boycotted the Swiss corporation Nestlé, in order to protest its marketing of substitutes for breast milk to mothers in developing countries. Today, a growing movement calls for colleges and universities—including (and especially?) Catholic ones—to boycott investing in fossil fuel companies that knowingly exacerbate climate change.

Boycotts are not the exclusive province of "liberals" or "conservatives," especially in today's controversies over abortion and same-sex marriage. In 2013, the Archdiocese of New Orleans called upon Catholics to boycott contractors involved in building a new Planned Parenthood facility in the city. In 2014, there were rumors that the National Football League might refuse to patronize (boycott?) the state of Arizona for the Super Bowl, if the governor signed a bill that expanded rights of business owners to withhold service from (boycott?) customers on religious grounds. In 2015, there were rumblings that the NCAA Final Four would boycott the state of Indiana, which had recently enacted a law protecting religious freedom. The NCAA worried that the law would give legal cover to businesses that wished to discriminate against same-sex couples. But what, exactly, *is* a boycott? And how do we analyze the morality of engaging in a boycott? These questions are important, and in sore need of greater, careful reflection.

We know that the central case of a boycott is when consumers refuse to patronize a particular business because of its stance or behavior. What about the reverse situation? Does it count as a boycott when a business owner refuses service to a patron because the business owner does not agree with the patron's public stance on a particular moral or political issue? For example, a gay hairdresser refused to cut the hair of the governor of New Mexico because he vehemently disagreed with her stance against gay marriage (which has since changed). Are the two situations morally analogous? Or are different issues raised when a business refuses service to a particular customer on moral grounds than when customers refuse to patronize businesses on moral grounds? In my view, while there are analogies, the two situations raise different issues. Generally speaking, a particular client (even a governor) is more vulnerable than a corporation. Furthermore, putting pressure on a political officeholder who comes to see a vendor in a personal capacity risks pitting her personal good (a flattering haircut) against what she believes is her political duty.

Does refusing to patronize a particular store for a moral or political reason count as a boycott, albeit as a private little boycott? It seems to me that a boycott needs to have a public element, since a key goal of any boycott is consciousness-raising. Practically, boycotters aim to communicate their grievances to a targeted business so that the business considers changing its practice(s). Strategically, boycotters aim to raise the profile of a particular moral or political issue in the community at large, who will learn of the boycott through the media. Tactically, boycotters aim to educate other potential customers of the targeted business about the moral issue at stake, in order to convince them to join the boycott. This is important because the numbers matter —boycotters aim to change a company's practices through financial pressure, but such pressure often requires significant numbers of participants.

It is these practical, strategic and tactical elements that help us distinguish situations of boycott, on the one hand, and situations of avoiding what Catholic moralists call "unacceptable cooperation with evil," on the other. A particular individual may decide not to shop at a local mom-and-pop restaurant notorious for discriminating against its non-white customers. She may think that it is wrong for her family to contribute to this restaurant's success—and future discriminatory acts. But that decision, in and of itself, is not a boycott, since it does not satisfy the above practical, strategic, and tactical criteria.

When a group of well-organized activists publicize their refusal to do any business with a big box store whose suppliers use child labor, it *is* a boycott. But that does not mean that shopping at those stores is engaging in wrongful cooperation with evil. In fact, for many people, shopping at that big box store chain is likely *not* to be impermissible cooperation with evil. The causal, temporal connection between their individual purchases and the wrongdoing is extremely attenuated. Moreover, their individual decisions to buy their goods elsewhere will make very little difference in the purchasing decisions of the chain in question. Finally, a traditional cooperation with evil analysis looks not only at the wrongdoing that cooperation facilitates, but also at the good that it achieves. It may be, for example, that some of these consumers are financially strapped, and can best provide for the material needs of their families by shopping at big box stores rather than at more expensive stores.

So a decision to avoid morally unacceptable cooperation with evil may overlap, but is not identical with, the decision to stage a boycott. The latter decision raises distinct practical and moral questions. Practically, one has to ask whether the boycott is focused enough to succeed, or will it simply dissipate and disappear. Morally, it is important to ask who will be harmed by the boycott, and whether that harm is justifiable. This latter question is particularly important in *indirect boycotts*, where one targets not the corporation that is actually engaged in wrongdoing, but other corporations that do business with it.

The boycott called for by the Archdiocese of New Orleans is an indirect boycott: it asks Catholics not to avoid patronizing Planned Parenthood (which it would claim they ought not to do in any case) but rather to avoid patronizing those whose work is helping to build a new Planned Parenthood facility: contractors, plumbers, electricians, office and medical supply stores. Before deciding upon this course of action, one has to ask several key questions, such as whether the boycott is fair to those workers. Fairness, in my view, not only involves asking whether those workers will be able to support themselves and their families. It also involves asking whether we want to put these people in the bulls-eye of these social and political battles. A boycott easily generates a counter-boycott. Suppose, for example, that supporters of Planned Parenthood retaliate by saying that they won't hire anyone who does work for the Archdiocese? Needless to say, this pattern of expanding boycotts can easily contribute to widespread social divisiveness and instability.

Considering whether, when, and how to boycott requires us to engage in careful moral analysis on a number of fronts. We need to face the wrongdoing that the potential target of our boycott is perpetuating or facilitating. But we also need to consider whether the boycott is likely to succeed. Finally, we need to consider the harm that our boycott may inflict upon innocent third parties, as well as upon the common good itself.

Sources

Berman, Mark. "What Does the NFL Have to Do with Arizona's Bill Letting Businesses Refuse Service to Gay People?" *Washington Post* (Post Nation), February 24, 2014. Available at http://www.washingtonpost.com/news/post -nation/wp/2014/02/24/what-does-the-nfl-have-to-do-with-arizonas-bill -letting-businesses-refuse-service-to-gay-people/.

Burns, Stewart, ed. *Daybreak of Freedom: The Montgomery Bus Boycott.* Chapel Hill, NC: University of North Carolina Press, 1997.

CNA/EWTN News. "New Orleans Archdiocese to Boycott Abortion Clinic Collaborators." *Catholic News Agency*, February 10, 2014. Available at http:// www.catholicnewsagency.com/news/new-orleans-archdiocese-to-boycott -abortion-clinic-collaborators/.

Demeo, Doug. "Getting Out of Oil: Catholic Universities Can Make a Difference through Divestment." *America*, April 21, 2014.

Fossil Free. "Fossil Free." 2014. Available at http://gofossilfree.org/.

Klöpping, Laura. *Nestlé: A Global Company Comes under Fire.* Norderstedt, Germany: GRIN Verlag, 2011.

Forever Young
The Trouble with the "Ashley Treatment"

How far ought we to go in transforming our bodies so that they better correspond to our psyches? This question is particularly vexing when the body we are transforming is not our own, but a vulnerable human being for whom we are responsible. No controversy raised this set of questions more than that surrounding the "Ashley Treatment"—a series of medical procedures performed at Seattle Children's Hospital in 2004 on a profoundly mentally and physically disabled six-year-old girl in order to insure that she would remain small, portable, and prepubescent.

Disability rights advocates and others argue that deliberately stunting Ashley's growth, as well as removing her uterus and breast buds, violated her right to mature in the same manner as a normal child. Her parents and doctors respond that the procedures improved Ashley's quality of life by sparing her the difficulties of puberty and making it possible for them to care for her at home.

It is easy to dismiss Ashley's case as a sensational ethical dilemma with little bearing on most people's lives, but if we look more closely, we can see deep parallels between Ashley's situation and our own. In fact, we can see that Ashley's parents wanted for her something that most of us want for ourselves and for our loved ones: a close and harmonious correspondence between our "insides" and our "outsides," between our bodies and our minds.

Ashley's parents and doctors wanted to make her body correspond, at least roughly, to her mental state. As one of her physicians, Dr. Daniel Gunther, explained to *Time*: "Ashley will always have the mind of an infant, and she will be able to stay where she belongs—in the arms of the family that loves her." Ashley's family elaborated on its blog: "Ashley has all of a baby's needs, including being entertained and engaged, and she calms down at the sounds of family voices.

240

Furthermore, given Ashley's mental age, a nine-and-a-half-year-old body is more appropriate and more dignified than a fully grown female body."

If we see Ashley's story as a dramatic attempt to make a person's body correspond with her mind and heart, it becomes more intelligible—though perhaps not ultimately defensible. After all, many people make changes to their bodies to make them reflect their psychic identity. Some cases, fairly common now, are nearly as dramatic as Ashley's. For example, transsexuals believe that their sexual organs do not accurately reflect the gender of their minds and hearts. Some transgendered persons not only take heavy doses of hormones, but also undergo sex reassignment surgery in order to bring their bodies into line with their psyches. They seek liberation through what many people believe to be a horrible form of mutilation.

For most of us, though, the major dissonance between mind and body occurs as we age. Many people find themselves looking and feeling older physically, but not psychically. So they take steps, some of them quite invasive, to bridge the gap. Someone who has "normal" hips and knees for a seventy-year-old might obtain hip and knee replacements in order to continue activities they enjoyed when they were thirty. Someone who "feels young" on the inside might obtain a face-lift, a tummy tuck, or liposuction to "look young."

How should Christians think about all this? The tradition provides an ethical framework for dealing with these questions, even if it doesn't provide answers for each and every hard case. Christian anthropology validates the quest for harmony of body and mind; it sees human beings as psychosomatic unities. At the same time, it provides a strong caution against trying to achieve perfect harmony anytime before the Second Coming. The tensions between body and soul, exemplified by suffering and death, will only be vanquished with the coming of God's kingdom. In the meantime, we need to be vigilant that our quest for harmony between body and soul doesn't lead us to harm, denigrate, or ignore those who don't currently possess it—a category of people that will include all of us as we age. We need to accept a certain amount of messiness in the relationship between body and soul.

We shouldn't try to neaten up everything according to contemporary standards of what's normal. Most important, we need to resist the temptation to narrow our concept of acceptable dependency. It's a big challenge: we live in a society that accepts, even welcomes, dependency in babies and small children—but not in adults. The sight of a completely dependent grownup with the mental age of a baby is disconcerting, if not frightening, to most people. In this context, it is entirely understandable that Ashley's parents tried to keep her a child—a "pillow angel." But as the years pass, she won't be a child, despite the Ashley Treatment. She will be a profoundly dependent teenager, adult, and finally, an old woman with the mind of a baby. We need to find a way to affirm the value of her life—and to provide her with necessary care—without requiring her to look like the baby we want her to be.

Sources

Allen, David B., Michael Kappy, Douglas Diekema, and Norman Frost. "Growth-Attenuation Therapy: Principles for Practice." *Pediatrics* 123, no. 6 (2009): 1556–61.

Copeland, M. Sean. *Enfleshing Freedom: Body, Race, and Being.* Philadelphia, PA: Fortress Press, 2009.

Gibbs, Nancy. "Pillow Angel Ethics," *Time*, January 22, 2007.

Gunther, Daniel F., and Douglas S. Diekema. "Attenuating Growth in Children with Profound Developmental Disability: A New Approach to an Old Dilemma." *Archives of Pediatrics & Adolescent Medicine* 160, no. 10 (2006): 1013–17.

McDonald, Anne. "The Other Story from a 'Pillow Angel': Been there. Done That. Preferred to Grow." *Seattle pi*, June 16, 2007. Available at http://www.seattlepi.com/local/opinion/article/The-other-story-from-a-Pillow-Angel-1240555.php#page-1.

Moltmann-Wendel, Elisabeth. *I Am My Body: A Theology of Embodiment.* London, UK: Bloomsbury Academic, 1995.

Vanier, Jean. *Jean Vanier: Essential Writings.* Introduction by Carolyn Whitney-Brown. Maryknoll, NY: Orbis, 2008.

Risk and Responsibility

Why Insurance Is the Wrong Way to Think about Health Care

The passage of the Patient Protection and Affordable Care Act of 2010 was a tremendous achievement that will help improve the health status of millions of Americans in the years to come. Nonetheless, it is not all that it could be. Political pressures transformed President Barack Obama's healthcare reform plan into a health insurance reform plan. Some commentators have protested that this transformation has resulted in a reform package that is far too limited in scope. I think the problem is more fundamental. We shouldn't be thinking of our duty to provide health care as a matter of insurance in the first place, because the logic of insurance leads us to avoid those who most need our help—the sick, the old, and the medically vulnerable.

The basic idea of insurance—making provision for risk of loss—is very old; it began with merchants making provision for the loss of their wares during transit. The Code of Hammurabi provided that merchants borrowing money to fund their ventures could pay an additional sum for loan forgiveness if their goods were lost. The Middle Ages saw the development of actual insurance contracts among ship owners, who paid wealthy individuals a premium to cover the costs of a ship lost at sea. It made sense for the merchants to throw in their lots together. All ships appeared to be equally at risk from the arbitrary cruelties of the wind and waves; no one could predict in advance whose ship would be lost.

The core of insurance is the rational transfer of the risk of a large, unmanageable loss or expense in exchange for a manageable fee—a premium. Insurance underwriters have become extremely sophisticated at estimating risk, and pricing premiums (or declining coverage) accordingly. Ironically, the closer they get to predicting the future accurately, the closer they get to making their jobs obsolete.

A true crystal ball, which eliminates risk entirely in favor of certain prediction, would be the death of insurance. No one is going to insure someone against a certain or virtually certain harm—the price of the premium would be the price of the payout.

We can now see why the idea of health insurance is so problematic. Death is a certainty for us all, and periods of disability and illness are highly likely occurrences for most of us. The question isn't whether our bodies will fail; it is when and how. Moreover, it doesn't take an actuary to predict with some degree of accuracy who is at low risk and who is at high risk—hence we have what insurers call the "moral hazard" problem, in which people try to buy insurance only when they think they will need it. So the young decide—quite rationally—that paying the rent is more important than buying health insurance.

Insurance companies face equal and contrary temptations. They can try to "cherry pick" those they cover by attracting healthy populations (free gym membership, anyone?) and excluding those who will run up high medical bills. Developments in medical diagnosis and genetic testing give them powerful new tools for medical underwriting. From the insurer's perspective, it is simply good business to exclude the baby girl born with the BRCA-1 gene from the coverage she will need most—for she has a preexisting condition indicating the potential for breast cancer even before she develops breasts. Employers face analogous temptations. Those employers who have a healthy group of workers in a low-risk environment may choose to cover medical bills themselves rather than join an insurance pool with other employers whose workers are likely to need more medical care. Quite rationally, they don't want to throw in their lots with companies likely to have higher medical bills.

Moreover, understanding health care through an insurance framework leads to other morally troublesome conclusions. Viewed purely from a bottom-line perspective, a health insurer's best customer is someone who leads a productive, sedentary, risk-free life until age fifty, and who then dies suddenly from a massive heart attack just as he receives his AARP card and schedules his first colonoscopy. The ugly fact is that a quick death is always cheaper for a health insurer than a prolonged period of debilitating illness. But this fact has been hidden since 1965 through the Medicare program, when the federal government started to cover the cost of health care for those most likely to need it.

By its very logic, the concept of health insurance pits the self-interest of the young and healthy against the interests of the sick and the old. One might object that young people's conception of self-interest may be too narrow; they will be old one day, too. True enough. But the objection does not go far enough—why should anyone pay for diseases that she knows she has escaped—say, juvenile diabetes?

The Affordable Care Act can avoid many of these problems by enabling regulations that prohibit, say, medical underwriting practices that charge exorbitant amounts to those with pre-existing conditions, or charge vastly higher rates to older people with chronic illnesses. Yet until we tackle the root conceptual problem, we will not be able to explain why those regulations are just rather than unjust.

People who don't (and won't) need healthcare ought to contribute to the care others need for the same reason that people who don't have children, or whose children are grown, ought to contribute to the education of the next generation—it's part of providing for the common good. A good society is one that honors the inherent dignity of all persons, no matter what their physical disability. The concepts at the center of healthcare reform need to be solidarity and vulnerability, not risk and its rational transfer.

Sources

Altman, Stuart, and David Shactman. *Power, Politics, and Universal Health Care: The Inside Story of a Century-Long Battle.* Foreword by John Kerry. Amherst, NY: Prometheus Books, 2011.

Cahill, Lisa Sowle. *Theological Bioethics: Participation, Justice, and Change.* Washington, DC: Georgetown University Press, 2005.

Hoffman, Beatrix. *Health Care for Some: Rights and Rationing in the United States Since 1930.* Chicago, IL: University of Chicago Press, 2012.

Rejda, George E., and Michael McNamara. *Principles of Risk Management and Insurance.* 12th ed. Upper Saddle River, NJ: Prentice Hall, 2013.

A Horrific Crime
But Is Execution the Answer?

It is one thing to have an opinion about a moral issue in the abstract. It is another thing to have that opinion tested in a crucible with facts presented by a hard case. My own moral opposition to the death penalty was so tested by the horrific murders in Cheshire, Connecticut, in July 2007.

Steven Hayes and Joshua Komisarjevsky broke into the suburban home of the Petit family in the dead of the night, beat the father senseless with a baseball bat, raped the mother, and terrorized the two daughters, one seventeen years old and the other just eleven. The little girl was also raped. When morning came, the two men forced the mother to withdraw fifteen thousand dollars from the bank, promising to release the family if she complied with their demands. Despite the fact that she managed to alert the authorities, help came too late. She was murdered within an hour of the timestamp marking her appearance on the grainy footage from the bank camera. Most horrible of all was the fate of the two girls. They died of smoke inhalation after the criminals tied them to their beds doused with accelerant and set the house ablaze.

Hayes and Komisarjevsky were tried and convicted of multiple counts of capital felony in separate trials. In November 2010, the jury recommended that Hayes receive the death penalty, which the Court followed. About a year later, a different jury made the same recommendation with respect to Komisarjevsky, which was also followed. Both men were sent to death row in the state of Connecticut, which abolished the death penalty prospectively in 2012. In August 2015, however, the Connecticut Supreme Court declared the death penalty unconstitutional, sparing their lives.

Having gone to graduate school in Connecticut, I followed the case closely. And when the verdicts were announced, I felt nothing but relief. So I struggle to reconcile my response in this case to my moral opposition to the death penalty.

As the saying goes, hard cases make bad law. This case is not representative of the death-row docket. Over forty persons with some degree of mental retardation were executed between 1984 and 2001. Moreover, there is a good deal of evidence suggesting that the practice of capital punishment is racist. The penalty is far more likely to be imposed in the case of a black perpetrator, especially if his victim is white. Finally, as improvements in DNA technology have demonstrated, many innocent persons have spent time on death row. Doubtless some have been executed for a crime they didn't commit.

Nonetheless, hard cases keep ethical reflection honest. They press us to clarify just why we hold the positions we hold. By making us uncomfortable, they also make us think. Here's what this case brought to my mind.

It's not enough to oppose the death penalty. As John Paul II acknowledged in *Evangelium vitae*, we also have to ensure that the appropriate structures are in place to keep dangerous men and women from harming others. Both Hayes and Komisarjevsky committed this crime while on parole. Furthermore, parole board members approved Komisarjevsky's early release without reviewing records that included a judge's description of him as a "cold, calculating predator." Many Catholics, on both the left and the right, emphasize that building a culture of life requires not merely banning abortion but also putting in place social structures that reduce the demand for it. We need to acknowledge that the same goes for capital punishment.

Two traditional goals of punishment are retribution and deterrence. But the evildoing in this case calls both those goals into question. From the perspective of the *lex talionis*, a quick, painless execution would be far too lenient a punishment to achieve retribution. Moreover, once a certain threshold of brutality has been crossed, the death penalty ceases to function as a deterrent: after they had raped and killed the mother, what more did the defendants have to lose? They could only be executed once.

The hard fact is that society cannot impose a condign punishment, or an effective deterrent to these monstrous acts, without in some sense recreating and participating in the brutality of the criminals themselves. And viewed more broadly, that fact suggests how we should think about the death penalty. We need to ask not what it does to the criminals, but what it does to us as a society. The execution is a separate event from the crime. At the moment of execution, a criminal is helpless before the power of the state. We strap him to a gurney and snuff out his life. Can a society engage in this ritual while meaningfully advancing a commitment to the unconditional dignity of every human being?

The best argument in favor of capital punishment is that it irrevocably separates criminals from the society they have betrayed. A quick, painless execution may not serve retribution, but it effectively dispatches evildoers from our midst. Aquinas memorably analogized a criminal to a gangrenous limb that needs to be cut off for the sake of the body politic.

The difficulty with this argument, however, is that it fails to face the terrifying fact that these evildoers *are* part of our society. In fact, Komisarjevsky grew up in a wealthy family and had lived near the victims. What prompted him to go so wrong? Nature or nurture? Was there anything that could have been done to correct his course? Executing Komisarjevsky only allows us to avoid these important questions.

How can people do such things to one another? I finally realized that this case haunts me not because of the problem of capital punishment but because of the problem of evil itself.

Sources

Bedau, Hugo Adam, and Paul G. Cassell, eds. *Debating the Death Penalty: Should America Have Capital Punishment? The Experts on Both Sides Make Their Case.* New York: Oxford University Press, 2004.

Benson, Michael. *Murder in Connecticut: The Shocking Crime That Destroyed a Family and United a Community.* Guilford, CT: Globe Pequot Press, 2008.

Fernandez, Manny, and Alison Leigh Cowan. "When Horror Came to a Connecticut Family." *New York Times*, August 7, 2007.

HBO. *The Cheshire Murders: An HBO Documentary.* 2013. Available at http://www.hbo.com/documentaries/the-cheshire-murders#/.

Otis, Ginger Adam. "First Picture of Baby Boy Born to Doctor 6 Years after His Wife, Daughters Were Murdered." *Daily News*, November 28, 2013. Available at http://www.nydailynews.com/news/national/picture-baby-boy-born-connecticut-doctor-years-wife-daughters-murdered-article-1.1531806.

Pope John Paul II. *Evangelium vitae* (1995).

State of Connecticut v. Santiago, SC 17413 (2015).

Could the Church Have Gotten It Wrong?
Let's Look at the Facts

Reading the *Catechism of the Catholic Church*, one is left with the impression that Catholic moral teaching is comprehensive, definite, and unchanging across the centuries. It is a comforting idea, but not an accurate one. As John Noonan recounts in detail in *A Church That Can and Cannot Change* (2005), the church's moral teaching has evolved in a number of key areas, such as slavery, religious liberty, usury, and the dissolubility of marriage. The changes are significant. As Noonan notes, what was morally permitted (owning another person) became absolutely prohibited; what was endorsed as a moral and political good (burning heretics) came to be seen as a moral and political evil. What was prohibited as intrinsically wrong (lending money at interest) became permissible. And what was seen as impossible (papal dissolution of marriages where one or both of the parties is not baptized) became possible.

What are the ramifications of Noonan's work for moral theology and ecclesiology? Catholics will be slow to grapple with those ramifications, I fear, because doing so will require us to confront three hard existential questions.

First, why did it take us so long to see the truth? According to the Venerable Bede, Pope Gregory the Great (590-604) decided to evangelize England when he came across some exotic white-skinned British boys for sale while browsing in the slave market in Rome. As Noonan notes, "Gregory's heart-felt emotion is not distress at their enslavement by slavetraders, but at their enslavement to the devil." It was not until fourteen hundred years later that the act of enslaving another human being was first declared by the magisterium to be intrinsically evil (by John Paul II in *Veritatis splendor*). The year before John Paul issued that encyclical, he visited the former "house of slaves" on the island of Gorée, Senegal, where he proclaimed, "It is fitting that there be confessed in all truth and humility this sin of man against man, this sin of man against God." Noonan wryly observes, "What this confession did not remark was how recently the sin had been discovered." How could Christians fail for so long to be moved by the pain, suffering, and degradation slavery inflicted on fellow human beings made in the image and likeness of God?

Second, what moral matters might we be wrong about today? To say that enslaving another person is an intrinsic evil is to say that it is always and everywhere objectively morally wrong. Yet, as horrifying as slavery seems to us now, it does not follow that those who failed to condemn it were wicked. In fact, some of them, like Gregory the Great, were saints. Nonetheless, they were trapped by the limitations of their own eras, their judgment impaired by unquestioned assumptions about the morality of certain inherited practices. What does that historical fact imply about us? Can we say for sure that we are not similarly trapped today? Can we say that there are no matters of enduring and grave moral import that have simply escaped our attention? Can we say that we ourselves will not be judged morally blind by our heirs in the faith?

Third, can moral teaching degenerate as well as develop? The notion of development suggests not only change, but also improvement. Doubtless most people will think that the changes in moral teaching that Noonan describes are not only welcome, but long overdue. Who today would doubt that religious liberty is morally preferable to justifying the burning of heretics? Yet depending on where one stands in history, doctrinal change can be for the worse as well as for the better. The church did not start out persecuting, or justifying persecution; rather, she was persecuted herself. Thanks in part to intellectual luminaries such as Augustine and Aquinas, Christian doctrine evolved— or rather devolved—over centuries to justify the use of force against heretics. How do we account for these substantial "wrong turns" our tradition took in its interpretation of the gospel? How do we distinguish legitimate development from potential "wrong turns" in our own time?

In dealing with these three questions we need to avoid both naive trust and hardened cynicism about the church's capacity to perceive moral truth. We must also avoid the temptation to think that all problems of mistaken moral perception are in the past. Pope John Paul II apologized over and over again for sins committed by Catholics—on the watch of other popes. But it never seemed to occur to him that his own—and our own—capacity to perceive moral truths might be analogously limited by cultural and historical blinders. We need to keep searching for the appropriate balance of confidence and humility in the face of the lessons of history. *Lumen gentium*, Vatican II's *Dogmatic Constitution on the Church*, articulates the problem in a nutshell: "The church . . . clasping sinners to her bosom, at once holy and always in need of purification, follows constantly the path of penance and renewal."

Sources

Noonan, John T., Jr. *A Church That Can and Cannot Change*. Notre Dame, IN: University of Notre Dame Press, 2005.
Pope John Paul II. *Veritatis splendor* (1993).
Vatican II. *Lumen gentium* (1995).

Conclusion
Tradition and Transformation

Running throughout the five parts of this book has been a consistent and fundamental theme: Religious traditions do not need to choose, as John Murray Cuddihy provocatively but mistakenly suggested, between assimilating to the broader culture and defiantly maintaining distinct communal boundaries against cultural incursions. They do not need to immerse themselves either in the culture of openness, on the one hand, or in the culture of identity, on the other. There is a third possibility, which I have labeled the culture of engagement, which is reducible to neither of the other two cultures. More specifically, the culture of openness is mistaken in implying that religious traditions should adopt most aspects of the surrounding culture in an unavoidable project of "updating." The culture of identity rightly opposes this sort of uncritical dissolution of a religious tradition into the solvent of the broader culture. At the same time, and unfortunately, the positive strategy proposed by the culture of identity ultimately falls prey to the same problem that it critiques. Defining one's identity over and against the broader culture is ultimately just another way of defining one's identity in terms of the culture—but doing so in a negative manner.

In my view, the many and different points of contact between a religious tradition and the broader culture in which its adherents live their lives can be understood as offering fruitful possibilities for interchange and interaction. In contrast to Cuddihy, who sees the compartmentalization of belief and overlapping social and political identities of modern life as excruciating for traditional religious communities, I propose that it can be energizing and empowering, provided those communities are equipped for the challenges involved. The crisscross of ideas and people provides new material, new concepts, and new patterns of living for the religious tradition to encounter, assess, and incorporate as its leaders and adherents see fit.

A reader might well object: It is one thing to formulate three labels, roughly distinguishing three ways of approach the challenges contemporary culture poses for adherents of religious traditions. It is another thing entirely to provide a sufficiently rich and detailed understanding of the culture of engagement, which this book advocates. Such a reader may complain that I have not in fact provided a sufficient outline of the methodology proper to the culture of engagement, or a clear path for adherents to follow as they confront new cases. My response to this objection is multifaceted: at its core is the claim that there is no comprehensive methodology for either developing a tradition or bringing it into conversation with another tradition. There is no moral "MapQuest" that will get adherents of a tradition from their current position to their future position, because there is no predetermined or predeterminable destination. We can, however, highlight certain skills that are necessary for the tradition's wayfarers, as well as certain signposts that merit deep consideration in plotting their journeys.

Working within the culture of engagement, as I understand it, is doubly demanding. Bringing two or more traditions into conversation with one another requires a deep familiarity and facility with both of them. As Alasdair MacIntyre described the process, it requires something like the skills of a cultural and linguistic translator. Such translators must have a good understanding not merely of the meaning of words and phrases and sentences considered in the abstract; they also need to understand the rich symbolic context adding depth and context to those words. Moreover, as MacIntyre argues, a fully competent speaker of a language has a certain creative, poetic capacity, which is the ability to develop the language; "to go on and to go further" in order to develop the language's vocabulary and conceptual structure in order to address new situations and questions.[1]

MacIntyre writes specifically of moral traditions that train young people to read texts that embody to an exemplary degree the capacity to go on and go further. Yet he would of course acknowledge that a tradition is not only composed of and carried forward by its philosophical and legal treatises, but also by its symbols, stories, and practices. So, for example, to fully understand the values embedded in the American moral and political tradition means knowing what the Statue of Liberty has come to symbolize in our nation's self-understanding as a nation of immigrants. To fully understand Catholic sensibilities about welcoming and protecting unwanted babies requires imaginative attention to liturgical and familial practices around the crèche at Christmas time.

Is there bedrock to a tradition? In other words, can we find some sort of indisputable basic law that supports and structures the entire edifice and is beyond all critique and reformulation? If we mean bedrock of general first principles, akin to the "do good and avoid evil" that Aquinas recognized as the foundation of the natural law, then perhaps.[2] If, however, we mean some sort of clear, detailed, and specific statement of a tradition that is rooted in general first principles but particular enough to be practically useful in the heat of every controversial case,[3] then I don't think so.

Someone might respond that the Constitution is to be treated as the immutable practical foundation of the American tradition of liberal democratic republicanism. Yet a moment's reflection reveals that this response is itself deeply flawed. First, the Constitution is an element of human law, and as such, subject to human change. Additionally, the Constitution has repeatedly been subject to scrutiny. Nineteenth-century American abolitionists criticized the Constitution as a "covenant with death" for endorsing and protecting slavery.[4] Twentieth-century prolife activists critiqued the Supreme Court for having extended constitutional protection to a woman's choice to have an abortion.[5] Neither set of activists rested content with the nation's foundational document or deferred to its duly recognized interpreters. To say that a document is foundational, or that an interpretation is authoritative, does not mean that it is immune from critique or correction on particular, very important issues.

What about the Roman Catholic moral tradition, which some might claim is unchangeable by virtue of its proximity to God's eternal law? Although the tradition may indeed be rooted in a bedrock of indisputable first principles (e.g., "God is love," 1 John 4:8), the Roman Catholic moral tradition has always been in many ways an evolving moral system. The Christian moral tradition began with a dispute about fundamentals—Peter and Paul disagreed about whether Gentiles needed to convert to Judaism before being admitted into Christian fellowship.[6]

Over the centuries, Christian teaching has developed on key moral issues: St. Paul admonished slaves to be subject to their masters *as they would to Christ*;[7] St. Thomas Aquinas considered slavery to be a useful addition to the natural law;[8] and the Jesuits owned slaves in the United States well into the nineteenth century.[9] As the eminent historian John T. Noonan, Jr., has pointed out, owning slaves was not categorically condemned by the Catholic Church until Pope John Paul II did so in 1993.[10] It was not the Roman Catholic Church that took the lead in the movement to abolish slavery in the United States (or worldwide); it was Evangelical Protestantism.

How do adherents of a tradition discern whether a particular issue is a ripe issue for development? Again, there is no clear path of decision. According to MacIntyre, a certain epistemological humility is warranted. He writes:

> It follows that the only rational ways for the adherents of any tradition to approach intellectually, culturally, and linguistically alien rivals is one that allows for the possibility that in one or more areas the other may be rationally superior to it in respect precisely of that in the alien tradition which it cannot as yet comprehend.[11]

MacIntyre's statement holds true in the abstract. He does not, in my view, sufficiently account for the way in which concrete experience may provide assistance in moving beyond this salutary openness to correction on the part of adherents to a tradition. More specifically, MacIntyre's account of communication among competing traditions places great emphasis upon the possibility of untranslatability; he stresses the fact that the key words, ideas, values, or practices of one tradition may be untranslatable into the matrix of another tradition. While untranslatability may be a fact, it is not a fate, particularly in situations where adherents of different traditions live side by side. In such situations, rival languages (and rival traditions) borrow from one another. Children, who pick up languages more easily than adults, not only learn a second language to communicate with their playmates and schoolmates, they also bring useful concepts from that language back home, so to speak. Their own tradition develops from close proximity and experience with other traditions.

This type of development by experience, I think, is the unique contribution that life in the pluralistic context of the United States can contribute to religious traditions, which are all now grappling with the challenges of globalization. Consider, for example, the development of Roman Catholic teaching on religious liberty. That development is tremendously indebted to the experience of Catholics living in America, who found that they did not need an established church in order to flourish. Ordinary American Catholics regularly encountered people of other faiths and found that they were people of good will. John Murray Cuddihy's theory notwithstanding, for many Americans, crisscross was not crucifixion but enrichment.

Aware of this insight, Cuddihy's distant cousin, John Courtney Murray, developed his defense of religious liberty by reflecting in a disciplined way upon the experience of American Catholics. He drew upon this experience to show how Catholic teaching could be developed in a way that was both organic and yet thoroughly innovative. What he did, in a nutshell, was reframe the debate. The older doctrine, which pressed for a religious establishment of Roman Catholicism as ideal, proclaimed that "*error* has no rights." Murray sidestepped that argument by emphasizing that *people* do have rights—even if the religious views they hold are in error. His defense of religious liberty focused on the dignity of the human person—which is reflected in the Latin name of the document from the Second Vatican Council endorsing his views.[12] The American experience did not lead Murray to reject the Catholic tradition, but instead to search its depths for a new way of approaching the matter of church-state relations.

I do not mean to paint a totally rosy picture of the effect of American values upon religious traditions; to do that would come perilously close to the inadequacies of the culture of openness. Let me also emphasize, therefore, that the first part of the twentieth century also offers instances where the Catholic Church was right in resisting a tidal wave of popular moral sentiment. For example, consider the eugenics movement, which actually began in the United States as a tool to improve the fitness of our own population long before it ended in Nazi atrocities.[13] Roman Catholics were among the most adamant opponents of this movement, which included legally sanctioned practices such as compulsory sterilization, forced institutionalization of the "unfit," restrictions on marriages, and quotas on immigration applied to population groups thought to be inferior.[14]

How do we determine, then, whether a development in a particular tradition is sound or not? At the end of his magisterial book, *A Church That Can and Cannot Change*, Noonan offers not a rule but a mnemonic device, recognizing that "in law and morals there is ABLE development.[15] A is for analogy; new cases are decided by reference to older, similar cases.[16] But analogy is never perfect. We also need B— for balance. "Balance refers to the vital business of organic functions necessary to sustain life in a living organism. Like it or not, balance limits logic in any legal or moral system."[17] This criterion has sobering implications: "Like it or not—and today none of us like it—balance once limited the rights of baptized slaves in the Christian community. . . . The organism was thought to need more growth to accommodate such a social upheaval."[18] L is for logic; working out the logical implications of a premise is a key method of development. But not the only method: "Who says A must say B, but may not be allowed to get further in the alphabet if the vital balance of the organism is affected."[19] And E is for experience—"understood broadly to include empathy, identification with the experience of the other."[20]

Noonan says that ABLE encapsulates the "tools of teaching," but does not define either the content or the rule of development in either law or morals.[21] Is there, then, a rule of development? Yes and no. Turning to the Catholic moral tradition, he claims "that development runs by no rule except the rule of faith, which is encapsulated in Jesus's command of the "double love of God and neighbor." Noonan concludes: "Development proceeds directed by this rule. The love of God generates, reinforces, and seals the love of neighbor. What is required is found in the community's experience as it tests what is vital. On the surface, contradictions appear. At the deepest level, the course is clear."[22] I myself think that the double commandment of love of God and love of neighbor can function similarly with regard to the development of the American political and legal tradition—provided that believers remember that the neighbors we are called upon to love may not understand God the same way that we do, or even believe in God at all. Nonetheless, we are still called to love them.

In the sixty or so essays comprising this book, I have attempted to illustrate what stepping into the culture of engagement might look like for an American and a Roman Catholic in the first decades of the third millennium. Using the tools of analogy, balance, logic, and experience, I have tried to work out what love of God and love of neighbor might concretely require here and now—in our time, place, and circumstances. I do not claim to have the decisive insight or the last word. I do hope, however, to have contributed in some positive way to the development, improvement, and flourishing of both traditions in which I have been called and enabled to participate. And I find myself deeply encouraged in this project by Pope Francis, who prods us to move past "engagement" with others coming from different perspectives, in order to "encounter" them as persons beloved to Jesus Christ.

Notes

1. Alasdair MacIntyre, *Whose Justice? Which Rationality?* (Notre Dame, IN: University of Notre Dame Press, 1988), 382.

2. Thomas Aquinas, *Summa Theologiae*, I-II, q. 94.

3. See Daniel Mark Nelson, *The Priority of Prudence: Virtue and Natural Law in Thomas Aquinas and the Implications for Modern Ethics* (University Park, PA: The University of Pennsylvania Press, 1992). There, Nelson argues that the precepts of the natural law are too general to be helpful in specific situations. As such, he argues that the natural law always requires the virtue of prudence by which a person utilizes practical reason to discern what the natural law requires in a particular situation.

4. See Paul Finkelman, "Garrison's Constitution: The Covenant with Death and How It Was Made," *Prologue Magazine* 32:4 (2000), available at http://www.archives.gov/publications/prologue/2000/winter/garrisons-constitution-1.html.

5. *Roe v. Wade*, 410 U.S. 113 (1973).

6. The debate about whether Gentile converts to Christianity needed to convert to Judaism took place at the "Council of Jerusalem." That council is often said to be discussed in Acts 15 and Galatians 2, although there is some scholarly dispute about whether the two passages refer to the same event.

7. See, e.g., Ephesians 6:5: "Slaves, obey your earthly masters with fear and trembling, in singleness of heart, as you obey Christ. . . ."

8. Thomas Aquinas, *Summa Theologica*, I-II, q. 94, art. 5, rep. ob. 3: "In this sense, 'the possession of all things in common and universal freedom' are said to be of the natural law, because, to wit, the distinction of possessions and slavery were not brought in by nature, but devised by human reason for the benefit of human life. Accordingly the law of nature was not changed in this respect, except by addition."

9. See Thomas Murphy, *Jesuit Slaveholding in Maryland, 1717–1838* (New York: Routledge, 2001).

10. Pope John Paul II, *Veritatis splendor* (1993); John T. Noonan, Jr., *A Church That Can and Cannot Change* (Notre Dame, IN: University of Notre Dame Press, 2005), 122.

11. MacIntyre, *Whose Justice?*, 388.

12. John Courtney Murray, *We Hold These Truths: Catholic Reflections on the American Proposition* (Lanham, MD: Rowman and Littlefield, 2005); Vatican II, *Dignitatis humanae* (1965).

13. See, e.g., Paul A. Lombardo, *A Century of Eugenics in America: From the Indiana Experiment to the Human Genome Era* (Bloomington, IN: Indiana University Press, 2011); Edwin Black, *War against the Weak: Eugenics and America's Campaign to Create a Master Race*, exp. ed. (New York: Dialog Press, 2012).

14. Sharon M. Leen, *An Image of God: The Catholic Struggle with Eugenics* (Chicago, IL: University of Chicago Press, 2013).

15. Noonan, *A Church That Can and Cannot Change*, 219.

16. Ibid.

17. Ibid.

18. Ibid.

19. Ibid., 220.

20. Ibid.

21. Ibid.

22. Ibid., 222.

Suggestions for Further Reading

Part 1: Law As a Teacher

Amaya, Amalia, and Ho Hock Lai, eds. *Law, Virtue and Justice*. Portland, OR: Hart Publishing, 2013.

Aquinas, Thomas. *Treatise on Law*, translated by Richard J. Regan. Indianapolis, IN: Hackett Publishing Company, 2000. See especially I–II, qq. 90–2, 95–7.

Farrelly, Colin, and Lawrence Solum. *Virtue Jurisprudence*. New York: Palgrave Macmillan, 2008.

Kaveny, Cathleen. *Law's Virtue: Fostering Autonomy and Solidarity in American Society*. Washington, DC: Georgetown University Press, 2012.

Wacks, Raymond. *Understanding Jurisprudence: An Introduction to Legal Theory*. 3rd ed. New York: Oxford University Press, 2012. http://dx.doi.org /10.1093/he/9780199608263.001.0001.

1. Rules Are Not Enough: Why Judges Need Empathy

Brooks, Peter, and Paul Gewirtz. *Law's Stories: Narrative and Rhetoric in the Law*. New Haven, CT: Yale University Press, 1996.

Dorf, Michael C. *Constitutional Law Stories*. 2nd ed. New York: Thomson Reuters/Foundation Press, 2009.

Dubber, Markus Dirk. *The Sense of Justice: Empathy in Law and Punishment*. New York: New York University Press, 2006.

Lai, Ho Hock. "Virtuous Deliberation on the Criminal Verdict." In *Law, Virtue and Justice*, edited by Amalia Amaya and Ho Hock Lai, 241–63. Portland, OR: Hart Publishing, 2013.

Modak-Truran, Mark C. "Corrective Justice and the Revival of Judicial Virtue." *Yale Journal of Law & the Humanities* 12, no. 2 (2000): 249–98.

Richards, Diana A. "Judicial Virtues in the XXIst Century: Awareness, Empathy, and Respect for Plurality." In *Philosophical Challenges of Plurality in a Globalized World*, edited by David Diaz-Soto, Delia Manaanero, and Bianca Thoilliez. Cambridge, UK: Cambridge Scholars Publishing, 2014.

Solum, Lawrence B. "Virtue Jurisprudence: A Virtue-Centered Theory of Judging." *Metaphilosophy* 34, no. 1-2 (2003): 178–213. http://dx.doi.org/10.1111 /1467-9973.00268.

2. Teacher or Remedy: What Is the Law for?

Brinig, Margaret F. *Family, Law, and Community: Supporting the Covenant*. Chicago, IL: University of Chicago Press, 2010. http://dx.doi.org/10.7208 /chicago/9780226075020.001.0001.

Caroben, June, and Naomi Cahn. *Marriage Markets: How Inequality Is Remaking the American Family*. New York: Oxford University Press, 2014.

Cherlin, Andrew J. *The Marriage-Go-Round: The State of Marriage and the Family in America Today*. New York: Vintage Books, 2010.

Devlin, Patrick. *The Enforcement of Morals*. New York: Oxford University Press, 1996.

Finnis, John. *Aquinas: Moral, Political, and Legal Theory*. Oxford: Oxford University Press, 1998. See especially VIII.I., "Law as Primary Means of Co-ordinating Civil Society," 255–58.

Fuller, Lon L. *The Morality of Law*. Rev. ed. New Haven, CT: Yale University Press, 1969.

George, Robert P. *Making Men Moral: Civil Liberties and Public Morality*. New York: Oxford University Press, 1995. http://dx.doi.org/10.1093/acprof:oso /9780198260240.001.0001.

Hart, H.L.A. *Law, Liberty, and Morality*. Stanford, CA: Stanford University Press, 1963.

Himma, Kenneth Einar. "Philosophy of Law." Internet Encyclopedia of Philosophy. n.d. Available at http://www.iep.utm.edu/law-phil/.

Lind, Goran. *Common Law Marriage: A Legal Institution for Cohabitation*. New York: Oxford University Press, 2008. http://dx.doi.org/10.1093/acprof: oso/9780195366815.001.0001.

Marmor, Andrei. *Philosophy of Law (Princeton Foundations of Contemporary Philosophy)*. Princeton, NJ: Princeton University Press, 2011.

Pleck, Elizabeth H. *Not Just Roommates: Cohabitation after the Sexual Revolution*. Chicago, IL: University of Chicago Press, 2012. http://dx.doi.org /10.7208/chicago/9780226671055.001.0001.

Wacks, Raymond. *The Philosophy of Law: A Very Short Introduction*. New York: Oxford University Press, 2006. http://dx.doi.org/10.1093/actrade /9780192806918.001.0001.

3. Letter versus Spirit: Why the Constitution Needs Interpreting

Amar, Akhil Reed. *America's Unwritten Constitution: The Precedents and Principles We Live By*. New York: Basic Books, 2012.

Balkin, Jack M. *Living Originalism*. Cambridge, MA: Belknap Press of Harvard University Press, 2011. http://dx.doi.org/10.4159/harvard.9780674063037.

Barber, Sotirios A., and James E. Fleming. *Constitutional Interpretation: The Basic Questions*. New York: Oxford University Press, 2007. http://dx.doi .org/10.1093/acprof:oso/9780195328578.001.0001.

Epps, Garret. "Constitutional Myth #1: The Right Is 'Originalist,' Everyone Else Is 'Idiotic.'" *Atlantic*, May 25, 2011. Available at http://www.theatlantic.com /national/archive/2011/05/constitutional-myth-1-the-right-is-originalist -everyone-else-is-idiotic/239291/.

Lepore, Jill. "The Commandments: The Constitution and Its Worshippers." *The New Yorker*, January 2011.

Levy, Leonard W. *Original Intent and the Framers' Constitution*. New York: Macmillan, 1988.

Perry, Michael J. *Constitutional Rights, Moral Controversy, and the Supreme Court*. New York: Cambridge University Press, 2009.

Tribe, Laurence, and Joshua Matz. *Uncertain Justice: The Roberts Court and the Constitution*. New York: Henry Holt, 2014.

4. Remember the Mormons: Thinking about the Nature of Marriage

Bottum, Joseph. "Engagement or Retreat? Catholicism & Same-Sex Marriage." *Commonweal*, June 13, 2014.

Bottum, Joseph. "The Things We Share: A Catholic's Case for Same-Sex Marriage." *Commonweal*, September 13, 2013.

Douthat, Ross. "Engagement or Retreat? Catholicism & Same Sex Marriage." *Commonweal*, June 13, 2014.

Editors, *Commonweal*. "The Future of Marriage." *Commonweal*, November 22, 1991.

Elshtain, Jean Bethke. "Against Gay Marriage II: Accepting Limits." *Commonweal*, November 22, 1991.

Girgis, Sherif, Ryan T. Anderson, and Robert P. George. *What Is Marriage? Man and Woman: A Defense*. New York: Encounter Books, 2012.

Gordon, Sarah Barringer. *The Mormon Question: Polygamy and Constitutional Conflict in Nineteenth-Century America*. Chapel Hill, NC: University of North Carolina Press, 2002.

Hartinger, Brent. "A Case for Gay Marriage: In Support of Loving & Monogamous Relationships," *Commonweal*, November 22, 1991.

Laycock, Douglas, Jr., Anthony Picarello, and Robin Fretwell Wilson. *Same-Sex Marriage and Religious Liberty: Emerging Conflicts*. Lanham, MD: Rowman & Littlefield, 2008.

Manson, Jamie L. "Engagement or Retreat? Catholicism & Same-Sex Marriage." *Commonweal*, June 13, 2014.

O'Brien, Dennis. "Against Gay Marriage I: What Heterosexuality Means." *Commonweal*, November 22, 1991.

Pierceson, Jason. *Same-Sex Marriage in the United States: The Road to the Supreme Court and Beyond*. Lanham, MD: Rowman & Littlefield, 2013.

United States Conference of Catholic Bishops. "Same-Sex Unions." 2014. Available at http://www.usccb.org/issues-and-action/human-life-and-dignity/same-sex-unions/.

5. Regulating Abortion: What Did the Roberts Court Do?

Dyer, Justin Buckley. *Slavery, Abortion, and the Politics of Constitutional Meaning*. New York: Cambridge University Press, 2014.

Griffith, Marie. "Roe v. Wade at 40: An Interview with Legal Scholar and Theologian Cathleen Kaveny." *Religion & Politics*. January 23, 2013. Available at http://religionandpolitics.org/2013/01/23/roe-v-wade-at-40-an-interview-with-legal-scholar-and-theologian-cathleen-kaveny/.

Halfmann, Drew. *Doctors and Demonstrators: How Political Institutions*

Shape Abortion Law in the United States, Britain, and Canada. Chicago, IL: University of Chicago Press, 2011. http://dx.doi.org/10.7208/chicago /9780226313443.001.0001.

Hull, N.E.H., and Peter Charles, eds. *Roe v. Wade: The Abortion Rights Controversy in American History.* 2nd ed. Lawrence, KS: University Press of Kansas, 2010.

United States Conference of Catholic Bishops. "Abortion" (2014). Available at http://www.usccb.org/issues-and-action/human-life-and-dignity/abortion /index.cfm.

West, Robin, Justin Murray, and Meredith Esser. *In Search of Common Ground on Abortion: From Culture War to Reproductive Justice.* Burlington, VT: Ashgate, 2014.

6. Caught in the Gap: What Hostility to Health-Care Reform Has Wrought

Catholic Health Association of the United States. "Affordable Care Act." Catholic Health Association of the United States. 2014. Available at https://www .chausa.org/affordable-care-act/overview.

Davidson, Stephen. *A New Era in U.S. Health Care: Critical Next Steps under the Affordable Care Act.* Stanford, CA: Stanford University Press, 2013.

Emanuel, Ezekiel J. *Reinventing American Health Care: How the Affordable Care Act Will Improve Our Terribly Complex, Blatantly Unjust, Outrageously Expensive, Grossly Inefficient, Error Prone System.* New York: PublicAffairs (Perseus Books), 2014.

Hoffman, Beatrix. *Health Care for Some: Rights and Rationing in the United States since 1930.* Chicago, IL: University of Chicago Press, 2012. http:// dx.doi.org/10.7208/chicago/9780226348056.001.0001.

McDonough, Mary J. *Can a Health Care Market Be Moral? A Catholic Vision.* Washington, DC: Georgetown University Press, 2007.

Roy, Avik. *How Medicaid Fails the Poor (Encounter Broadside No. 36).* New York: Encounter Books, 2013.

Selker, Harry P., and June S. Wasser, eds. *The Affordable Care Act as a National Experiment: Health Policy Innovations and Lessons.* New York: Springer, 2014. http://dx.doi.org/10.1007/978-1-4614-8351-9.

United States Conference of Catholic Bishops. "Health Care Reform." 2015. Available at http://www.usccb.org/issues-and-action/human-life-and-dignity /health-care/.

United States Conference of Catholic Bishops. "The USCCB and Health Care Reform." June 2010. Available at http://www.usccb.org/issues-and-action /human-life-and-dignity/health-care/.

7. "Peaceful and Private": Montana's Supreme Court Rules on Assisted Suicide

Catholic Health Association of the United States. "Physician-Assisted Suicide: CHA Amicus Brief." *Health Progress (Saint Louis, Mo.)* 78, no. 3 (1997): 35–47.

Gloth, F. Michael. "Physician-Assisted Suicide: The Wrong Approach to End of Life Care." United States Conference of Catholic Bishops, n.d. Available at http://www.usccb.org/about/pro-life-activities/respect-life-program/physici anassisted-suicide-the-wrong-approach-to-end-of-life-care.cfm.

Gorsuch, Neil M. *The Future of Assisted Suicide and Euthanasia*. Princeton, NJ: Princeton University Press, 2006.

Hehir, Bryan J. "Physician-Assisted Suicide: Political, Pastoral Challenges Ahead." *Health Progress (Saint Louis, Mo.)* 95, no. 1 (2014): 7–10.

Jackson, Emily, and John Keown. *Debating Euthanasia*. Portland, OR: Hart Publishing, 2012.

New York State Task Force on Life and the Law. *When Death Is Sought: Assisted Suicide and Euthanasia in the Medical Context*. New York: New York State Task Force on Life and the Law, 1994.

Pope John Paul II, *Evangelium vitae* (1995).

United States Conference of Catholic Bishops. "Assisted Suicide." United States Conference of Catholic Bishops, n.d. Available at http://www.usccb.org /issues-and-action/human-life-and-dignity/assisted-suicide/.

8. More Than a Refuge: Why Immigration Officials Should Steer Clear of Churches

Bau, Ignatius. *This Ground Is Holy: Church Sanctuary and Central American Refugees*. Mahwah, NJ: Paulist Press, 1985.

Rabben, Linda. *Give Refuge to the Stranger: The Past, Present, and Future of Sanctuary*. Walnut Creek, CA: Left Coast Press, 2011.

Rose, Ananda. *Showdown in the Sonoran Desert: Religion, Law, and the Immigration Controversy*. New York: Oxford University Press, 2014.

United States Conference of Catholic Bishops. "Immigration," n.d. Available at http://www.usccb.org/issues-and-action/human-life-and-dignity /immigration/.

Wild, Kara L. "The New Sanctuary Movement: When Moral Mission Means Breaking the Law, and the Consequences for Churches and Illegal Immigrants." Selected Works. 2009. Available at http://works.bepress.com/kara_wild/1/.

9. Justice or Vengeance: Is the Death Penalty Cruel and Unusual?

Bedau, Hugo Adam, and Paul G. Cassell. *Debating the Death Penalty: Should America Have Capital Punishment? The Experts on Both Sides Make Their Case*. New York: Oxford University Press, 2005.

Brugger, E. *Christian. Capital Punishment and Roman Catholic Moral Tradition*. 2nd ed. Notre Dame, Indiana: University of Notre Dame Press, 2014.

Holland, Joe, and D. Michael McCarron. *Beyond the Death Penalty: The Development in Catholic Social Teaching*. Charleston, SC: BookSurge, 2007.

Hopcke, Robert H. *Catholics and the Death Penalty: Six Things Catholics Can Do to End Capital Punishment*. Cincinnati, OH: St. Anthony Messenger Press, 2004.

Mandery, Evan J. *A Wild Justice: The Death and Resurrection of Capital Punishment in America*. New York: W.W. Norton & Co, 2013.

Martino, Renato Raffaele. "Death Penalty Is Cruel and Unnecessary." *L'Osservatore Romano*, February 24, 1999, 2–3.

Prejean, Helen. *Dead Man Walking: The Eyewitness Account of the Death Penalty That Sparked a National Debate*. New York: Random House, 1993.

Sarat, Austin. *Gruesome Spectacles: Botched Executions and America's Death Penalty*. Stanford, CA: Stanford Law Books, 2014.

Schieber, Vicki, Trudy D. Conway, and David Matzko McCarthy, eds. *Where Justice and Mercy Meet: Catholic Opposition to the Death Penalty*. Collegeville, MN: Liturgical Press, 2013.

United States Conference of Catholic Bishops. "Death Penalty / Capital Punishment." 2014. Available at http://www.usccb.org/issues-and-action/human-life-and-dignity/death-penalty-capital-punishment/.

10. Undue Process: The Evisceration of Habeas Corpus

Duker, William F. *A Constitutional History of Habeas Corpus (Contributions in Legal Studies)*. Westport, CT: Greenwood Press, 1980.

Farrell, Brian. "The Rights of Detainees: Prisoners at Guantanamo Are Entitled to Habeas Corpus." *America*, April 16, 2007.

Gregory, Anthony. *The Power of Habeas Corpus in America: From the King's Prerogative to the War on Terror*. New York: Cambridge University Press, 2013. http://dx.doi.org/10.1017/CBO9781139567640.

Halliday, Paul D. *Habeas Corpus: From England to Empire*. Cambridge, MA: Belknap Press of Harvard University Press, 2012.

King, Nancy J., and Joseph L. Hoffmann. *Habeas for the Twenty-First Century: Uses, Abuses, and the Future of the Great Writ*. Chicago, IL: University of Chicago Press, 2011. http://dx.doi.org/10.7208/chicago/9780226436968.001.0001.

Sadowski, Dennis. "Religious, Rights Groups Applaud Supreme Court in Habeas Corpus Case." Catholic News Service. June 16, 2008. Available at http://www.catholicnews.com/data/stories/cns/0803184.htm.

11. Bad Evidence: Not Only Is Torture Immoral, It Doesn't Work

Argon, Kemal. "What Can the Salem Witch Museum Teach American Muslims?" *Huffington Post*. June 26, 2012. Available at http://www.huffingtonpost.com/kemal-argon/what-can-the-salem-witch-_b_1602909.html.

Cavanaugh, William T. *Torture and Eucharist*. Malden, MA: Blackwell Publishing, 1998.

Ginbar, Yuval. *Why Not Torture Terrorists? Moral, Practical, and Legal Aspects of the Justification for Torture*. New York: Oxford University Press, 2010.

McCoy, Alfred W. *Torture and Impunity: The U.S. Doctrine of Coercive Interrogation*. Madison, WI: University of Wisconsin Press, 2012.

Scarry, Elaine. *The Body in Pain: The Making and Unmaking of the World*. New York: Oxford University Press, 1985.

12. Perverted Logic: Behind the Bush Administration's "Torture Memo"

Goldsmith, Jack. *The Terror Presidency: Law and Judgment inside the Bush Administration*. New York: W. W. Norton & Company, 2009. See especially Chapter 5: "Torture and the Dilemmas of Presidential Lawyering"; and Chapter 6: "The Terror Presidency."

Levinson, Sanford. *Torture: A Collection*. New York: Oxford University Press, 2004.

United States Conference of Catholic Bishops. "Human Rights / Torture." 2014. Available at http://www.usccb.org/issues-and-action/human-life-and -dignity/torture/.

13. Regret Is Not Enough: Why the President Should Read Paul Ramsey

Brooks, David. "Obama, Gospel and Verse." *New York Times*, April 26, 2006.

Carnahan, Kevin. *Reinhold Niebuhr and Paul Ramsey: Idealist and Pragmatic Christians on Politics, Philosophy, Religion, and War*. Lanham, MD: Lexington Books, 2010.

Niebuhr, Reinhold. *The Children of Light and the Children of Darkness: A Vindication of Democracy and a Critique of Its Traditional Defense*. Chicago, IL: University of Chicago Press, 2011. http://dx.doi.org/10.7208/chicago /9780226584010.001.0001.

Niebuhr, Reinhold. *Moral Man and Immoral Society: A Study in Ethics and Politics*. 2nd ed. Foreword by Cornel West. Louisville, KY: Westminster John Knox Press, 2013.

Ramsey, Paul. *Basic Christian Ethics. Louisville, KY*. Westminster: John Knox Press, 1993.

Ramsey, Paul. *The Just War: Force and Political Responsibility*. Lanham, MD: Rowman & Littlefield, 2002.

Ramsey, Paul. *War and the Christian Conscience: How Shall Modern War Be Conducted Justly?* Durham, NC: Duke University Press, 1961.

Part 2: Religious Liberty and Its Limits

Berg, Thomas C., ed. *The Free Exercise of Religion Clause: The First Amendment (Bill of Rights Series)*. Amherst, NY: Prometheus Books, 2007.

Cookson, Catharine. *Regulating Religion: The Courts and the Free Exercise Clause*. New York: Oxford University Press, 2001. See especially Chapter 6: "A Critique of the Court's Free Exercise Clause Jurisprudence in the U.S. Supreme Court Case of *Employment Division v. Smith*," 118–148.

Corbett, Michael, Julia Corbett-Hemeyer, and J. Matthew Wilson. *Politics and Religion in the United States*, 2nd ed. New York: Routledge, 2014. See especially Chapter 6: "The Free Exercise Clause," 150–77.

Evans, Bette Novit. *Interpreting the Free Exercise of Religion: The Constitution and American Pluralism*. Chapel Hill, NC: University of North Carolina Press, 1997.

Greenawalt, Kent. *Free Exercise and Fairness*. Vol. 1 of *Religion and the Constitution*. Princeton, NJ: Princeton University Press, 2009.

Hammond, Phillip E. *With Liberty for All: Freedom of Religion in the United States*. Louisville, KY: Westminster John Knox Press, 1998.

Laycock, Douglas. The Free Exercise Clause. Vol. 2 of *Religious Liberty*. Grand Rapids, MI: Wm. B. Eerdmans, 2011.

Regan, Richard J. *The American Constitution and Religion*. Washington, DC: The Catholic University of America Press, 2013.

Second Vatican Council. *Dignitatis humanae* (1965).

Smith, Steven D. *The Rise and Decline of American Religious Freedom*. Cambridge, MA: Harvard University Press, 2014. http://dx.doi.org/10.4159/9780674730137.

United States Conference of Catholic Bishops. "Religious Liberty." United States Conference of Catholic Bishops. 2014. Available at http://www.usccb.org/issues-and-action/religious-liberty/index.cfm.

14. The Right to Refuse: How Broad Should Conscience Protections Be?

Buttiglione, Rocco. "Comment: Freedom of Conscience and Religion as Fundamental Human Rights: A Commentary." In *Catholic Social Doctrine and Human Rights: The Proceedings of the 15th Plenary Session*, edited by Roland Minnerath, Ombretta Fumagalli Carulli, and Vittorio Possenti, 317–23. Vatican: Pontifical Academy of Social Sciences, 2010.

Carulli, Ombretta Fumagalli. "Freedom of Conscience and Religion as Fundamental Human Rights: Their Importance for Interreligious Dialogue." In *Catholic Social Doctrine and Human Rights: The Proceedings of the 15th Plenary Session*, edited by Roland Minnerath, Ombretta Fumagalli Carulli, Vittorio Possenti, 278–316. Vatican: Pontifical Academy of Social Sciences, 2010.

Nelson, William A., and Cedric K. Dark. "Evaluating Claims of Conscience." In *Managing Healthcare Ethically: An Executive's Guide, Second Edition (ACHE Management)*, edited by William A. Nelson and Paul B. Hoffman, 99–102. Chicago, IL: Health Administration Press, 2010.

Rogers, Alan. *The Child Cases: How America's Religious Exemption Laws Harm Children*. Amherst, MA: University of Massachusetts Press, 2014.

United States Conference of Catholic Bishops. "Current Federal Laws Protecting Conscience Rights." January 2015. Available at http://webcache.google usercontent.com/search?q=cache:HTDLRbJEj70J:www.usccb.org/issues-and -action/religious-liberty/conscience-protection/upload/Federal-Conscience -Laws.pdf+&cd=2&hl=en&ct=clnk&gl=us.

U.S. Department of Health & Human Services. "Fact Sheet—Your Rights under the Federal Health Care Provider Conscience Protection Laws." U.S. Department of Health & Human Services. May 2012. Available at June 2, 2014. http://webcache.googleusercontent.com/search?q =cache:Cs843z2VSzoJ:www.hhs.gov/ocr/civilrights/provider_conscience _factsheet.pdf+&cd=1&hl=en&ct=clnk&gl=us.

Watt, Helen. *Cooperation, Complicity & Conscience: Problems in Healthcare, Science, Law and Public Policy*. Oxford, UK: The Linacre Centre, 2006.

15. The Bishops and Religious Liberty: Are Catholics Becoming a Sect?

Allhoff, Fritz, and Mark Hall, eds. *The Affordable Care Act Decision: Philosophical and Legal Implications.* New York: Routledge, 2014. See especially Flanigan, Jessica. "Employers' Rights and the Affordable Care Act," 150–64; Affolter, Jacob. "Moral Pluralism and Federal Authority," 165–178; and Lemmons, R. and Mary Hayden. "The Affordable Care Act and Religious Liberty: Principles of Adjudication," 179–92.

Aquinas, Thomas. *Treatise on Law,* edited by Richard J. Regan. Indianapolis, IN: Hackett Publishing Company, 2000. See especially I–II, qq. 90–92, 95–97.

Augustine. *On Free Choice of the Will,* edited by Anna S. Benjamin and L.H. Hackstaff. Translated by Thomas Williams. Indianapolis, Indiana: Hackett Publishing Company, 1993. See especially Augustine's consideration of unjust law in Book One, 8.

Bevans, Stephen B., and Jeffrey Gros. *Evangelization and Religious Freedom: Ad gentes, Dignitatis Humanae.* Mahwah, NJ: Paulist Press, 2009.

Davies, Michael. *The Second Vatican Council and Religious Liberty.* Charlotte, NC: Neumann Press, 1992.

Glendon, Mary Ann. *Rights Talk: The Impoverishment of Political Discourse.* New York: Free Press, 1991.

King, Jr. Martin Luther. "Letter from a Birmingham Jail." In *I Have a Dream: Writings and Speeches That Changed the World,* edited by James M. Washington, 83–100. New York: HarperOne, 2003. See especially King's discussion of just and unjust laws, 88–90.

16. Is the Government "Defining Religion"? The Bishops' Case against the Mandate

Appleby, R. "Scott. "Pluralism: Notes on the American Catholic Experience." In *Gods in America: Religious Pluralism in the United States,* edited by Charles L. Cohen and Ronald L. Numbers, 125–40. New York: Oxford University Press, 2013. http://dx.doi.org/10.1093/acprof:oso/9780199931903.003.0005.

Benestad, J. Brian. *Church, State, and Society: An Introduction to Catholic Social Doctrine.* Washington, DC: The Catholic University of America Press, 2011.

Issel, William. *Church and State in the City: Catholics and Politics in Twentieth-Century San Francisco (Urban Life, Landscape and Policy).* Philadelphia, PA: Temple University Press, 2013.

Murray, John Courtney. *Religious Liberty: Catholic Struggles with Pluralism,* edited by J. Leon Hooper. Louisville, KY: Westminster John Knox Press, 1993.

Olsen, Glenn W. *On the Road to Emmaus: The Catholic Dialogue with America and Modernity.* Washington, DC: The Catholic University of America Press, 2012.

Rhonheimer, Martin. *The Common Good of Constitutional Democracy: Essays in Political Philosophy and on Catholic Social Teaching.* Trans. William F. Murphy. Washington, DC: The Catholic University of America Press, 2013.

Steinfels, Margaret O'Brien. *American Catholics and Civic Engagement: A Distinctive Voice*. Vol. 1 of *American Catholics in the Public Square*. Lanham, MD: Rowman & Littlefield, 2004.

Steinfels, Margaret O'Brien, ed. *American Catholics, American Culture: Tradition and Resistance*. Vol. 2 of *American Catholics in the Public Square*. Lanham, MD: Rowman & Littlefield, 2004.

Winters, Michael Sean. "Catholic Health Association Says It Can Live with HHS Mandate." *National Catholic Reporter*, July 9, 2013. Available at http://ncronline.org/blogs/distinctly-catholic/breaking-cha-can-live-hhs-mandate.

Yamane, David A. *The Catholic Church in State Politics: Negotiating Prophetic Demands and Political Realities*. Lanham, MD:Rowman & Littlefield, 2005.

17. Defining Exemptions Does Not Equal Defining Religion: A Category Mistake

Ogilvie, M.H. *Religious Institutions and the Law in Canada (Essentials of Canadian Law)*. Toronto, ON: Irwin Law, 2010.

Serritella, James A., Thomas C. Berg, W. Cole Durham, Jr., Edward McGlynn Gaffney, and Craig B. Mousin, eds. *Religious Organizations in the United States: A Study of Identity, Liberty, and the Law*. Durham, NC: Carolina Academic Press: 2006.

Tracey, Paul, Nelson Phillips, and Michael Lounsbury. *Religion and Organization Theory (Research in the Sociology of Organizations)*. Cambridge, MA: Emerald Group Publishing, 2014.

Winters, Michael Sean. "Contra Kaveny." *National Catholic Reporter*, January 14, 2013. Available at http://ncronline.org/blogs/distinctly-catholic/contra-kaveny.

18. An Evolving Accommodation: Religious Minorities and the Common Good

Banchoff, Thomas, ed. *Democracy and the New Religious Pluralism*. New York: Oxford University Press, 2007. http://dx.doi.org/10.1093/acprof:oso/9780195307221.001.0001.

Kozinski, Thaddeus J. *The Political Problem of Religious Pluralism: And Why Philosophers Can't Solve It*. Lanham, MD: Lexington Books, 2010.

Lippy, Charles H. "From Consensus to Struggle: Pluralism and the Body Politic in Contemporary America." In *Gods in America: Religious Pluralism in the United States*, edited by Charles L. Cohen and Ronald L. Numbers, 297–319. New York: Oxford University Press, 2013. http://dx.doi.org/10.1093/acprof:oso/9780199931903.003.0013.

McGraw, Barbara A., and Jo Renee Formicola, eds. *Taking Religious Pluralism Seriously: Spiritual Politics on America's Sacred Ground*. Waco, TX: Baylor University Press, 2005.

Monsma, Stephen V. *Pluralism and Freedom: Faith-Based Organizations in a Democratic Society*. Lanham, MD: Roman & Littlefield, 2013.

Mookherjee, Monica. *Democracy, Religious Pluralism and the Liberal Dilemma of Accommodation (Studies in Global Justice)*. New York: Springer, 2012.

Peach, Lucinda. *Legislating Morality: Pluralism and Religious Identity in Lawmaking*. New York: Oxford University Press, 2002. http://dx.doi.org/10.1093/019514371X.001.0001.

Roof, Wade Clark, ed. *Religious Pluralism and Civil Society (The ANNALS of the American Academy of Political and Social Science Series)*. Thousand Oaks, CA: Sage Publications, 2007.

Volokh, Eugene. *Sebelius v. Hobby Lobby: Corporate Rights and Religious Liberties*. Washington, DC: Cato Institute, 2014. Kindle edition.

19. *Employment Division v. Smith*: The Eye of the Storm

Banka, Jeana. *Employment Division of the Department of Human Resources of Oregon v. Smith: Case Brief (Court Case Briefs)*. Washington, DC: Washington Book Publishers, 2014.

Echo-Hawk, Walter R. *In The Courts of the Conqueror: The 10 Worst Indian Law Cases Ever Decided*. Golden, CO: Fulcrum Publishing, 2010. See especially Chapter 11: "*Employment Division V. Smith*: Taking the Religion," 273–324.

Long, Carolyn N. *Religious Freedom and Indian Rights: The Case of* Oregon v. Smith. Lawrence, KS: University Press of Kansas: 2000.

Urofsky, Melvin I. *The Public Debate over Controversial Supreme Court Decisions*. Thousand Oaks, CA: CQ Press, 2005.

20. *Smith*, RFRA, and the Bishops' Claims: Neutral Laws of General Applicability?

Berg, Thomas C. *The State and Religion in a Nutshell*. St. Paul MN: West Group, 2004. See especially Chapter 3, C.2: "Federal Legislation: RFRA and RLUIPA," 132–37.

DeGirolami, Marc O. *The Tragedy of Religious Freedom*. Cambridge, MA: Harvard University Press, 2013. http://dx.doi.org/10.4159/harvard.9780674074118.

Federal Register (Vol. 73, No. 245, 78072–78101). "Ensuring That Department of Health and Human Services Funds Do Not Support Coercive or Discriminatory Policies or Practices in Violation of Federal Law." Available at http://webcache.googleusercontent.com/search?q=cache:Dw0gntBi8ekJ:www.gpo.gov/fdsys/pkg/FR-2008-12-19/html/E8-30134.htm+&cd=1&hl=en&ct=clnk&gl=us.

Lee, Francis Graham. *Church-State Relations*. Westport, CT: Greenwood Press, 2002. See especially Chapter 8: "Congress and Free Exercise: The Religious Freedom Restoration Act," 185–216.

Sullivan, Winnifred Fallers. *The Impossibility of Religious Freedom*. Princeton, NJ: Princeton University Press, 2007.

United States Conference of Catholic Bishops. "Why We Need the Health Care Conscience Rights Act." September 18, 2013. Available at http://webcache

.googleusercontent.com/search?q=cache:KqvCy-XgA1MJ:www.usccb.org
/issues-and-action/religious-liberty/conscience-protection/upload/why-we
-need-the-hccra-sept2013.pdf+&cd=1&hl=en&ct=clnk&gl=us.

21. The Key Supreme Court Case for the Mandate: *U.S. v. Lee*

Berg, Thomas C. *The State and Religion in a Nutshell*. St. Paul MN: West Group,
  1998. See especially Chapter 3, B.3.b.: "Compelling Interest and Least Restrictive Means," 106–11; and 4: "The End of Compelling Accommodations?
  Employment Division v. Smith," 112–13.
Ferrara, Peter J. "Social Security and Taxes." In *The Amish and the State*, edited
  by Donald B. Kraybill and Martin E. Marty, 125–43. Baltimore, MD: The
  Johns Hopkins University Press, 2003.
Guinn, David E. *Faith on Trial: Communities of Faith, the First Amendment,
  and the Theory of Deep Diversity*. Lanham, MD: Lexington Books, 2006. See
  especially Chapter 5: "Deep Diversity and Religious Freedom," 117–35.
Kraybill, Donald B., Karen M. Johnson-Weiner, and Steven M. Nolt. *The Amish*.
  Baltimore, MD: The Johns Hopkins University Press, 2013. See especially
  Chapter 16: "Business," pp. 291–311.

22. Reading the Tea Leaves: Why the Supreme Court Is Unlikely to Block the Contraception Mandate

Brown, Mark R. "Marijuana and Religious Freedom in the United States." In
  *Prohibition, Religious Freedom, and Human Rights: Regulating Traditional
  Drug Use*, edited by Beatriz Caiuby Labate and Clancy Cavnar, 45–63. New
  York: Springer-Verlag Berlin Heidelberg, 2014. http://dx.doi.org/10.1007
  /978-3-642-40957-8_3.
Feeney, Kevin. "Peyote, Race, and Equal Protection in the United States." In
  *Prohibition, Religious Freedom, and Human Rights: Regulating Traditional
  Drug Use*, edited by Beatriz Caiuby Labate and Clancy Cavnar, 65–88. New
  York: Springer-Verlag Berlin Heidelberg, 2014. http://dx.doi.org/10.1007
  /978-3-642-40957-8_4.
"*Gonzales v. O Centro Espirita Beneficente União do Vegetal (2006)*." In *Ency-
  clopedia of Drug Policy*, edited by Mark A. R. Kleiman and James E. Hawdon,
  323–24. Thousand Oaks, CA: Sage Publications, 2011.
Pevar, Stephen L. *The Rights of Indians and Tribes*, 4th ed.. New York: Oxford
  University Press, 2012. See especially Chapter 13: "Civil Rights of Indians,"
  221–40.

23. A Minefield: The Troubling Implications of the *Hobby Lobby* Decision

Clements, Jeffrey D. *Corporations Are Not People: Reclaiming Democracy from
  Big Money and Global Corporations*. 2nd ed. San Francisco, CA: Berrett-
  Koehler Publishers, 2014.
Clements, Jeffrey D. *Corporations Are Not People: Why They Have More Rights*

Than You Do and What You Can Do about It. San Francisco, CA: Berrett-Koehler Publishers, 2012.

Colombo, Ronald J. *The First Amendment and the Business Corporation.* New York: Oxford University Press, 2014. http://dx.doi.org/10.1093/acprof:oso/9780199335671.001.0001.

Green, David, and Dean Merrill. *More Than a Hobby: How a $600 Startup Became America's Home and Craft Superstore.* Nashville, TN: Thomas Nelson, 2005.

Hamilton, Marci A. *God vs. the Gavel: The Perils of Extreme Religious Liberty.* New York: Cambridge University Press, 2014. http://dx.doi.org/10.1017/CBO9781316104286.

Gonzales v. O Centro Espirita Beneficente União do Vegetal (2006)." In *Encyclopedia of Drug Policy,* edited by Mark A. R. Kleiman and James E. Hawdon, 323–4. Thousand Oaks, CA: Sage Publications, 2011.

Murray, Celia L. *Contracts, Commercial Law and Business Organizations: For Georgia Paralegals.* Wrightsville, GA: Ostrup Press, LLC, 2014. See especially Chapter 1.4, "The First Amendment and Business," which discusses *Burwell v. Hobby Lobby* on pp. 11–12.

Volokh, Eugene. *Sebelius v. Hobby Lobby: Corporate Rights and Religious Liberties.* Washington, DC: Cato Institute, 2014. Kindle edition.

Waltman, Jerold L. *Congress, the Supreme Court, and Religious Liberty: The Case of* City of Boerne v. Flores. New York: Palgrave Macmillan, 2013. Kindle edition. http://dx.doi.org/10.1057/9781137300645.

Waltman, Jerold L. *Religious Free Exercise and Contemporary American Politics: The Saga of the Religious Land Use and Institutionalized Persons Act of 2000.* New York: Continuum, 2010.

Wells, Trish. *How Hobby Lobby Changed My Life.* Seattle, WA: CreateSpace, 2014.

Part 3: Conversations about Culture

Bretherton, Luke. *Christianity and Contemporary Politics: The Conditions and Possibilities of Faithful Witness.* Malden, MA: Blackwell Publishing, 2010. http://dx.doi.org/10.1002/9781444317824.

Hellwig, Monika K. *Public Dimensions of a Believer's Life: Rediscovering the Cardinal Virtues.* Lanham, MD: Rowman & Littlefield, 2005.

Himes, Michael J., and Kenneth R. Himes. *Fullness of Faith: The Public Significance of Theology.* Mahwah, NJ: Paulist Press, 1993.

Hughson, Thomas. *Connecting Jesus to Social Justice: Classical Christology and Public Theology.* Lanham, MD: Rowman & Littlefield, 2013.

Krason, Stephen M. *The Public Order and the Sacred Order: Contemporary Issues, Catholic Social Thought, and the Western and American Traditions.* Lanham, MD: Scarecrow Press, 2009.

Matthewes, Charles T. *A Theology of Public Life.* Cambridge, UK: Cambridge University Press, 2008.

Niebuhr, H. *Richard. Christ and Culture*. New York: HarperCollins, 2001.

Tracy, David. *The Analogical Imagination: Christian Theology and the Culture of Pluralism*. New York: Crossroad, 1998.

Volf, Miroslav. *A Public Faith: How Followers of Christ Should Serve the Common Good*. Grand Rapids, MI: Brazos Press, 2013.

24. Watch Your Mouth: Sage Advice from St. James

Berry, Jeffrey M., and Sarah Sobieraj. *The Outrage Industry: Political Opinion Media and the New Incivility*. New York: Oxford University Press, 2014.

Boone, Dan. *A Charitable Discourse: Talking about the Things That Divide Us*. Kansas City, MO: Beacon Hill Press of Kansas City, 2011.

Carter, Stephen. *Civility: Manners, Morals, and the Etiquette of Democracy*. New York: Basic Books, 1998.

Crowley, Sharon. *Toward a Civil Discourse: Rhetoric and Fundamentalism*. Pittsburgh, PA: University of Pittsburgh Press, 2006.

Esper, Joseph M. *Saintly Solutions to Life's Common Problems: From Anger, Boredom, and Temptation to Gluttony, Gossip, and Greed*. Manchester, NH: Sophia Institute Press, 2001. See especially "Argumentativeness," 15–20; "Gossip," 161–66.

Malone, Matt. "Pursuing the Truth in Love." *America*, June 3–10, 2013.

Mouw, Richard W. *Uncommon Decency: Christian Civility in an Uncivil World*. Downers Grove, IL: InterVarsity Press, 2010.

Rodin, Judith, and Stephen P. Steinberg. *Public Discourse in America: Conversation and Community in the Twenty-First Century*. Philadelphia, PA: University of Pennsylvania Press, 2003.

Rountree, Clarke, ed. *Venomous Speech: Problems with American Political Discourse on the Right and Left*. Santa Barbara, CA: Praeger, 2013.

Sistare, Christine T., ed. *Civility and Its Discontents: Civic Virtue, Toleration, and Cultural Fragmentation*. Lawrence, KS: University Press of Kansas, 2004.

Tannen, Deborah. *The Argument Culture: Stopping America's War of Words*. New York: Ballantine Books, 1998.

25. Model Atheist: Jeffrey Stout and the Culture Wars

Heclo, Hugh, Theda Skocpol, Mary Jo Bane, et al. *Christianity and American Democracy*. Cambridge, MA: Harvard University Press, 2007. http://dx.doi.org/10.4159/9780674027053.

Maritain, Jacques. *Christianity and Democracy, and the Rights of Man and Natural Law*. San Francisco, CA: Ignatius Press, 2011.

Mendieta, Eduardo, and Jonathan Van Antwerpen, eds. *The Power of Religion in the Public Sphere*. New York: Columbia University Press, 2011.

Ratzinger, Joseph, and Jürgen Habermas. *The Dialectics of Secularization: On Reason and Religion*. San Francisco: Ignatius Press, 2007.

Wolfe, Alan, and Ira Katznelson, eds. *Religion and Democracy in the United*

States: Danger or Opportunity? Princeton, NJ: Princeton University Press, 2010. http://dx.doi.org/10.1515/9781400836772.

Wolterstorff, Nicholas, and Robert Audi. *Religion in the Public Square: The Place of Religious Convictions in Political Debate.* Lanham, MD: Rowman & Littlefield, 1997.

26. Bishops and Politics: Lessons from Australia

Cafaradi, Nicholas P. *Voting and Holiness: Catholic Perspectives on Political Participation.* Mahwah, NJ: Paulist Press, 2012.

Gaillardetz, Richard. "The Limits of Authority." To be read with Weinandy (below) *Commonweal*, August 13, 2010.

Heyer, Kristin E., Mark J. Rozell, and Michael A. Genovese, eds. *Catholics and Politics: The Dynamic Tension between Faith and Power.* Washington, DC: Georgetown University Press, 2008.

Weinandy, Thomas G. "The Bishops and the Right Exercise of Authority." United States Conference of Catholic Bishops. 2010. Available at http://www.usccb .org/issues-and-action/human-life-and-dignity/health-care/gaillardetz-response.cfm. To be read with Gaillardetz (above).

Yamane, David A. *The Catholic Church in State Politics: Negotiating Prophetic Demands and Political Realities.* Lanham, MD: Sheed & Ward, 2005.

27. Moving beyond the Culture Wars: Why a Bioethics Council Needs Diversity

Barry, Vincent. *Bioethics in a Cultural Context: Philosophy, Religion, History, Politics.* Boston, MA: Wadsworth, Cengage Learning, 2012.

Charles, Daryl J. *Retrieving the Natural Law: A Return to Moral First Things (Critical Issues in Bioethics).* Grand Rapids, MI: Eerdmans, 2008.

Charlesworth, Max. *Bioethics in a Liberal Society.* New York: Cambridge University Press, 1993. http://dx.doi.org/10.1017/CBO9780511552120.

Engelhardt, Tristram H. *Bioethics and Secular Humanism: The Search for a Common Morality.* Harrisburgh, PA: Trinity Press, 1991.

Engelhardt, Tristram H. *Global Bioethics: The Collapse of Consensus.* Beverly, MA: M & M Scrivener Publishing, 2006.

Have, H.A. Ten, and Hans-Martin Sass, eds. *Consensus Formation in Healthcare Ethics.* Hingham, MA: Kluwer Academic Publishers, 2010.

Hester, Micah D., and Toby Schonfeld, eds. *Guidance for Healthcare Ethics Committees.* New York: Cambridge University Press, 2012. http://dx.doi .org/10.1017/CBO9780511846441.

Lachman, Vick. *Ethical Challenges in Health Care: Developing Your Moral Compass.* New York: Springer, 2009.

O'Rourke, Kevin D, ed. *A Primer for Health Care Ethics: Essays for a Pluralistic Society.* 2nd ed. Washington, DC: Georgetown University Press, 2000.

Shelp, E.E. *Secular Bioethics in Theological Perspective. Reprint.* New York: Springer, 2011.

Spicker, Stuart F. *The Healthcare Ethics Committee Experience: Selected Readings from Hec Forum*. Malabar, FL: Krieger, 1997.

Viafora, C. *Clinical Bioethics: A Search for the Foundations*. New York: Springer, 2005.

28. A Flawed Analogy: Prochoice Politicians and the Third Reich

Condit, Celeste. *Decoding Abortion Rhetoric: Communicating Social Change*. Champaign, IL: University of Illinois Press, 1990.

Mall, David, ed. *When Life and Choice Collide: Essays on Rhetoric and Abortion*. Eagan, MN: Kairos Books, 1993.

Schuman, Sharon. *Freedom and Dialogue in a Polarized World*. Lanham, MD: University of Delaware Press, 2014.

Smith, Leslie Dorrough. *Righteous Rhetoric: Sex, Speech, and the Politics of Concerned Women for America*. New York: Oxford University Press, 2014. http://dx.doi.org/10.1093/acprof:oso/9780199337507.001.0001.

Wagner, Stephen. *Common Ground without Compromise*. Signal Hill, CA: Stand to Reason Press, 2008.

29. Sick Minds: What Can We Do to Prevent Another Tucson?

Executive Office of the President of the United States. *Progress Report on the President's Executive Actions to Reduce Gun Violence*. Damascus, MD: Pennyhill Press, 2013.

Rogers, Anne, and David Pilgrim. *A Sociology of Mental Health and Illness*. 4th ed. New York: Open University Press, 2010.

Torry, E. Fuller. *American Psychosis: How the Federal Government Destroyed the Mental Illness Treatment System*. New York: Oxford University Press, 2014.

Tsemberis, Sam. *Housing First Manual: The Pathways Model to End Homelessness for People with Mental Illness and Addiction*. Center City, MN: Hazelden, 2010.

Webster, Daniel W., Jon S. Vernick, and Michael R. Bloomberg. *Reducing Gun Violence in America: Informing Policy with Evidence and Analysis*. Baltimore, MD: Johns Hopkins University Press, 2013.

Zandler, John C., ed. *Mass Shootings and Gun Violence in America: Issues and Perspectives*. Baltimore, MD: Johns Hopkins University Press, 2013.

30. Crime or Tragedy? Murder and Suicide at Villanova

Albers, Robert H., William H. Meller, and Steven D. Thurber, eds. *Ministry with Persons with Mental Illness and Their Families*. Minneapolis, MN: Fortress Press, 2012.

Ashley, Benedict M., OP, Jean deBlois,CSJ, and Kevin D. O'Rourke, OP. *Health Care Ethics: A Catholic Theological Analysis*. 5th ed. Washington, DC: Georgetown University Press, 2006. See especially Chapter 5: "Mental Health: Ethical Perspectives," 125–62.

Greene-McCreight, Kathryn. *Darkness Is My Only Companion: A Christian Response to Mental Illness.* Grand Rapids, MI: Brazos Press, 2006.

Hermes, Kathryn J. *Prayers for Surviving Depression.* Dedham, MA: Pauline Books & Media, 2004.

Kendall-Tackett, Kathleen A. *Depression in New Mothers: Causes, Consequences, and Treatment Alternatives.* 2nd ed. New York: Routledge, 2010.

Kheriaty, Aaron, and John Cihak. *Catholic Guide to Depression.* Manchester, NH: Sophia Institute Press, 2012.

McKee, Geoffrey R. *Why Mothers Kill: A Forensic Psychologist's Casebook.* New York: Oxford University Press, 2006.

NCPD Council on Mental Illness. Janice L. Benton and Dorothy Coughlin. *Welcomed and Valued: Building Faith Communities of Support and Hope with People with Mental Illness and Their Families.* Washington, DC: National Catholic Partnership on Disability, 2009. For more from the National Catholic Partnership on Disability, see http://ncpd.org/.

Pope Benedict, X.V.I. "Message of His Holiness Benedict XVI for the 14th World Day of the Sick." December 8, 2005. Available at http://www.vatican .va/holy_father/benedict_xvi/messages/sick/documents/hf_ben-xvi_mes _20051208_world-day-of-the-sick-2006_en.html.

Simpson, Amy. *Troubled Minds: Mental Illness and the Church's Mission.* Downers Grove, IL: InterVarsity Press, 2013.

Singer, Jonathan. *The Special Needs Parent Handbook: Critical Strategies and Practical Advice to Help You Survive and Thrive.* Tenafly, NJ: Clinton+Valley Publishing, 2012.

Tessman, Lisa. *Burdened Virtues: Virtue Ethics for Liberatory Struggles.* New York: Oxford University Press, 2005. http://dx.doi.org/10.1093/0195179145 .001.0001.

Twomey, Teresa M, ed. *Understanding Postpartum Psychosis: A Temporary Madness.* Westport, CT: Praeger, 2009.

Velasquez, Leticia. *A Special Mother Is Born: Parents Share How God Called Them to the Extraordinary Vocation of Parenting a Special Needs Child.* Bloomington, IN: WestBow Press, 2011.

31. Dignity and the End of Life: How Not to Talk about Assisted Suicide

Ashley, Benedict M., OP, Jean deBlois, CSJ and Kevin D. O'Rourke, OP. *Health Care Ethics: A Catholic Theological Analysis.* 5th ed. Washington, DC: Georgetown University Press, 2006. See especially Chapter 6.6: "Suicide, Assisted Suicide, Euthanasia," 178–81.

Dworkin, Ronald. *Life's Dominion: An Argument about Abortion, Euthanasia, and Individual Freedom.* New York: Vintage Books, 1994.

Jackson, Emily, and John Keown. *Debating Euthanasia.* Oxford, UK: Hart Publishing, 2012.

May, William E. *Catholic Bioethics and the Gift of Human Life,* 3rd ed.

Huntington, IN: Our Sunday Visitor, 2013. See especially Chapter 7: "Euthanasia, Assisted Suicide, and Care of the Dying," 251–92.

Pappas, Demetra M. *The Euthanasia/Assisted-Suicide Debate (Historical Guides to Controversial Issues in America)*. Santa Barbara, CA: Greenwood, 2012.

Tollefsen, Christopher, ed. *John Paul II's Contribution to Catholic Bioethics*. Norwell, MA: Springer, 2004. http://dx.doi.org/10.1007/978-1-4020-3130-4.

Wildes, Kevin William, and Alan Mitchell, eds. *Choosing Life: A Dialogue on Evangelium vitae*. Washington, DC: Georgetown University Press, 1997.

32. The Right Questions: Catholic Colleges and Pop Culture

Benedict, XVI Pope. *Family: Spiritual Thoughts Series*. Edited by the United States Conference of Catholic Bishops. Washington, DC: USCCB Publishing, 2009.

Cahill, Lisa Sowle. *Family: A Christian Social Perspective*. Minneapolis, MN: Augsburg Fortress, 2000.

Cloutier, David, ed. *Leaving and Coming Home: New Wineskins for Catholic Sexual Ethics*. Eugene, OR: Wipf and Stock, 2010.

Farley, Margaret. *Just Love: A Framework for Christian Sexual Ethics*. New York: Continuum, 2006.

Freitas, Donna. *The End of Sex: How Hookup Culture Is Leaving a Generation Unhappy, Sexually Unfulfilled, and Confused about Intimacy*. New York: Basic Books, 2013.

Freitas, Donna. *Sex and the Soul: Juggling Sexuality, Spirituality, Romance, and Religion on America's College Campuses*. New York: Oxford University Press, 2008.

Gaillardetz, Richard R. *Daring Promise: A Spirituality of Christian Marriage*. Rev. ed. Liguori, MO: Liguori/Triumph, 2007.

Rubio, Julie Hanlon. *A Christian Theology of Marriage and Family*. Mahwah, NJ: Paulist Press, 2003.

Salzman, Todd A., and Michael G. Lawler. *Sexual Ethics: A Theological Introduction*. Washington, DC: Georgetown University Press, 2012.

Stepp, Laura Sessions. *Unhooked: How Young Women Pursue Sex, Delay Love and Lose at Both*. New York: Penguin Books, Ltd, 2007.

West, Christopher. *Theology of the Body for Beginners: A Basic Introduction to Pope John Paul II's Sexual Revolution*. Rev. ed. West Chester, PA: Ascension Press, 2009.

33. Either/Or? Catholicism Is More Complex

D'Antonio, William V., Michele Dillon, and Mary L. Gautier. *American Catholics in Transition*. Lanham, MD: Rowman & Littlefield, 2013.

Fowler, James W. *Stages of Faith: The Psychology of Human Development and the Quest for Meaning*. New York: HarperCollins, 1995.

Gautier, Mary L., Paul M. Perl, and Stephen J. Fichter. *Same Call, Different Men: The Evolution of the Priesthood since Vatican II*. Collegeville, MN: Liturgical Press, 2012.

Hetherington, Marc J., and Jonathan D. Weiler. *Authoritarianism and Polarization in American Politics*. New York: Cambridge University Press, 2009. http://dx.doi.org/10.1017/CBO9780511802331.

Powell, Timothy, ed. *Beyond the Binary: Reconstructing Cultural Identity in a Multicultural Context*. Piscataway, NJ: Rutgers University Press, 1999.

Richardson, Ronald W. *Polarization and the Healthier Church: Applying Bowen Family Systems Theory to Conflict and Change in Society and Congregational Life*. Seattle, WA: CreateSpace, 2012.

Rohr, Richard. *The Naked Now: Learning to See As the Mystics See*. New York: Crossroad, 2009.

Schneider, Kirk J. *The Polarized Mind: Why It's Killing Us and What We Can Do about It*. Colorado Springs, CO: University Professors Press, 2013.

Part 4: Conversations about Belief

Clark, Christopher, and Wolfram Kaiser, eds. *Culture Wars: Secular-Catholic Conflict in Nineteenth-Century Europe*. New York: Cambridge University Press, 2003. http://dx.doi.org/10.1017/CBO9780511496714.

D'Antonio, William V., Steven A. Tuch, and Josiah R. Baker. *Religion, Politics, and Polarization: How Religiopolitical Conflict Is Changing Congress and American Democracy*. Lanham, MD: Rowman & Littlefield, 2013.

Hasson, Kevin Seamus. *The Right to Be Wrong: Ending the Culture War over Religion in America*. San Francisco, CA: Encounter Books, 2005.

Hollenbach, David. "S.J. "Commentary on *Gaudium et spes* (Pastoral Constitution on the Church in the Modern World)." In *Modern Catholic Social Teaching: Commentaries and Interpretations*, edited by Kenneth R. Himes, 266–91. Washington, DC: Georgetown University Press, 2005.

Jones, Robert P. *Progressive & Religious: How Christian, Jewish, Muslim, and Buddhist Leaders Are Moving beyond the Culture Wars and Transforming American Public Life*. Lanham, MD: Rowman & Littlefield, 2008.

Lawler, Michael G., Todd A. Salzman, and Eileen Burke-Sullivan. *The Church in the Modern World: Gaudium et spes Then and Now*. Collegeville, MN: Michael Glazier, 2014.

Lorentzen, Lois Ann. "Gaudium et spes." In *The New Dictionary of Catholic Social Thought*, edited by Judith Dwyer, 406–17. Collegeville, MN: Liturgical Press, 1994.

Francis, Pope. *A Big Heart Open to God: A Conversation with Pope Francis*. New York: HarperCollins, 2013.

Second Vatican Council. *Gaudium et spes* (1965).

Woods, Thomas E. *The Church Confronts Modernity: Catholic Intellectuals and the Progressive Era*. New York: Columbia University Press, 2004.

34. Family Feuds: What's Keeping Catholics Apart?

Allen, Jr. John. *Common Ground in a Global Key: International Lessons in Catholic Dialogue*. New York: National Pastoral Life Center, 2004. Response

by Mary Ann Glendon. Available at http://www.catholiccommonground.org
/response-2004-murnion-lecture.

Catholic Common Ground Initiative. *Church Authority in American Culture: The Second Cardinal Bernardin Conference.* New York: Crossroad, 1999.

Conway, Jill Ker. *Where to Look for Common Ground.* New York: National Pastoral Life Center, 2007. Response by Rev. James Bacik. Available at http:// www.catholiccommonground.org/response-2007-murnion-lecture.

Davidson, James D., ed. *The Search for Common Ground: What Unites and Divides Catholic Americans.* Huntington, IN: Our Sunday Visitor, 1997.

Dulles, Avery R. *Dialogue, Truth, and Communion.* New York: National Pastoral Life Center, 2001.

Johnson, Elizabeth A., ed. *The Church Women Want: Catholic Women in Dialogue.* New York: Crossroad, 2002.

Komonchak, Joseph A. *Dealing with Diversity and Disagreement: Vatican II and Beyond.* New York: National Pastoral Life Center, 2003. Response by Most Rev. Daniel E. Pilarczyk. Available at http://www.catholiccommonground .org/response-2003-murnion-lecture.

Ruddy, Christopher. *Tested in Every Way: The Catholic Priesthood in Today's Church.* New York: Crossroad, 2007.

Smith, Christian, Kyle Longest, Jonathan Hill, and Kari Christoffersen. *Young Catholic America: Emerging Adults In, Out of, and Gone from the Church.* New York: Oxford University Press, 2014. http://dx.doi.org/10.1093/acprof: oso/9780199341078.001.0001.

Warfel, Michael. "Catholic Common Ground Initiative: Journey to Communion in Christ." Catholic Common Ground Initiative. 2010. Available at http:// www.catholiccommonground.org/transcript-catholic-common-ground -initiative-journey-communion-christ#overlay-context=transcript-catholic -common-ground-initiative-journey-communion-christ.

Weisgerber, James. *Building a Church of Communion.* New York: National Pastoral Life Center, 2005.

Yankelovich, Daniel. *The Magic of Dialogue.* New York: Simon & Schuster, 1999.

35. The Martyrdom of John Roberts: Catholic Squabbling, Then and Now

Abramowitz, Alan I. *The Disappearing Center: Engaged Citizens, Polarization, and American Democracy.* New Haven, CT: Yale University Press, 2011.

Ahua, Sunil. *Congress Behaving Badly: The Rise of Partisanship and Incivility and the Death of Public Trust.* Santa Barbara, CA: Praeger, 2008.

Fiorina, Morris P., Samuel J. Abrams, and Jeremy C. Pope. *Culture War? The Myth of a Polarized America.* 3rd ed. New York: Longman, 2010.

Hilley, John L. *The Challenge of Legislation: Bipartisanship in a Partisan World.* Washington, DC: Brookings Institution Press, 2007.

Huntsman, Jon, and Joe Manchin. *No Labels: A Shared Vision for a Stronger America.* New York: Diversion Books, 2014.

Snowe, Olympia. *Fighting for Common Ground: How We Can Fix the Stalemate in Congress*. New York: Weinstein Books, 2013.

Thomas, Cal, and Bob Beckel. *Common Ground: How to Stop the Partisan War That Is Destroying America*. New York: HarperCollins, 2009.

Ullman, Harlan. *America's Promise Restored: Preventing Culture, Crusade and Partisanship from Wrecking Our Nation*. New York: Carroll & Graf, 2006.

Wald, Kenneth D., and Allison Calhoun-Brown. *Religion and Politics in the United States*. 7th ed. Lanham, MD: Rowman & Littlefield, 2014.

36. No Academic Question: Should the CTSA Seek "Conservative" Views?

Copeland, M. Shawn. *Enfleshing Freedom: Body, Race and Being*. Philadelphia, PA: Fortress Press, 2009.

Dulles, Avery, S.J. *The Assurance of Things Hoped For: A Theology of Christian Faith*. New York: Oxford University Press, 1994.

Dulles, Avery, S.J. *The Magisterium: Teacher and Guardian of the Faith*. Washington, DC: Catholic University of America Press, 2010.

Gaillardetz, Richard R. *By What Authority? Primer on Scripture, the Magisterium, and the Sense of the Faithful*. Collegeville, MN: Liturgical Press, 2003.

Griffiths, Paul J. *Intellectual Appetite: A Theological Grammar*. Washington, DC: Catholic University of America Press, 2009.

Gutierrez, Gustavo. *A Theology of Liberation: History, Politics, and Salvation. 15th anniversary edition*. Trans. Caridad Inda and John Eagleson. Maryknoll, NY: Orbis Books, 1988.

Hopkins, Dwight N., and Edward P. Antonio, eds. *The Cambridge Companion to Black Theology*. Cambridge, UK: Cambridge University Press, 2012. http://dx.doi.org/10.1017/CCOL9780521879866.

Isasi-Diaz, Ada Maria. *Mujerista Theology: A Theology for the Twenty-First Century*. Maryknoll, NY: Orbis Books, 1996.

Kilby, Karen. *Balthasar: A (Very) Critical Introduction*. Grand Rapids, MI: Eerdmans, 2012.

Kilby, Karen. *A Brief Introduction to Karl Rahner*. New York: Crossroad, 2007.

Lindbeck, George A. *The Nature of Doctrine. 25th anniversary edition*. Introduction by Bruce D. Marshall. Louisville, KY: Westminster John Knox Press, 2009.

McGrath, Alister E. *The Christian Theology Reader*. Malden, MA: Wiley-Blackwell, 2011.

Mueller, J. J., S.J., ed. *Theological Foundations: Concepts and Methods for Understanding Christian Faith*. 2nd ed. Winona, MN: Anselm Academic, 2011.

Nichols, Aidan. O.P. *The Shape of Catholic Theology: An Introduction to Its Sources, Principles, and History*. Collegeville, MN: Liturgical Press, 1991.

Parsons, Susan Frank, ed. *The Cambridge Companion to Feminist Theology*. Cambridge, UK: Cambridge University Press, 2002. http://dx.doi.org/10.1017/CCOL052166327X.

Pope Benedict XVI. *Theological Highlights of Vatican II*. Mahwah, NJ: Paulist Press, 2009.

Rowland, Christopher, ed. *The Cambridge Companion to Liberation Theology*. Cambridge, UK: Cambridge University Press, 2007. http://dx.doi.org/10 .1017/CCOL0521868831.

Sullivan, Francis A. S.J. *Creative Fidelity: Weighing and Interpreting Documents of the Magisterium*. Eugene, OR: Wipf & Stock, 2003.

Tracy, David. *The Analogical Imagination: Christian Theology and the Culture of Pluralism*. New York: Crossroad, 1998.

37. The "New" Feminism: John Paul II and the 1912 Encyclopedia

Bachiochi, Erika, ed. *Women, Sex, and the Church: A Case for Catholic Teaching*. Boston, MA: Pauline Books & Media, 2010.

Beattie, Tina. *The New Catholic Feminism: Theology, Gender Theory, and Dialogue*. Abingdon, Oxon: Routledge, 2006.

Bucar, Elizabeth M. *Creative Conformity: The Feminist Politics of U.S. Catholic and Iranian Shi'i Women*. Washington, DC: Georgetown University Press, 2011.

Butler, Sara. M.S.B.T. *The Catholic Priesthood and Women: A Guide to the Teaching of the Church*. Mundelein, IL: Hillenbrand Books, 2007.

Curran, Charles E., Margaret A. Farley, and Richard A. McCormick, S.J., eds. *Feminist Ethics and the Catholic Moral Tradition (Readings in Moral Theology, No. 9)*. Mahwah, NJ: Paulist Press, 1996.

Henold, Mary J. *Catholic and Feminist*. Chapel Hill, NC: University of North Carolina Press, 2008.

Hogan, Linda, and A.E. Orobator, eds. *Feminist Catholic Theological Ethics: Conversations in the World Church (Catholic Theological Ethics in the World Church)*. Maryknoll, NY: Orbis Books, 2014.

Johnson, Elizabeth A. *She Who Is: The Mystery of God in Feminist Theological Discourse*. New York: Crossroad, 2002.

O'Reilly, Barbara A. *Grace under Pressure: The Roles of Women—Then and Now—in The Catholic Church*. Bloomington, IN: WestBow Press, 2012.

Schneiders, Sandra M. *Beyond Patching: Faith and Feminism in the Catholic Church*. Rev. ed. Mahwah, NJ: Paulist Press, 2004.

Schumacher, Michele M., ed. *Women in Christ: Toward a New Feminism*. Grand Rapids, MI: Eerdmans, 2004.

38. Catholic Kosher: Is the Ban on Contraception Just an Identity Marker?

Arbuckle, Gerald A. *Catholic Identity or Identities?: Refounding Ministries in Chaotic Times*. Collegeville, MN: Liturgical Press, 2013.

Burtchaell, James Tunstead. *The Dying of the Light: The Disengagement of Colleges and Universities from Their Christian Churches*. Grand Rapids, MI: Eerdmans, 1998.

Butler, Francis J., ed. *American Catholic Identity: Essays in an Age of Change*. Lanham, MD: Sheed & Ward, 1994.

Catholic Health Association of the United States. "By Their Fruits You Will Know Them: Mission Assessment and Measurement." Catholic Health Association of the United States. n.d. Available at http://www.chausa.org /missionassessment/.

Catholic Health Association of the United States. "Mission: Overview." Catholic Health Association of the United States. n.d. Available at https://www .chausa.org/mission/overview

Cook, Timothy J. *Architects of Catholic Culture: Designing & Building Catholic Culture in Catholic Schools*. Arlington, VA: National Catholic Educational Association, 2001.

Dillon, Michele. *Catholic Identity: Balancing Reason, Faith, and Power*. New York: Cambridge University Press, 1999. http://dx.doi.org/10.1017/CBO 9780511752728.

Donovan, Daniel. *Distinctively Catholic: An Exploration of Catholic Identity*. Mahwah, NJ: Paulist Press, 1997.

Estanek, Sandra M., and Michael J. James. *Principles of Good Practice for Student Affairs at Catholic Colleges and Universities*. 2nd ed. Washington, DC: Association of Catholic Colleges and Universities, 2009., Available at http:// www.accunet.org/i4a/pages/index.cfm?pageid=3681.

Gallin, Alice. *Negotiating Identity: Catholic Higher Education since 1960*. South Bend, IN: University of Notre Dame Press, 2001.

Greer, Peter, Chris Horst, and Anna Haggard. *Mission Drift: The Unspoken Crisis Facing Leaders, Charities, and Churches*. Bloomington, MN: Bethany House Publishers, 2014.

Griese, Orville N. *Catholic Identity in Health Care: Principles and Practice*. Washington, DC: National Catholic Bioethics Center, 1987.

Morey, Melanie M., and John J. Piderit. *Catholic Higher Education: A Culture in Crisis*. New York: Oxford University Press, 2010.

Muldoon, Timothy P., ed. *Catholic Identity and the Laity (Annual Publication of the College Theology Society)*. Maryknoll, NY: Orbis Books, 2009.

Stabile, Carol C. *Ensuring Catholic Identity in Catholic Schools*. Arlington, VA: National Catholic Educational Association, 2000.

United States Conference of Catholic Bishops Committee on Education (Bishops' and Presidents' Subcommittee). *Catholic Identity in Our Colleges and Universities: A Collection of Defining Documents*. Washington, DC: USCCB Publishing, 2006.

Van Beeck, Frans Jozef. *Catholic Identity after Vatican II: Three Types of Faith in the One Church*. Chicago, IL: Loyola Press, 1985.

39. The Big Chill: *Humane Vitae* Dissenters Need to Find a Voice

Bachiochi, Erkia, ed. *Women, Sex, and the Church: A Case for Catholic Teaching*. Boston, MA: Pauline Books & Media, 2010.

Cahill, Lisa Sowle. *Between the Sexes: Foundations for Christian Ethics of Sexuality*. Philadelphia, PA: Fortress Press, 1985.

Cloutier, David. *Love, Reason, and God's Story: An Introduction to Catholic Sexual Ethics*. Winona, MN: Anselm Academic, 2008.

Farley, Margaret A. *Just Love: A Framework for Christian Sexual Ethics*. New York: Continuum, 2006.

Franks, Angela. *Contraception and Catholicism: What the Church Teaches and Why*. Boston, MA: Pauline Books & Media, 2013.

Freitas, Donna. *Sex and the Soul: Juggling Sexuality, Spirituality, Romance, and Religion on America's College Campuses*. New York: Oxford University Press, 2008.

Gudorf, Christine E. *Body, Sex, and Pleasure: Reconstructing Christian Sexual Ethics*. Cleveland, OH: Pilgrim Press, 1994.

Kalbian, Aline H. *Sex, Violence, and Justice: Contraception and the Catholic Church*. Washington, DC: Georgetown University Press, 2014.

May, William E., Ronald Lawler, O.F.M. Cap., and Joseph Boyle, Jr. *Catholic Sexual Ethics: A Summary, Explanation, & Defense*. 3rd ed. Huntington, IN: Our Sunday Visitor, 2011.

Rubio, Julie Hanlon. *A Christian Theology of Marriage and Family*. Mahwah, NJ: Paulist Press, 2003.

Salzman, Todd A., and Michael G. Lawler. *Sexual Ethics: A Theological Introduction*. Washington, DC: Georgetown University Press, 2012.

40. How about NOT Firing Her? Moral Norms and Catholic School Teachers

Brinig, Margaret F., and Nicole Stelle Garnett. *Lost Classroom, Lost Community: Catholic Schools' Importance in Urban America*. Chicago, IL: University of Chicago Press, 2014. http://dx.doi.org/10.7208/chicago/9780226 122144.001.0001.

Byrne, Gareth. *Toward Mutual Ground: Pluralism, Religious Education and Diversity in Irish Schools*. Ed. Patricia Kieran. Dublin: Columba Press, 2013.

Cook, Timothy J. *Architects of Catholic Culture: Designing & Building Catholic Culture in Catholic Schools*. Washington, DC: National Catholic Educational Association, 2001.

Dwyer-McNulty, Sally Dwyer. *Common Threads: A Cultural History of Clothing in American Catholicism*. Chapel Hill, NC: University of North Carolina Press, 2014.

Francis, Pope. *The Church of Mercy: A Vision for the Church*. Chicago, IL: Loyola Press, 2014.

Francis, Pope. *Only Love Can Save Us: Letters, Homilies, and Talks of Cardinal Jorge Bergoglio*. Huntington, IN: Our Sunday Visitor, 2013.

Pope Francis. *Evangelii Gaudium* (2013).

Shaugnessy, Mary Angela. *The Law and Catholic Schools: A Guide to Legal Issues for the Third Millennium*. 2nd ed. Washington, DC: National Catholic Educational Association, 2005.

Vallely, Paul. *Pope Francis: Untying the Knots*. London, UK: Bloomsbury, 2013.

41. Truth or Consequences: In Ireland, Straying Far from the Mental Reservation

Augustine. *On Lying*. Mitchellville, MD: Fig Publishing, 2013.

Bretzke, James T. *A Morally Complex World: Engaging Contemporary Moral Theology*. Collegeville, MN: Michael Glazier, 2004.

Curran, Charles E. *The Development of Moral Theology: Five Strands*. Washington, DC: Georgetown University Press, 2013. See especially Chapter 3, "Strand Three: Natural Law," 73–147.

Dorszynski, Julius A. *Catholic Teaching about the Morality of Falsehood*. Seattle, WA: CreateSpace Independent Publishing Platform, 2011.

Griffiths, Paul J. *Lying: An Augustinian Theology of Duplicity*. Ada, MI: Brazos Press, 2004.

Keenan, James F. *A History of Catholic Moral Theology in the Twentieth Century*. New York: Continuum, 2010.

Porter, Jean. "The Virtue of Justice (IIa IIae, qq. 58-122)." In *The Ethics of Aquinas*, edited by Stephen J. Pope, 272–286. Washington, DC: Georgetown University Press, 2002. See especially q. 110.

Ryan, John A., and Henry Davis. "Birth Control: The Perverted Faculty Argument." In *The Historical Development of Fundamental Moral Theology*, edited by Charles E. Curran and Richard A. McCormick, 120–34. Mahwah, NJ: Paulist Press, 1999.

Tollefsen, Christopher O. *Lying and Christian Ethics*. New York: Cambridge University Press, 2014. See especially Chapter 3, "The Christian Case for Lying: Cassian, Bonhoeffer, and Niebuhr," 57–78. http://dx.doi.org/10.1017/CBO9781107447745.

42. Unspeakable Sins: Why We Need to Talk about Them

Beck, Elizabeth, Nancy P. Kropf, and Pamela Blume Leonard. *Social Work and Restorative Justice: Skills for Dialogue, Peacemaking, and Reconciliation*. New York: Oxford University Press, 2010. http://dx.doi.org/10.1093/acprof:oso/9780195394641.001.0001.

Lee, Philip J. *Communication and Reconciliation: Challenges Facing the 21st Century*. Geneva, Switzerland: World Council of Churches, 2001.

Miller, Susan L. *After the Crime: The Power of Restorative Justice Dialogues between Victims and Violent Offenders*. New York: NYU Press, 2011.

Schreiter, Robert J. *The Ministry of Reconciliation: Spirituality & Strategies*. Maryknoll, NY: Orbis Books, 1998.

Tutu, Desmond. *No Future without Forgiveness*. New York: Image, 2000.

Umbreit, Mark, and Marilyn Peterson Armour. *Restorative Justice Dialogue: An Essential Guide for Research and Practice*. New York: Spring Publishing Company, 2011.

Vos, Betty, Robert B. Coates, Katherine A. Brown, et al. *Facing Violence: The Path of Restorative Justice and Dialogue*. Monsey, NY: Criminal Justice Press, 2003.

Waldron, Vincent R., and Douglas L. Kelley. *Communicating Forgiveness.* Thousand Oaks, CA: Sage Publications, Inc, 2008. http://dx.doi.org/10.4135 /9781483329536.

43. A Darkening: Why a Church Scandal Does More Harm Than the New Atheism

Balboni, Jennifer M. *Clergy Sexual Abuse Litigation: Survivors Seeking Justice.* Boulder, CO: Lynne Rienner Publishers, 2011.

Bartunek, Jean M., Mary Ann Hinsdale, and James F. Keenan, eds. *Church Ethics and Its Organizational Context: Learning from the Sex Abuse Scandal in the Catholic Church (Boston College Church in the 21st Century Series).* Lanham, MD: Sheed & Ward, 2006.

D'Antonio, Michael. *Mortal Sins: Sex, Crime, and the Era of Catholic Scandal.* New York: Thomas Dunne Books, 2013.

Doyle, Thomas P., A.W. Richard Sipe, and Patrick J. Wall. *Sex, Priests, and Secret Codes: The Catholic Church's 2,000 Year Paper Trail of Sexual Abuse.* Los Angeles, CA: Volt Press, 2006.

Higgins, Michael W., and Peter Kavanagh. *Suffer the Children Unto Me: An Open Inquiry into the Clerical Sex Abuse Scandal.* Toronto, Ontario: Novalis, 2010.

Jenkins, Philip. *Pedophiles and Priests: Anatomy of a Contemporary Crisis.* New York: Oxford University Press, 2001.

Mooney, Tom. *All the Bishops' Men: Clerical Abuse in an Irish Diocese.* Wilton, Rep. of Ireland: Collins Press, 2011.

Podles, Leon J. *Sacrilege: Sexual Abuse in the Catholic Church.* Baltimore, MD: Crossland Press, 2008.

Ridge, Martin. *Breaking the Silence: One Man's Quest to Find the Truth about One of the Most Horrific Series of Sex Abuse Cases in Ireland.* Dublin, Ireland: Gill & Macmillan, 2008.

Survivors Network of Those Abused by Priests. "SNAP: Survivors Network of Those Abused by Priests." Survivors Network of Those Abused by Priests. June 19, 2014. Available at http://www.snapnetwork.org/.

United States Conference of Catholic Bishops. "Charter for the Protection of Children and Young People." United States Conference of Catholic Bishops. 2014. Available at http://www.usccb.org/issues-and-action/child-and-youth -protection/charter.cfm.

44. The Long Goodbye: Why Some Devout Catholics Are Leaving the Church

Home, Catholics Come. Inc. "Catholics Come Home." Catholics Come Home, Inc. 2013. Available at http://www.catholicscomehome.org/.

Douglas, Jean K. *Why I Left the Church, Why I Came Back, and Why I Just Might Leave Again.* Barberville, FL: Fortuity Press, 2013.

Duquin, Lorene Hanley. *Recovering Faith: Stories of Catholics Who Came Home.* Huntington, IN: Our Sunday Visitor Publishing Division, 2011.

Field, Bill, Ed Griffin, and Kerry Griffin Gergeron, eds. *Why We Walked Away.* Seattle, WA: CreateSpace Independent Publishing Platform, 2013.

Francis, Pope. *The Church of Mercy.* Chicago, IL: Loyola Press, 2014.

Gauss, James F. *The Catholic Church: Why I Left It.* Seattle, WA: CreateSpace Independent Publishing Platform, 2012.

Kemp, Carrie. *Catholics Can Come Home Again!: A Guide for the Journey of Reconciliation with Inactive Catholics.* Mahwah, NJ: Paulist Press, 2001.

Madrid, Patrick. *Why Be Catholic?: Ten Answers to a Very Important Question.* New York: Image, 2014.

Peterson, Tom. *Catholics Come Home: God's Extraordinary Plan for Your Life.* New York: Image, 2013.

Rigney, Melanie, and Anna M. LaNave. *When They Come Home: Ways to Welcome Returning Catholics.* New London, CT: Twenty-Third Publications, 2009.

45. That '70s Church: What It Got Right

Cavalletti, Sofia. *The Religious Potential of the Child: Experiencing Scripture and Liturgy with Young Children.* Chicago, IL: Liturgy Training Publications, 1992.

Congregation for the Clergy. *General Directory for Catechesis.* Washington, DC: United States Conference of Catholic Bishops, 1998.

Congregation for the Clergy. *The Religious Potential of the Child: 6 to 12 Years Old.* Chicago, IL: Liturgy Training Publications, 2007.

Hart, Mark. *Blessed Are the Bored in Spirit: A Young Catholic's Search for Meaning.* Cincinnati, OH: Servant Books, 1994.

Lillig, Tina. *The Catechesis of the Good Shepherd in a Parish Setting.* Chicago, IL: Liturgy Training Programs, 1998.

Schonborn, Cardinal Christoph, ed. *Youcat: Youth Catechism of the Catholic Church.* San Francisco, CA: Ignatius Press, 2010.

United States Conference of Catholic Bishops. *National Directory for Catechesis.* Washington, DC: United States Conference of Catholic Bishops, 2005.

Vost, Kevin. *Memorize the Reasons! Defending the Faith with the Catholic Art of Memory.* San Diego, CA: Catholic Answers, 2013.

Walch, Timothy. *Parish School: American Catholic Parochial Education from Colonial Times to the Present.* Washington, DC: National Catholic Educational Association, 2003.

Wuerl, Donald W. *New Evangelization: Passing on the Catholic Faith Today.* Huntington, IN: Our Sunday Visitor, 2013.

Part 5: Cases and Controversies

Ashley, Benedict M., Jean deBlois, and Kevin D. O'Rourke. *Health Care Ethics: A Catholic Theological Analysis.* 5th ed. Washington, DC: Georgetown University Press, 2006.

Ashley, Benedict M., and Kevin D. O'Rourke. *Ethics of Health Care: An*

Introductory Textbook. 3rd ed. Washington, DC: Georgetown University Press, 2002.

Austriaco, Nicanor Pier Giorgio. *Biomedicine and Beatitude: An Introduction to Catholic Bioethics.* Washington, DC: The Catholic University of America Press, 2011.

Cahill, Lisa Sowle. *Theological Bioethics: Participation, Justice, and Change.* Washington, DC: Georgetown University Press, 2005.

Cates, Diana Fritz, and Paul Lauritzen, eds. *Medicine and the Ethics of Care.* Washington, DC: Georgetown University Press, 2002.

Corkery, Padraig. *Bioethics and the Catholic Moral Tradition.* Dublin: Veritas Publications, 2010.

Fisher, Anthony. *Catholic Bioethics for a New Millennium.* New York: Cambridge University Press, 2012.

Hamel, Ronald P., Laurence J. O'Connell, and Edwin R. Dubose, eds. *A Matter of Principles? Ferment in U.S. Bioethics.* Valley Forge, PA: Trinity Press International, 1994.

Kane, Brian. *The Blessing of Life: An Introduction to Catholic Bioethics.* Lanham, MD: Lexington Books, 2013.

Keenan, James F. *Moral Wisdom: Lessons and Texts from the Catholic Tradition.* Lanham, MD: Sheed & Ward, 2010.

Kelly, David F, Gerard Magill, and Henk ten Have. *Contemporary Catholic Health Care Ethics.* Washington, DC: Georgetown University Press, 2013.

May, William E. *Catholic Bioethics and the Gift of Human Life.* 3rd ed. Huntington, IN: Our Sunday Visitor, 2013.

Morris, John F. *Medicine, Health Care, & Ethics: Catholic Voices.* Washington, DC: The Catholic University of America Press, 2007.

Panicola, Michael R., David M. Belde, John Paul Slosar, et al. *Health Care Ethics: Theological Foundations, Contemporary Issues, and Controversial Cases.* Winona, MN: Anselm Academic, 2011.

Pellegrino, Edmund D., and Alan I. Faden, eds. *Jewish and Catholic Bioethics: An Ecumenical Dialogue.* Washington, DC: Georgetown University Press, 2000.

Ryan, Maura A. *Ethics and Economics of Assisted Reproduction: The Cost of Longing.* Washington, DC: Georgetown University Press, 2003.

Scarnecchia, D. Brian. *Bioethics, Law, and Human Life Issues: A Catholic Perspective on Marriage, Family, Contraception, Abortion, Reproductive Technology, and Death and Dying.* Lanham, MD: Rowman & Littlefield, 2010.

Walter, James J., and Thomas A. Shannon. *Contemporary Issues in Bioethics: A Catholic Perspective.* Lanham, MD: Sheed & Ward, 2005.

46. The Consistent Ethic: An Ethic of "Life," Not "Purity"

Bernardin, Joseph. *The Seamless Garment: Writings on the Consistent Ethic of Life,* edited by Thomas A. Nairn. Maryknoll, NY: Orbis Books, 2008.

Nairn, Thomas A., ed. *The Consistent Ethic of Life: Assessing Its Reception and*

Relevance. Maryknoll, NY: Orbis Books, 2008.
For additional resources, see the chapter "Why Prolife? It's about People, Not Abstractions."

47. Contraception, Again: Where Can We Find Compromise?

Cahill, Lisa Sowle. *Sex, Gender, & Christian Ethics*. New York: Cambridge University Press, 1996. See especially Chapter 6, "Sex, Marriage, and Family in Christian Tradition," 166–216.

Curran, Charles E. *Loyal Dissent: Memoir of a Catholic Theologian*. Washington, DC: Georgetown University Press, 2006.

Gaillardetz, Richard R. *Daring Promise: A Spirituality of Christian Marriage*. Rev. ed. Liguori, MO: Liguori/Triumph, 2007. See especially Chapter 5, "Marriage and Sexuality," 69–92.

Kalbian, Aline H. *Sex, Violence, and Justice: Contraception and the Catholic Church*. Washington, DC: Georgetown University Press, 2014.

May, William E., Ronald Lawler, and Joseph Boyle, Jr. *Catholic Sexual Ethics: A Summary, Explanation, & Defense*. 3rd ed. Huntington, IN: Our Sunday Visitor, 2011.

McClory, Robert. *Turning Point: The Inside Story of the Papal Birth Control Commission and How* Humanae Vitae *Changed the Life of Patty Crowley and the Future of the Church*. New York: Crossroad, 1997.

Noonan. John T., Jr. *Contraception: A History of Its Treatment by the Catholic Theologians and Canonists*. Cambridge, MA: Harvard University Press, 1986.

Salzman, Todd A., and Michael G. Lawler. *The Sexual Person: Toward a Renewed Catholic Anthropology*. Washington, DC: Georgetown University Press, 2008.

Tentler, Leslie Woodcock. *Catholics and Contraception: An American History*. Ithaca, NY: Cornell University Press, 2004.

Wooden, Cindy. "Vatican Publishes Reflection on Discerning Essentials of Faith." *National Catholic Reporter*, June 20, 2014. Available at http://ncronline.org/news/theology/vatican-publishes-reflection-discerning-essentials-faith.

48. When Does Life Begin? Two Prolife Philosophers Disagree

Ashley, Benedict M., and Kevin D. O'Rourke. *Ethics of Health Care: An Introductory Textbook*. 3rd ed. Washington, DC: Georgetown University Press, 2002.

Austriaco, Nicanor Pier Giorgio. *Biomedicine and Beatitude: An Introduction to Catholic Bioethics*. Catholic Moral Thought. Washington, DC: The Catholic University of America Press, 2011.

Cahill, Lisa Sowle. *Theological Bioethics: Participation, Justice, and Change*. Washington, DC: Georgetown University Press, 2005.

Corkery, Pádraig. *Bioethics and the Catholic Moral Tradition*. Dublin: Veritas Publications, 2010. See especially Chapter 3: "Embryonic Stem Cell Research," 59–78.

Fisher, Anthony. *Catholic Bioethics for a New Millennium*. New York: Cambridge University Press, 2012.

Grisez, Germain. *Abortion: The Myths, the Realities, and the Arguments*. New York: Corpus Books, 1970.

Kane, Brian. *The Blessing of Life: An Introduction to Catholic Bioethics*. Lanham, MD: Lexington Books, 2013.

May, William E. *Catholic Bioethics and the Gift of Human Life*. 3rd ed. Huntington, IN: Our Sunday Visitor, 2013.

O'Rourke, Kevin D, ed. *A Primer for Health Care Ethics: Essays for a Pluralistic Society*. 2nd ed. Washington, DC: Georgetown University Press, 2000.

Panicola, Michael R., David M. Belde, John Paul Slosar, et al. *Health Care Ethics: Theological Foundations, Contemporary Issues, and Controversial Cases*. Winona, MN: Anselm Academic, 2011.

Ramsey, Paul. "Abortion: A Review Article." *Thomist* 37 (1973): 174–226.

Walter, James J., and Thomas A. Shannon. *Contemporary Issues in Bioethics: A Catholic Perspective*. Lanham, MD: Sheed & Ward, 2005.

49. Why Prolife? It's about People, Not Abstractions

Bernardin, Joseph. *Consistent Ethic of Life: Joseph Cardinal Bernardin*, edited by Thomas G. Fuechtmann. Lanham, MD: Sheed & Ward, 1988.

Bernardin, Joseph. *The Seamless Garment: Writings on the Consistent Ethic of Life*, edited by Thomas A. Nairn. Maryknoll, NY: Orbis Books, 2008.

Duffy, Regis, and Angelus Gambatese, eds. *Made in God's Image: The Catholic Vision of Human Dignity*. Mahwah, NJ: Paulist Press, 1999.

Groppe, Elizabeth. "Climate for Change: What the Church Can Do about Global Warming." *America*, March 26, 2012.

Gushee, David P. *The Sacredness of Human Life: Why an Ancient Biblical Vision Is Key to the World's Future*. Grand Rapids, MI: Eerdmans, 2013.

Kateb, George. *Human Dignity*. Cambridge, MA: Harvard University Press, 2011.

Meilaender, Gilbert. *Neither Beast Nor God: The Dignity of the Human Person*. New York: Encounter Books, 2009.

Nairn, Thomas A., ed. *The Consistent Ethic of Life: Assessing Its Reception and Relevance*. Maryknoll, NY: Orbis Books, 2008.

Waldron, Jeremy. *Dignity, Rank, & Rights. The Berkeley Tanner Lectures*. New York: Oxford University Press, 2012. http://dx.doi.org/10.1093/acprof:oso/9780199915439.001.0001.

50. The ACLU Takes on the Bishops: Tragedy Leads to a Misguided Lawsuit

Ashley, Benedict M., Jean DeBlois, and Kevin D. O'Rourke. *Health Care Ethics: A Catholic Theological Analysis*. Washington, DC: Georgetown University Press, 2006.

Corsi, Jerome R. *Bad Samaritans: The ACLU's Relentless Campaign to Erase Faith from the Public Square*. Nashville, TN: Thomas Nelson, 2013.

Fisher, Anthony. *Catholic Bioethics for a New Millennium*. Cambridge, UK: Cambridge University Press, 2012.

Furton, Edward J., and Peter J. Cataldo, eds. *Catholic Health Care Ethics: A Manual for Practitioners*. 2nd ed. Philadelphia, PA: National Catholic Bioethics Center, 2009.

Kutulas, Judy. *The American Civil Liberties Union and the Making of Modern Liberalism, 1930–1960*. Chapel Hill, NC: University of North Carolina Press, 2006.

Lapidus, Lenora M., Emily J. Martin, and Namita Luthra. *The Rights of Women: The Authoritative ACLU Guide to Women's Rights*. 4th ed. New York: New York University Press, 2009.

Palm, Daniel C., and Thomas L. Krannawitter. *A Nation under God?: The ACLU and Religion in American Politics*. New York: Rowman & Littlefield, 2005.

Walch, Timothy. *Parish School: American Catholic Parochial Education from Colonial Times to the Present*. Washington, DC: National Catholic Educational Association, 2003.

Walker, Samuel. *In Defense of American Liberties: A History of the ACLU*. 2nd ed. Carbondale, IL: Southern Illinois University Press, 1999.

51. Co-Opted by Evil? Abortion and Amnesty International

Ashley, Benedict M., Jean deBlois, and Kevin D. O'Rourke. *Health Care Ethics: A Catholic Theological Analysis*. 5th ed. Washington, DC: Georgetown University Press, 2006.

Ashley, Benedict M., and Kevin D. O'Rourke. *Ethics of Health Care: An Introductory Textbook*. 3rd ed. Washington, DC: Georgetown University Press, 2002.

Austriaco, Nicanor Pier Giorgio. *Biomedicine and Beatitude: An Introduction to Catholic Bioethics*. Washington, DC: The Catholic University of America Press, 2011.

Bretzke, James T. *Handbook of Roman Catholic Moral Terms*. Washington, DC: Georgetown University Press, 2013. See especially "Causality," "Compromise and compromise/cooperation with lesser evil"; "Lesser evil"; "*Minus malum*"; "Proportionate reason"; and "Tolerance."

Bretzke, James T. "The Lesser Evil: Insights from the Catholic Moral Tradition." *America*, March 26, 2007.

Bretzke, James T. *A Morally Complex World: Engaging Contemporary Moral Theology*. Collegeville, MN: Michael Glazier, 2004.

Corkery, Pádraig. *Bioethics and the Catholic Moral Tradition*. Dublin, Ireland: Veritas Publications, 2010. See especially Chapter 6, "Embryonic Stem Cell Research," 59–78, which discusses cooperation with evil.

Fisher, Anthony. *Catholic Bioethics for a New Millennium*. New York: Cambridge University Press, 2012.

Kaveny, M. Cathleen. "Catholics as Citizens." *America*, November 1, 2010.

Scarnecchia, D. Brian. *Bioethics, Law, and Human Life Issues: A Catholic*

Perspective on Marriage, Family, Contraception, Abortion, Reproductive Technology, and Death and Dying. Lanham, MD: Rowman & Littlefield, 2010.

52. Boycotts in a Pluralistic Society: How and Where Do We Draw Moral Lines?

Friedman, Monroe. *Consumer Boycotts: Effecting Change through the Market-place and Media.* New York: Routledge, 1999.

Glickman, Lawrence B. *Buying Power: A History of Consumer Activism in America.* Chicago, IL: The University of Chicago Press, 2009. http://dx.doi .org/10.7208/chicago/9780226298665.001.0001.

Harrison, Rob, Terry Newholm, and Deirdre Shaw, eds. *The Ethical Consumer.* Thousand Oaks, CA: SAGE Publications Inc, 2005.

Hilton, Matthew. *Prosperity for All: Consumer Activism in an Era of Globalization.* Ithaca, NY: Cornell University Press, 2009.

McFarland, Andrew. *Boycotts and Dixie Chicks: Creative Political Participation at Home and Abroad.* Boulder, CO: Paradigm Publishers, 2013.

McKibben, Bill. "The Case for Fossil-Fuel Divestment: On the Road with the New Generation of College Activists Fighting for the Environment." *Rolling Stone*, February 22, 2013. Available at http://www.rollingstone.com/politics /news/the-case-for-fossil-fuel-divestment-20130222.

Micheletti, Michele. *Political Virtue and Shopping: Individuals, Consumerism, and Collective Action.* New York: Palgrave Macmillan, 2003. http://dx.doi .org/10.1057/9781403973764.

Minda, Gary. *Boycott in America: How Imagination and Ideology Shape the Legal Mind.* Carbondale, IL: Southern Illinois University Press, 1999.

Richter, Judith. *Holding Corporations Accountable: Corporate Conduct, International Codes, and Citizen Action.* New York: Zed Books Ltd, 2001.

Robinson, Jo Ann. *Montgomery Bus Boycott and the Women Who Started It: The Memoir of Jo Ann Gibson Robinson*, edited by David J. Garrow. Knoxville, TN: The University of Tennessee Press, 1987.

53. Forever Young: The Trouble with the "Ashley Treatment"

Burns, Patout. *Theological Anthropology.* Minneapolis, MN: Fortress Press, 1981.

Cahill, Lisa Sowle. *Sex, Gender, and Christian Ethics.* New York: Cambridge University Press, 1996. http://dx.doi.org/10.1017/CBO9781139166584.

Cortez, Marc. *Theological Anthropology: A Guide for the Perplexed.* New York: T&T Clark International, 2010.

Harrison, Nonna Verna. *God's Many-Splendored Image: Theological Anthropology for Christian Formation.* Grand Rapids, MI: Baker Academic, 2010.

Madden, James D. *Mind, Matter, and Nature: A Thomistic Proposal for the Philosophy of Mind.* Washington, DC: The Catholic University of America Press, 2013.

Miller, Mark T. *The Quest for God and the Good Life: Lonergan's Theological Anthropology.* Washington, DC: The Catholic University of America Press, 2013. See especially Chapter 9, "Religious, Moral, and Intellectual Conversation," 149–75.

Pannenberg, Wolfhart. *Anthropology in Theological Perspective.* Louisville, KY: Westminster John Knox Press, 1985.

Ross, Susan A. *Anthropology (Engaging Theology: Catholic Perspectives).* Collegeville, MN: Liturgical Press, 2012.

Sachs, John R. *The Christian Vision of Humanity.* Collegeville, MN: Liturgical Press, 1991.

Schwarz, Hans. *The Human Being: A Theological Anthropology.* Grand Rapids, MI: Wm. B. Eerdmans Publishing Co, 2013.

54. Risk and Responsibility: Why Insurance Is the Wrong Way to Think about Health Care

Allhoff, Fritz, and Mark Hall, eds. *The Affordable Care Act Decision: Philosophical and Legal Implications.* New York: Routledge, 2014.

Bodenheimer, Thomas, and Kevin Grumbach. *Understanding Health Policy.* 6th ed. Columbus, OH: McGraw-Hill Education, 2012.

Fuchs, Victor R. *Who Shall Live?: Health, Economics and Social Choice.* 2nd ed. Singapore: World Scientific, 2011.

Hadler, Nortin M. *The Citizen Patient: Reforming Health Care for the Sake of the Patient, Not the System.* Chapel Hill, NC: The University of North Carolina Press, 2013.

Hansson, Sven Ove. *The Ethics of Risk: Ethical Analysis in an Uncertain World.* New York: Palgrave Macmillan, 2013. http://dx.doi.org/10.1057/9781137333650.

Harris, Dean M. *Ethics in Health Services and Policy: A Global Approach.* San Francisco, CA: John Wiley & Sons, Inc, 2011. http://dx.doi.org/10.4337/9780857931610.

Reid, T.R. *The Healing of America: A Global Quest for Better, Cheaper, and Fairer Health Care.* New York: Penguin Books, 2010.

Roberts, Marc, William Hsiao, Peter Berman, et al. *Getting Health Reform Right: A Guide to Improving Performance and Equity.* New York: Oxford University Press, 2008. http://dx.doi.org/10.1093/acprof:oso/9780195371505.001.0001.

Sorrell, Tom, ed. *Health Care, Ethics and Insurance.* New York: Routledge, 1998. http://dx.doi.org/10.4324/9780203274392.

Staff of the Washington Post. *Landmark: The Inside Story of America's New Health-Care Law—The Affordable Care Act—and What It Means for Us All.* New York: Public Affairs, 2010.

55. A Horrific Crime: But Is Execution the Answer?

Garnett, Richard W. "Criminal Law: 'Everlasting Splendours'—Death Row Volunteers, Lawyers' Ethics, and Human Dignity." In *Recovering Self-Evident*

Truths: Catholic Perspectives on American Law, edited by Michael A. Scaperlanda and Teresa Stanton Collett, 254–74. Washington, DC: The Catholic University of America Press, 2007.

King, Rachel. *Capital Consequences: Families of the Condemned Tell Their Stories*. Piscataway, NJ: Rutgers University Press, 2005.

King, Rachel. *Don't Kill in Our Names: Families of Murder Victims Speak Out against the Death Penalty*. Piscataway, NJ: Rutgers University Press, 2003.

Oliver, Willard M. *Catholic Perspectives on Crime and Criminal Justice*. Lanham, MD: Lexington Books, 2008.

Prejean, Helen. *Dead Man Walking: The Eyewitness Account of the Death Penalty That Sparked a National Debate*. New York: Vintage, 1994.

Skotnicki, Andrew. *Criminal Justice and the Catholic Church*. Lanham, MD: Rowman & Littlefield, 2007.

United States Conference of Catholic Bishops. "Criminal Justice—Restorative Justice." 2014. Available at http://www.usccb.org/issues-and-action/human -life-and-dignity/criminal-justice-restorative-justice/index.cfm.

United States Conference of Catholic Bishops. "Responsibility, Rehabilitation, and Restoration: A Catholic Perspective on Crime and Criminal Justice: A Statement of the Catholic Bishops of the United States." November 15, 2000. Available at http://www.usccb.org/issues-and-action/human-life-and-dig nity/criminal-justice-restorative-justice/crime-and-criminal-justice.cfm.

56. Could the Church Have Gotten It Wrong? Let's Look at the Facts

Curran, Charles E. *Catholic Moral Theology in the United States: A History*. Washington, DC: Georgetown University Press, 2008.

Curran, Charles E. *Catholic Social Teaching, 1891—Present: A Historical, Theological, and Ethical Analysis*. Washington, DC: Georgetown University Press, 2002.

Curran, Charles E. *The Development of Moral Theology: Five Strands*. Washington, DC: Georgetown University Press, 2013.

Espin, Orlando O., and Gary Macy, eds. *Futuring Our Past: Explorations in the Theology of Tradition*. Maryknoll, NY: Orbis Books, 2006.

Newman, John Henry. *Conscience, Consensus, and the Development of Doctrine*. New York: Image, 1992.

Noonan, John T. *A Church That Can and Cannot Change: The Development of Catholic Moral Teaching*. Notre Dame, IN: University of Notre Dame Press, 2005.

Thiel, John E. *Senses of Tradition: Continuity and Development in Catholic Faith*. New York: Oxford University Press, 2000.

About the Author

Cathleen Kaveny

Professor Cathleen Kaveny, a scholar who focuses on the relationship of law and morality, joined the Boston College faculty in January 2014 as the Darald and Juliet Libby Professor, a position that includes appointments in both the department of theology and the law school. She earned her AB summa cum laude from Princeton University and both her JD and her PhD from Yale University. A member of the Massachusetts Bar since 1993, Professor Kaveny clerked for the Honorable John T. Noonan Jr. of the U.S. Court of Appeals for the Ninth Circuit and worked as an associate at the Boston law firm of Ropes & Gray in its health-law group. Professor Kaveny teaches in both the Theology Department and the Law School at Boston College. She teaches contract law to first-year law students, as well as interdisciplinary seminars that explore the relationship between theology, ethics, and law. Professor Kaveny has been the president of the Society of Christian Ethics, the major professional society for scholars of Christian ethics and moral theology in North America. She has published over a hundred articles and essays, in journals and books specializing in law, ethics, and medical ethics. She serves on the masthead of *Commonweal* as a regular columnist. Her book, *Law's Virtues: Fostering Autonomy and Solidarity in American Society*, was published by Georgetown University Press in 2012 and won a first-place award in the category of "Faithful Citizenship" from the Catholic Press Association in 2013. She has served on editorial boards including *The American Journal of Jurisprudence*, the *Journal of Religious Ethics*, the *Journal of Law and Religion*, and the *Journal of the Society of Christian Ethics*. She has been a visiting professor at Princeton University, Yale University, and Georgetown University, and a visiting scholar at the University of Chicago. From 1995 until 2013 she taught law and theology at the University of Notre Dame, where she was a John P. Murphy Foundation Professor of Law.

Index

abortion: Amnesty International's prochoice position, 233–34; and "cooperation with evil," 137, 232–34; differences between the Nazi Holocaust and legalized, 140–42; Donohue/Levitt argument about legalization of, 227–28; Ethical and Religious Directives for Catholic Health Care Services, 229–31; and language of "unspeakable" sins, 194, 195–96; Partial Birth Abortion Act, 37–39; and physician-assisted suicide (PAS), 149–51; and postpartum depression and psychosis of Mine Ener at Villanova, 147–48; prolife arguments for conscience-clause protections, 72; Roberts Court decision in *Gonzales v. Carhart*, 37–39; *Roe v. Wade*, 4–5, 12, 31, 33, 37, 43, 66, 96–98, 117; U.S. bishops situating within an emerging "consistent ethic of purity," 216–17; and the USCCB voting guide, 216. *See also* prolife movement

Academy of Catholic Theology (ACT), 173–76

Adams, John and Abigail, 154

adoption: Catholic adoption agencies and same-sex couples, 77, 233; Pauline notion of, 13–14

Affordable Care Act (ACA), 82–84, 109, 219, 243–45; and concept of health insurance, 243–45; goals of, 106; Supreme Court's upholding of (and striking down the Medicaid expansion mandate), 40–42; U.S. bishops' opposition, 82–84. *See also* contraceptive mandate of the ACA

alcoholism, 22

Alito, Samuel, 113, 115–18

Alvaré, Helen, 183

American Academy of Pediatrics, 71

American Bill of Rights (1791), 50

American Civil Liberties Union (ACLU), 46, 229–30

American exceptionalism, 61–62

Amnesty International (AI), 233–34

Angel in the Waters (Doman), 217

Aquinas, Thomas, 8, 150, 186–87, 248; on marriage, 154; and "natural law" tradition, 22, 180, 186, 255–56, 259n8; on the qualities that sound law must demonstrate, 22; on slavery, 256, 259n8; *Summa Theologiae*, 128, 259n8; on unjust laws, 186

Arellano, Elvira, 47

"Ashley Treatment" and surgery on a mentally handicapped child, 240–42

atheism: Stout's atheist rebuttal to popular atheists, 130–32; a 2010 debate between Hitchens and D'Souza, 198–200

Augustine, St., 62, 122, 158; *Confessions*, 226; on the goods of marriage (*fides, proles*, and *sacramentum*), 13; on original sin, 226

Australian Catholics, 133–35

Awful Disclosures of Maria Monk, or, The Hidden Secrets of a Nun's Life in a Convent Exposed (1836), 165

Baltimore Catechism, 205, 208

Baxter v. Montana (2009), 43–45

Baze v. Reese (2008), 49–51

Bede, the Venerable, 249

Benedict XVI, Pope, 199, 201; on Catholic women, 177; and the church ban on contraception, 183; and culture of identity, 5

Bentham, Jeremy, 51

Bercovitch, Sacvan, 122

Bernardin, Joseph, 167, 215–17

Berrigan, Daniel, 120

Berrigan, Patrick, 120

bioethics councils and diversity, 136–39

birth control. *See* contraception; contraceptive mandate of the ACA

bishops. *See* U.S. Conference of Catholic Bishops (USCCB)

truth-and-reconciliation commissions, 196–97

Twenty-First Amendment, 22

UN Convention against Torture and Other Cruel, Inhuman, and Degrading Treatment, 58–59

United Methodist Church (Chicago), 47

United States v. Lee (1982), 78–80, 84, 104–9

Universal Declaration on Human Rights, 181

University of Notre Dame, 93–94, 153, 198, 223

"unspeakable" sins, language of, 194–97

U.S. Conference of Catholic Bishops (US-CCB), 43, 75–81; and an emerging "consistent ethic of purity," 216–17; criticism that the government is "defining religion," 82–84, 85–88; and ethical and religious directives for Catholic hospitals, 229–31; "Married Love and the Gift of Life" (2006 statement on contraception), 219; Migration and Refugee Services, 77, 78; opposition to the contraceptive mandate (and request for exemption on religious liberty grounds), 67, 76–80, 82–99, 100–102, 111–12, 119, 216, 219; and same-sex marriage, 12, 77, 216–17; statement of the Ad Hoc Committee for Religious Liberty, 95–96; statement on physician-assisted suicide, 149; voting guide ("Forming Consciences for Faithful Citizenship"), 216

U.S. Court of Appeals for the District of Columbia, 52

The Vagina Monologues (Ensler), 152–53

Van Wagoner, Richard, 34–35; *Mormon Polygamy*, 34

Veritatis splendor (John Paul II), 230, 249–50

Villanova University's memorial to Mine Ener, 146–48

virtue theorism, 165, 202–3

Volstead Act (1919), 35

war on terror: Bush administration and the "torture memo," 58–60; Bush's Military Commissions Act and detention of unlawful enemy combatants, 52–54; habeas corpus, 52–54; Obama administration, 61–63; torture and coercive interrogations of terrorism suspects, 55–57, 58–60

Warren, Earl, 32–33

Washington Times, 25

Watts v. Watts (1987), 28–30

Weaver, Robert C., Jr., 52

Weigel, George, 215

West, Cornel, 138

Wheaton College, 113–14, 117, 118

Winters, Michael Sean, 19n14

Wisconsin v. Yoder (1972), 75, 96, 100, 105, 110, 115

witchcraft trials and seventeenth-century Salem, 55–56

women, Catholic: Benedict XVI on, 177; CCD teachers of the 1970s, 208; and church teaching on sexual morality, 183; dissenters of the ban on contraception, 183–85; John Paul II's *Mulieris dignitatem* and efforts to formulate a "new feminism," 127, 177–79; the 1912 *Catholic Encyclopedia*'s article ("Woman"), 177–79; ordination of, 202

Zelikow, Philip, 56–57